Transformed in a Stroke

Transformed in a Stroke

*A Memoir of Brain Hemorrhage
and Recovery
in the United States and Japan*

LAUREL KAMADA

Foreword by Edward Nudelman

Toplight

Jefferson, North Carolina

ISBN (print) 978-1-4766-8604-2
ISBN (ebook) 978-1-4766-4382-3

LIBRARY OF CONGRESS AND BRITISH LIBRARY
CATALOGUING DATA ARE AVAILABLE

Library of Congress Control Number 2021036236

Front cover image: Leaving the nursing home in the U.S. to move to the next place.
My postmodern smile; my mother's hand calms me in the ICU.

Printed in the United States of America

Toplight is an imprint of McFarland & Company, Inc., Publishers

*Box 611, Jefferson, North Carolina 28640
www.toplightbooks.com*

I dedicate this book to my sister, Janice Seino, who called 911 when I passed out in her house on a visit from my home in Japan. Thank you for watching over me daily in the ICU as I struggled to hang on to life for weeks, as well as supporting me in rehabilitation afterward. I also dedicate this book to my dear, sweet little brother, Edward Nudelman, a mentor and constant support, who helped me reorganize my life by making contact with many of my associates in Japan. He has also greatly helped in reviewing and editing this manuscript, for which I am indebted, and his humor has kept me laughing even when everything looked dire. I cannot thank Eddie without also thanking his wife, my sister-in-law, Susie, who has always showed love and care to me, and of course my dear mom, who recently passed away. Susie and my 90-year-old mother would come visit me daily with Eddie and helped with encouragement and support while I was recovering in Seattle.

In addition, I dedicate this book to my cousin, Ronald Sidell, one of my role models for courage, who became a quadriplegic after contracting Guillain-Barré Syndrome. He, along with my aunt, Shirley Sidell, set up a website for people who are blind and those who are wheelchair-bound (see Appendix V).

Finally, I heartily dedicate this book to my husband, Kotaro, and my son, Jonah-Iori, who were there for me daily during the half-year that I spent recuperating in hospital in Japan and then back at our home. They remain a constant source of help and encouragement, going beyond what is to be expected from a husband and a son, including traveling over to the United States to bring me back home to Japan in my poor condition. My husband has been by my side throughout this journey, helping me to not fall down, even when going up and down stairs to the fourth floor of my Sendai apartment to recover items left there before my stroke; so many times he assisted my movements, aiding my progress, with my half-paralyzed body barely making headway (and often without handrails and on unstable ground). I extend gratitude, love and much more, beyond words, to Kotaro.

Table of Contents

Acknowledgments

First and foremost, even though I am not religious, I thank God for life itself and for allowing me to survive and to be reborn when many stroke victims do not make it. I have so much to be thankful for. I am blessed with two wonderful families: one in Seattle, Washington, and another in Hirosaki, Japan. I am grateful for my creative, tireless cognition and my strong right arm/hand and my right leg/foot. I thank God for giving me the innate passion to keep on going strong even when things get very tough, and I thank God for keeping me motivated and on track to pursue my goals. I am grateful for my ability to think, speak, and deconstruct and to type with just one finger for hours on end. Starry skies at night remain awesome to me. I am thrilled by freshly blooming flowers and the warmth of spring sunshine. I am charmed by animals, birds and other creatures.

My prayer: "Thank you, God, for helping me to survive and for giving me motivation and energy to keep on trying my best even when things got dire."

Since coming out of a stroke-induced coma several years ago, I have met many people and reconnected with others, including therapists, family, and friends. So many people told me that they were praying for me, and it seems their prayers have been heard and answered with blessings upon me.

First and foremost, I extend gratitude to my dear husband, Kotaro, and my beloved son, Jonah-Iori, in Japan, who have helped me daily. I also thank my Japanese family: *Obaasan* (Grandmother), *Ojiisan* (Grandfather), Siho, Katou, Yuujiro, Yuuko, and others.

So many thanks to my Jewish relatives and friends from Seattle, Portland, and Alaska who prayed for me, as well as some friends from Israel and my Muslim and Catholic nurses and aides in hospitals in Seattle and students and friends in Japan. There is also my Christian brother, Eddie, and his wife, Susie, along with their friends and relatives who prayed for me, including my little four-year-old great-nephew, Ethan, who delayed his family's dinner to make sure everyone present there prayed for me. He also prayed for my doctors, who had my life in their hands. God bless your loving heart, Ethan. I love you dearly.

My Krishnamuri, agnostic, atheist, Japanese Buddhist and Shintoist friends and family prayed for me; my spiritualist friend prayed for me, and others prayed for me in their own ways. You all have taught me how to pray for myself and others. Thank you, God, for putting all of these wonderful people around me, to help me and to love me, and for them allowing me to love them. This book honors all those who helped me over the first year or so of my rehabilitation, as well as other survivors and the families of those who did not survive.

Love and loving actions remain in one's heart forever. Love does not get consumed or depleted with use; on the contrary, love increases as it develops and is passed on. Gaotama Buddha similarly said, "Thousands of candles can be lighted from a single candle, and the life of the candle will not be shortened. Happiness [or love] never decreases by being shared."

At the same time that I express my gratitude, I apologize to those I have inadvertently inconvenienced in the process, including those public workers of Japan Railways who have been so helpful to me. (I was especially impressed by the special room on the platform of the Shinkansen, or the bullet train, in Sendai Station especially for wheelchair users.)

Next, I want to thank my doctors at Harborview Medical Center in Seattle, who were there when I arrived by ambulance and who performed surgery on my skull and saved my life. Thanks also go to Dr. Esselman and Dr. Slissinger, who watched over me in an intensive rehabilitation program there.

In addition, I extend my fondest gratitude to my doctors in Japan who have watched over me: Dr. Kamata at the Stroke Rehabilitation Center Hospital and afterward; the late Dr. Ishitoya for making me laugh; and Dr. Kitagawa for encouraging my hopes at Kibougaoka Home. Thanks also to the nurses and aides who took care of me in both the United States and Japan.

I extend my deepest thanks to all of my therapists, starting with Aaron and then Josh in the United States. I also have much gratitude for my therapists in Japan at the Hirosaki Stroke Rehabilitation Center Hospital: I want to say *arigatou* to Miyako, Yoko, Sato, Imai, and

Shiina. I likewise extend gratitude to my other therapists in Japan at Kibougaoka Home Day Service, starting with my therapist Mr. Kudo, along with Kabutomori, Kitabatake, Toyama, Marina, Fujita, Nakanuma Misaki and others who all have touched my body and my heart and who have given me hope, strength and courage to stand up from my wheelchair and walk a bit.

Mostly, I have an abundance of gratitude to the following family members: my sister, Janice Seino; my brother, Edward Nudelman, and his wife, Susan; my mom, Revella Nudelman; my cousins, Joel (and his wife, Liz) and Jimmy, along with my Aunt Jackie; my Aunt Shirley and Uncle Shelly, along with my cousin, Michael; my nieces, Lena (and her husband, Jake), Sarah (and her husband, Levi), Katie (and her husband, James), Momoko, and Reika; my nephew, Aaron (and his wife, Emily); Naoki; and, finally, my many great-nephews and great-nieces, who lent me their energy and joy of life.

Thanks to all of those who traveled from afar to visit me in the United States (Lillian and Kathleen came over from Japan and visited me in the nursing home in Seattle). Many people helped me heartfully, especially Gail O., Kathleen B., Lillian, Todd L., Diane N., Nikki Y., Fiona M., Marian Hara, and Edo. I also fondly thank all of my home helpers and care managers, especially Tashiro, Fukita, Mori, Kumagai, Kobayashi, and Shiroto, who are like mothers, sisters or friends to me.

I have a special place in my heart for my dearest women friends in Japan who have been so supportive and loving to me: Akko Villenueva-Kono, Nana, Emiko Maeda, Hiromi Arata and all of my sisters at the AFWJ: Gail Okuma, Nikki Y., Maria N., Diane Nagatomo, Louise, Norma, and Marian H., among others. I thank my Hirosaki friends for being there for me.

I extend a heartfelt "thank you" to all of the volunteers offering activities and entertainment at the nursing home in Seattle; thanks also go to the gospel singers who came to the Hirosaki Stroke Rehabilitation Center Hospital in Hirosaki, Japan, at Christmas. Those volunteers brought us some joy, and I want to give a shoutout to them and their work and organizations.

I want to thank a very good American friend, Diane Arrigoni, for giving me support and virtual hugs over email as she sheltered for a half-year in Vietnam during my writing and revising process. We reconnected, following my stroke, when she came out to visit me in Seattle and in Japan.

Many people caring for me or coming to visit me have also offered me their heartfelt advice, which I have tried to take to my heart. Thanks to my sister-in-law, Susie, for her advice to "appreciate even taking baby steps" in order to more carefully reach my goals, rather than trying to jump by flying leaps and bounds. I likewise appreciate the advice of Eddie, my dear brother, to "accept pain as gain," to "feel free to dip into your savings to spend on what you need for yourself now," and to remember that "you can't take it with you!" I thank my main nurse's aide caregiver in the Seattle nursing home, Ms. Israel (AKA Teresa), for her constant advice to "slow down" based on her experience of caring for her own stroke-survivor mother.

I also thank Marian and Dean, the certified nursing assistants (CNAs) who looked after me daily in the Seattle nursing home. I especially thank Dean, who listened to me when I was feeling mistreated. Dean always treated me with kindness and the respect of friendship and professional care.

Lastly, this book would never have gone to press without the meticulous help and technical assistance of several individuals. First, Clay Boutwell carefully read over the entire first draft, offering very good suggestions and guiding me to important improvements in the early stages of the manuscript. Also, I thank my primary beta reader and writing support, Diane Hawley Nagatomo in Japan, who gave me lots of support and advice. My brother, Eddie (a gifted writer with many books to his credit), offered advice and edited early manuscript drafts with great skill, in addition to tirelessly poring over final drafts with suggestions for organization, content and syntax/grammar. Finally, I would like to thank my editor and all the people at Toplight Books who made this dream come true.

Foreword

by the Author's Brother,
Edward Nudelman

When I got the call from my sister Janice that Laurel, my other sister, had collapsed, I didn't think much of it at first. She had probably fainted. But my wife Susie and I hurriedly packed up a few things and headed to the hospital emergency room. On the way, I learned a little more concerning Laurel's situation, and after about fifteen minutes in the waiting room, I heard nearly the worst scenario possible: Laurel had sustained a massive hemorrhaging stroke in the center of her brain and might not survive. The bleeding had almost stopped, but a mass of blood the size of a baseball had collected in the center of her brain. After hours in the ER, a hole was drilled in Laurel's head to drain fluids and relieve pressure. She was finally stabilized and moved into the Intensive Care Unit, though in critical condition and in a coma.

The next day, Laurel continued in a deep coma. Upon viewing the X-rays with the doctors, we were shown a very large white space in her brain, representing where the tissue had been pushed aside by the blood clot. We were told that the next 48 hours would tell the story one way or the other. We wanted to hope for the best, but we were told it could go either way.

After days of brain swelling and unresponsiveness, the doctors wondered whether Laurel would ever regain consciousness. But she surprised them. The first weeks were slow and arduous before she finally regained consciousness. At that point, we all wondered whether Laurel would ever "come back to Earth" and regain her cognition or have any ability to move her limbs. Again, Laurel surprised us all.

After more than half a year in hospitals and nursing homes in the United States, it wasn't clear how Laurel would make the transition from the United States to her home in northern Japan. Of course, Laurel surprised us again, making it back to Japan, albeit with much difficulty—a long and arduous trip—with her husband and son by her side.

Over the past couple of years, during which we have exchanged emails nearly every day and spoken over the phone, I have to say that I wondered whether Laurel would thrive in her new environment, having to give up her career as a professor that she had loved so much, say good-bye to her students, put her writing on hold (perhaps indefinitely), and, sadly, resign herself to no more dancing! However, and it gives me great pleasure and admiration to say, in the most profound sense, Laurel surprised us all, and continues to surprise us all—to impress, inspire, encourage us all—in so many ways, which I hope you'll discover as you read her book.

A hero or heroine is commonly understood to be someone admired or idealized for their courage, outstanding achievements or noble qualities. As I think back on Laurel's journey during these past several years, I can see all of these attributes fulfilled and vividly portrayed: her courage to look ahead in the face of overwhelming odds, and her outstanding achievements performed in writing, as evidenced by this exemplary book. Her continuing improvement is nothing short of a miracle, and her constant drive to work at getting better, to thrive in a mentally, physically, and emotionally trying situation, has been nothing short of heroic.

This book has been a labor of love for Laurel—not that she hasn't battled with formatting, organizing, focusing, striving for accuracy and the proper chronology of events, and so on. But having seen all of the early drafts, pages and pages of notes and burgeoning paragraphs, I can accurately affirm that she has learned and improved and really come to understand a new way of thinking and processing, of coping with the detrimental effects of her stroke. As an individual involved in biomedical research for the past 40 years, I don't take these triumphs lightly, and I don't think you should either. I think I know more than anyone else the kind of dogged energy, perseverance and downright pigheaded obsession needed to overcome the obstacles Laurel has faced, to be able to write such a sprawling account of her trials and tribulations, to provide academic aids and references from the relevant literature, and to make it all interesting and provocative—all elements and characteristics of an exemplary individual.

The manuscript itself grew and swelled (at one point to some 500 pages); then, through much cajoling and encouragement, she pared it down, keeping and improving the best material, and finally honing it to what you will find herein: fascinating and harrowing accounts, detailed critiques and comparisons of American and Japanese standards of practice (or lack thereof), references to Laurel's struggles and triumphs, and, significantly, useful academic discussions from her published work as a professor at a Japanese university.

I would like the reader to note an additional important point: This is Laurel's book. Many of us who have followed and come alongside Laurel could have directed her in other ways. We could have advised her to write her story purely from a biographical perspective, not including technical aspects or resource referencing. Or we could have pushed her toward more vivid and subjective accounts. I'd ask, "Is it really worth it, Laurel? Can't you eliminate this section? Or just don't mention that one. What's the point?" Along this journey, I have made both general and specific comments, suggestions and often downright imploring pleas to change the manuscript. A few things she'd change right away; some she'd say that she would change but never did. Most suggestions, however, were met with sheer opposition. More power to her! I loved and continue to love her dogged determination. And I believe it is noteworthy and unique to find here a pristine and undaunted account by a stroke survivor, written under considerable difficulty and duress. It's what makes this book a good read.

Whether you yourself are a stroke survivor, or are experiencing another type of disabling trial (whether physical or emotional), or are just curious about how an American living in Japan for most of her adult life, as a professor at major universities, has coped with a devastating stroke and flourished against overwhelming odds, you should take up this book and read it. You won't be sorry you did.

"When you are grateful, fear disappears
and abundance appears."
—*Anthony Robbins*

"Gratitude is the memory of the heart."
—*Jean Baptiste Massieu, letter to Abbe Sicard*

Introduction

You have just had a stroke that has left you disabled, and you have lost much of your physical ability. You are having trouble speaking and swallowing. Half of your body, vertically from head to toes, is weakened or paralyzed. Is your face dropped and/or crooked, so that you have lost your former attractiveness? Perhaps even smiling is not helpful, as your face sags on one side. Are you now ready to begin the hard work of recovering from your loss? Are you anxious to get started on your path to recovery? My guess is that you have already begun.

Or perhaps you are the primary caregiver of a loved one who has recently survived a stroke, and you are having trouble making decisions and caring for someone who has, up until now, been very independent. Perhaps you are a husband, and your wife is the stroke survivor; this may well be the first time you have had to switch roles and be the caregiver instead of being the recipient of care in your relationship. If any of these scenarios seem similar to your situation, congratulations to you for taking on your new role. Now you have a great opportunity to see the world from another perspective and to help another person, who will love you like never before and appreciate all your extraordinary efforts. Perhaps you are not sure of how to fulfill your new role. You could be an overwhelmed wife or a gainfully employed single male. Perhaps you are a professional caring for stroke survivors or helping others in long-term care. Do you work in a hospital, a nursing home, a rehabilitation facility, or some other hospital-like facility? Are you on the nursing staff? Are you on the rehabilitation staff? Are you a nurse's aide or a CNA (certified nursing assistant)? Or are you some other staff member caring for stroke survivors? Do you work in some kind of teaching facility that trains students in this field? Are you a student in training to one day work with stroke survivors?

If you can identify with any of those roles or job descriptions, then this book is designed and written for you. If you recently survived a stroke, and not long ago came out of a coma, it might be scary for you at this moment, but please maintain hope. The road ahead will be difficult, but it will also lead to recovery, and it will be filled with many awesome new experiences and relationships that you might otherwise have missed. I can say that for certain, based on my own experience of going through stroke rehabilitation in two countries—the United States and Japan—spending over a year incapacitated in hospital-like rehabilitation facilities after suffering a profound hemorrhagic stroke that bled into the center of my brain, leaving a hole about the size of a baseball. Here, I offer up all of the insights that I have gained over the seven years since I landed in a stroke-induced coma, in 2013, lying unconscious in an ICU in the United States, far from where I had been working as a professor and living with my husband and son in Japan for the latter half of my life. Through many varied situations, challenges, workarounds, and seemingly insurmountable obstacles, I have worked to overcome numerous difficulties, and during this period I even enjoyed the process quite often. I sincerely hope to share what I have learned with you, my readers, to make your journey much smoother and more familiar. This is a book that I wish I could have read early on after awakening from my coma, confused, irrational and basically uninformed. I felt a strong need to know as much as possible about my condition. It felt like being in a strange land where I did not speak the language and I had lost my way, wandering around, crippled and in a wheelchair.

Emotionally as well as physically, the task ahead for a stroke survivor is immense. But one should not despair and feel overwhelmed. If you are a parent, such a task must be even more emotionally difficult. However, stroke recovery and rehabilitation can be a very fantastic process, and in this book I will share all I have learned through my research, reading and experiences, so that you do not have to reinvent the wheel. This book is based on my rehabilitation experience in two countries with very different cultures and belief systems. I introduce problems in both settings and celebrate the best of both worlds. I introduce to my readers all of the things that I learned that ideally might contribute to reduced recovery time and an improvement in the quality of that experience for some people. I try to expose various problems in both contexts that I experienced, which, if attended to and solved, could make life for those recuperating in hospital-like facilities much better. In addition, I try here to advocate for those people who might be having problems in some facilities.

CHAPTER 1

An Overview
"You are very lucky!"

"Stroke is the leading cause of serious, long-term disability in the United States."
— *U.S. Centers for Disease Control and Prevention, 2009*

"In Japan, stroke now ranks third among all causes of death following cancer and heart disease. Approximately one in five men and women of middle age [in Japan] will experience a stroke in their remaining lifetime."
— *Tanvir Chowdhury Turin et al., 2010*

"You are very lucky," I was told repeatedly by many people. I had lost my ability to walk. I had lost my job. I could no longer put on my bra by myself.

"You are lucky to be alive," they all said. Besides being a university lecturer professor, I was also a writer, but I lost my ability to type quickly with two hands, and the process of assembling large drafts, though still preserved, was nevertheless much slower than before. I also lost my driver's license and my ability to drive. I could not even go grocery shopping.

"You came within a camel's hair of dying, but you were lucky and blessed," my brother informed me. I had lost my ability to go trekking in the foothills, forests and mountains. I could no longer swim or ski, and I had to give up doing Latin dance. For a long time, I stopped laughing, dancing, singing, doing sports, and going out with friends.

"You are so fortunate. So many people having strokes die, but you survived," I was told. I had lost my ability to dream. I lost hope for a while.

"You are very lucky, you know," I was told. I lost some of my friends; I lost my spirit of adventure. I lost my identity. I lost contact with my closest students. I lost academic associations built up over a career of a quarter-century, as I could not travel alone to conferences anymore.

"You are very lucky beyond words," I was told. I was no longer able to go places by myself. I was humiliated and mocked by nursing staff young enough to be my daughters, who were tasked with changing my diapers. I had to sacrifice going to parties, conferences, conventions and gatherings that I had wanted to attend but could not get myself to. I stopped going outside of the house at all, even to my backyard or to my garden.

I became dependent on others to help me travel, to go shopping and to get from one place to another. I needed help bathing and washing my hair. I stayed home alone most of the time.

But I indeed was very lucky, fortunate and blessed. I had the most precious of all things: I had my life still very much intact. After a season, I could think, talk and argue. I was alive and thriving. I had a surplus of creative ideas that often kept me from sleeping at night. I was otherwise healthy, motivated and ready to do many things and have new experiences. I could continue to learn, to read and to write. I could enjoy listening to music and small things around me in daily life. I could still love and appreciate those people who entered my world.

However, the road was full of challenges. Little things became huge. Having lost so much, even small things became very important to me, such as a phone call from home; someone causing me to laugh; being touched in any way; meeting up with good friends, even at my own house; attending conventions, conferences, parties and gatherings; being part of a group; and clinking glasses of red wine and saying, "To life" and "To walking again," while eating good cheese and other healthy Japanese appetizers before dinner with my husband. All of these were experiences of great pleasure, but still they did not come easily; they called for some workarounds, some extra thinking and maneuvering.

I soon got back on my feet, at first heavily guided by an aid worker, and I later learned how to walk, wobbling and stomping forward noisily with a too-tight leg brace and an unstable cane, performing some ten laps around my house under the guidance of my helpers. I learned how to get dressed, type out long manuscripts for hours on end, prepare meals, do the laundry, and take care of my longish hair by myself, all with just one hand. (I implore my able-bodied readers to try doing everything from morning until night for a day with just one hand and one leg, and you will understand the challenge facing hemiplegics, stroke survivors, and many other impaired individuals.) I became adept at maneuvering my wheelchair around, and I won first place in a wheelchair race at an indoor *undoukai* sports event for users/residents at a facility in Japan that I often used. I became humbled and vulnerable. I started loving or re-loving many people near me.

Rehabilitating and re-enabling oneself after a stroke is a process that can be navigated with success, and it also brings many positive experiences and creates chances to gain new relationships and to transcend one's earlier lifestyle. My own experiences as a stroke survivor in two countries can perhaps serve as an example of how progress can be achieved. Rehabilitation from stroke disability can be rewarding, enjoyable and meaningful, and the process is as inspiring as the goal. In addition, there is much for all to learn regarding this process of healing. How can we facilitate recovery for survivors of strokes (as well as other disabling diseases and scenarios that leave a person paralyzed, immobilized or injured in other ways)? How can we serve as role models and be a part of the solution? It's not easy, it doesn't come naturally, but it is perfectly within our grasp.

This book includes a memoir of my stroke and rehabilitation experiences in the United States and Japan. I compare differences between the dichotomous regions of the East and the West, regarding practices and philosophies of care and recovery over the first year or so of my rehabilitation process. I examine lessons for the institutions involved, such as hospitals, nursing homes, rehabilitation centers, and assisted-living homes. And I offer suggestions for the people involved: nurses, aides, *kaigo fukushi* (or NACs in Japan), facility directors, doctors, therapists, other staff, stroke survivors and their families. This story also includes my personal experiences of warping into "a parallel world" for weeks while I was in a coma, having a very vivid dream-experience in that world, and then having an "out-of-body" experience, which I feel helped shock me into realizing that my situation was serious and I needed to wake up and survive.

CHAPTER 2

My Stroke
Issues and Challenges

I was so hyped for that trip to the United States, especially the conference I was to attend in Los Angeles. I was so much looking forward to presenting my paper at the very special gathering called the 2013 Happa-Half Japan Festival. It was the first time for me ever to be invited to present a paper at an international U.S. conference (that was overseas from Japan), although I had attended the presentations of many others at scores of international conferences over my 25-year professional career. Being asked to present a main conference paper in the United States had been one of my goals. I had accomplished this goal in Japan already, some years earlier, when I was asked to present the opening plenary address at a local international conference in Tokyo. As for the LA conference presentation, I had received all of my expenses paid in transportation, hotel, and other fees while in Los Angeles (which was more a boost to my self-esteem than to my pocketbook).

I felt honored to be asked to present a paper at the University of Southern California in Los Angeles. I had already written the paper and submitted it to the conference chair and the discussant. I was looking forward to any feedback, and I was hoping to have some good discussions about my paper. I was also very much looking forward to connecting with my counterparts, my American colleagues in my narrow field of Japanese- and English-speaking (mostly Caucasian) hybridity and mixed ethnic identity. I was excited about the social events lined up for the festival as well, including films, art exhibits and parties. It was a great group of very connected people on both sides of the Pacific Ocean, and I felt extremely flattered to be included among them. Some of them I knew from related events in Japan, some I knew as writers and as colleagues in my field, but some of them I had not yet met in person. I was excited and nervous about my travel to Los Angeles, via Seattle, and back.

I expected to be back in my office in Japan in a few weeks to complete teaching my classes for the term before making grades. But, due to my devastating stroke, I did not make it back in early May 2013, as planned. Instead, I returned to Japan in August 2014—the following fiscal school year in Japan. But, as I was hospitalized in northern Japan at that time, I was not able to return to my office then either. It was so disorienting for me, missing the chance to finish up there. I had already planned my courses for the second term, which was to begin in September 2014, and I had carefully selected the textbooks for my eight classes, which the publishers had already prepared for me by sending the teacher's books to my office. I could not return for that term, to my great dismay, as, first of all, I was not able to find a barrier-free apartment near my university in Sendai. Second, I was unable to get support from my husband or from my doctor to live by myself in Sendai. I was still officially living in a fourth-floor apartment in Sendai with no elevator and even without handrails in many portions of the four flights of stairs (see the photo on page 167). I did not yet have a renewed driver's license, and I could not travel by myself then at all. Thus I could not return to my office as I had hoped, even though the people at my office were very supportive and treated me very fairly. They had arranged barrier-free access there for me and had construction work done to install a wheelchair barrier-free toilet near my office.

I had wanted to be back in my office before we were to make the move out of our temporary prefabricated facility and into our repaired office building (we had been using the temporary quarters for several years after the mega-quake of March 11, 2011, severely damaged our building). I had also planned to leisurely pack up my things by myself over the next few years before retirement; instead, my husband and some office staff had to help me do it in a great rush. Many of my things could not be easily located later, as they were quickly crammed into boxes and sealed without labels, left behind, or misplaced. Transition, workarounds, and seemingly huge roadblocks were everywhere upon my return to Japan. But first, let me review briefly what happened on that fateful day in Seattle in 2013.

I was staying with my sister in her two-bedroom home. All seemed normal, and thus the usual routines and outings were being planned, although I was exhausted from traveling from Japan. While we were out driving, I was even having a difficult time getting words out and feeling disoriented. I recall asking myself whether this feeling was more than fatigue. My sister recalls thinking I seemed really tired, but we attributed it to my recent traveling. Later that evening, I collapsed. Flash forward four weeks, after emergency surgery (when doctors placed a tube directly into my brain to ease draining and swelling) and several weeks in the ICU, when I finally woke up.

My first recollections are of my sister confirming my speculation that something was wrong. My brother later informed me that I was "inches from dying," an unsettling thought later confirmed by specialists handling my case. It turns out that hemorrhagic strokes can be much more difficult to manage than clots, which can often be addressed using "clot busters." With a bleeding stroke, especially in the brain, the only real therapeutic approach at the onset is to try to stop the bleeding and prevent pressure from building up in the brain, a rigid compartment that will not expand.

I was very determined from the start to get my life back in order before leaving Seattle, and that meant returning the borrowed wheelchair to the nursing home and standing up and walking by myself like before. But it was much easier said than done, even with scores of people helping me over many years. It is happening too slowly for me, so I have taken it upon myself to move on to the next step, even without that walking goal completely accomplished, as my goals are far too numerous to let any snags hold me back. So while I continue to work on my walking and getting my left hand to be more functional, I have continued writing.

I had wanted to continue my work as a university lecturer, but I was unable to do that given the mandatory retirement at age 65. Instead, I decided to write out some of those lectures as books, which I had wanted to continue discussing with students and others.

My rehabilitation following the stroke has been hard, but also very rewarding and even amazing at times. I sometimes feel like "my therapists are gods from another world." They breathe life back into me when I am very low or in much pain. There is nothing that compares to a good physical therapist or an occupational therapist. I would love to have therapy done all day if I could! I feel like I am normal again while doing physical therapy. Sometimes, especially when it is cold in northern Japan at night or in the early morning, in our large unheated house, my body gets very tight, tensed up, and painful. It seems that stress of any kind cruelly accumulates in the weakened limbs or joints of one's body. For me, that is the entire left side of my body. I become tense and feel lots of pain in ordinary movements or even while just sitting or lying in bed. My therapists can massage and stretch/pull my muscles, ligaments, joints and bones back into proper alignment, which makes me feel human again. Then, when they help me to stand upright and walk forward, they provide me with my only daily exercise, and that feels fantastic too. My body gets an internal self-massage through the exercise, even if just for fifteen minutes or so per session, a few times weekly. "Thank you for touching my body and helping me," I want to tell my therapists.

I think the hardest thing is being dependent on others to do things for me that I want to do myself. That includes driving, shopping, preparing dinner, housecleaning, bathing, washing dishes and traveling by myself. I dislike having to ask others to do such things for me. However, my brother has told me, in the true Christian spirit that he espouses, and informed by his own care of our mother in the late stages of dementia, "Helping others is one of the best human activities that we can do."

Lately, some of my home helpers have been pushing me to do more things myself, such as hanging up my wet laundry, standing up to brush my teeth or washing dishes at the kitchen sink. That practice has been helpful, since I hope to eventually be able to do everything by myself, as I did before the stroke. I had a bit of a setback, though, the first time I tried to stand up by myself at the kitchen sink while home alone. When I went to sit back down in my wheelchair, it moved backward, and I ended up on the floor, unable to get up by myself, but fortunately I was not injured at all. I was prepared to camp out there on the floor with the three blankets from my chair until my husband was expected to return, several hours later (usually after 9:00 p.m.), but he came home relatively early that night, within about two hours. He was certainly surprised to see me on the floor, calling for help.

Walking seems to be one of the most elusive of all goals, though. I often see others walking well at the facilities that I attend, people who are more frail, much older, or less motivated than I am. I think, "If they can walk, why can't I?" I am still very motivated to overcome the pain, fear, balance problems and whatever else it takes to walk by myself. At least I want more independence to be able to get away from my wheelchair and be mobile enough to walk for certain short distances. It is scary, painful, and potentially dangerous, and it takes a lot of stamina and strength, which I need to build up as I work to lose body fat and gain muscle. Those are some of my short- and long-term goals. Below are some points that may be helpful to keep in mind as you read this book.

Regarding my self-positioning, I am a Caucasian American woman, born, raised, and educated in Seattle. I spent the first half of my life in the northwestern United States and have since been residing in Japan. I am nearly fluent in Japanese, including reading.

In this story you will see many examples of my resistance and struggles in which I have tried to contest being marginalized. In both U.S. and Japanese cultures, since the stroke, I have found myself fighting others' tendency to see me as crazy, brain damaged and depressed. I believe that medical staff are sometimes led to expect such stereotypical conditions, and it is unnerving for those of us who are treated in a "cookie-cutter" fashion.

Additionally, in Japan, besides being disabled, I have also had to resist being marginalized within racist and gendered discourses of *gaijin* (foreigner) or "outsider" as a white foreigner in Japan.

While advocating for myself, I have worked hard through much pain, agony and loss. I have lost much of my physical prowess, seemingly permanently. My left side became extremely weak due to the massive stroke, and even after over seven years of rehabilitation work, I still cannot walk well by myself. My left hand remains curled tightly and is spastic (see the photo on page 15), and I had to type out this entire book using one finger of my right hand. I thank God for my robust right hand, though, and I also thank God for my cognition, which seems, for the most part, to be intact.

I found myself falling in love with so many people around me who showed me kindness or helped me, even when they were doing their jobs professionally. I also developed a newly realized love for my family. I have gained a deeper understanding of love and gratitude along with other life lessons. Illustrating the many differences of care, healing and recovery models between Japan and the United States is one of my main purposes in writing this book. I found that in this comparison, it is not about what the East should learn from the West, or vice versa, but rather how we can take the best of both worlds, coming up with better models so that we can learn from them and improve. I also researched many effective rehabilitation methods, practices and philosophies, which I hope to share with my readers here.

In this book you will hear me rant, complain, discuss and propose. Why have some people already healed completely, while I am left unable to walk, immobilized in a wheelchair? I will attempt to deconstruct and critique areas that I feel are in need of improvement. Why was I able to survive when others did not? Surely these are not questions we mortal

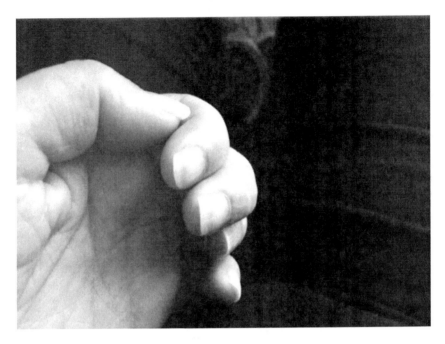

My badly curled hand, in 2015, two and a half years after the stroke—not much progress there (photograph by Edward Nudelman).

humans can answer. But I did survive this injury to tell my story. Here it is. I thank you for reading this story, and if you want to comment, ask questions or such, please contact me via my publisher.

Following are several central questions that I hope to address in this book:

1. How might stroke survivors come to better accept, enjoy and transcend their rehabilitation process?

2. What practices and philosophies of rehabilitation care for stroke survivors should be discontinued or changed in hospitals and rehabilitation facilities anywhere?

3. What practices and philosophies of rehabilitation care for stroke survivors would be good to incorporate into hospitals and rehabilitation facilities around the world?

4. What are the most important things to do and to keep in mind during stroke rehabilitation from the viewpoint of stroke survivors, staff, caregivers and families?

5. What can the East learn from the West? And what can the West learn from the East (or from "the Japan Model") in terms of

stroke rehabilitation, healing, wellness, and care in hospital-like facilities?

Dreams Do Come True

Shortly before my stroke, many dreams and aspirations that I had held for years became reality. I had wanted to be a full professor, and it happened at Aomori Akenohoshi Tandai College. My dream of being employed at an elite national university in Japan also came true when I became employed as a lecturer professor at Tohoku (National) University in Sendai (usually ranked the fourth-best university in Japan). I had wanted to complete my Ph.D. and write a book of the dissertation/thesis. I was delighted when my supervisors and outside oral examiner in England encouraged me to do so, saying it was the sort of dissertation conducive to making a good book, as it had a reader-friendly storyline to it. I also had hoped to have my work be recognized and to be of high enough quality to win a prize. These all came true for me, after much energy and work over ten years on that project.

Another dream was fulfilled when I was asked to make several important presentations at conferences on my work, both locally in Japan and overseas. I was honored to be asked to present the opening plenary address at the 2010 international JALT conference in Tokyo, Japan, and was further honored to be invited by both Kyoto University and the University of Southern California to go to the United States to present a paper in April 2013, but I collapsed from the stroke (in my first stopover in my hometown) just before I was about to go there. It was reaffirming to be recognized and to accomplish many of my dreams.

Even in my absence, another dream materialized when my proposal for a Japanese government-sponsored and -funded research project was accepted for a renewed three-year research extension, and I was to be awarded generous funding for that study. But this dream was squashed when my office superiors had to refuse the funding on my behalf after the stroke, due to me being out of my office on an extended sick leave. I may still try to find ways to complete the study, even without funding. For that project, I had hoped to continue to examine mixed-ethnic *haafu* (or "halves"—that is, hybrid people) in Japan. I wanted to examine more marginalized races/ethnicities, and the identities of youths of mixed ethnicity, that had not been included in my earlier work on hybrid adolescent girls in Japan of half–Japanese and half-white ancestry. For the newer project, I wanted to examine hybrid people of half–Japanese and half–black ethnicity/race, as well as half–Chinese, half–Iranian, half–Pakistani, and other mixes. I also wanted to further examine identities of "Japaneseness." In addition, I wanted to use some of the funding to allow me to get summaries of some of my research up to that point professionally translated into Japanese, so that it could be shared with the most obvious audience for the subject. I appreciated being recognized by the *Monkashou* (Japanese government selection committee) for this work and to have been offered the funding, even though it had to be refused. If I do not find a means to complete my projects within my lifetime, I hope to pass my work on to others (such as to the BSIG members of JALT) to complete it.

I still have lots of other new dreams and goals, which is perhaps why I was not ready to leave this "party" yet, allowing me to wake up from the coma and survive the stroke. If you are reading this book, you are seeing another of my dreams that has come true, and I thank you for your support. I keep a list of several other book titles that I hope to write next, in various genres from fiction to research-oriented studies and even textbooks. If this book is well enough received, I may even write a sequel, a prequel or a textbook.

CHAPTER 3

How Many Hours Does It Take?

In the book *Outlier: The Story of Success* (2008), author Malcolm Gladwell introduced the "10,000 Hour Rule." Basically, this rule states that it takes ten thousand hours of practice to master a skill or to achieve mastery in a field. I tried to think of all of the things in my life in which I had invested some 10,000 hours and mastered a particular skill, and then I also tried to determine which of those skills I am no longer able to utilize as a result of stroke weakness on the left side of my body and those skills that I can still do well in spite of the stroke impairment. I came up with a rather long list, pared down, as follows:

1. **Typing.** I used to be a very fast typist, at some eighty words per minute or more at my peak in high school, when I was at the top of my class. Indeed, I can still type, but it takes a lot of time, and I typed out this entire book manuscript and earlier drafts with just one finger. Those 10,000 hours have helped me today—even in my slower typing, I feel.

2. **Playing the guitar.** I used to play the guitar daily to relax, and I would sing songs (off-key) from the late 1960s or early 1970s, usually together with other friends. I must have played guitar for more than 10,000 hours, starting in high school. I have tried playing the guitar since the stroke, but I was not able to form the chords with my extremely weak left hand, so I cannot play it by strumming alone unless I can find a chord player of some sort. I still sing off-key loudly, but that does not help much to relieve my stress. There may be an electric smart guitar on the market where you can just push a button for the chord and strum with the right hand, and I will search for it (or perhaps send a plan to design one at quirky.com).

3. **Mountain climbing, hiking and ice climbing.** Growing up in Seattle, Washington, at the foothills of the Cascade mountain

range, I enjoyed trail and mountain hiking and camping since before the age of twelve. I also did trail and ice climbing for a few years starting at age 25. Among other practice climbs, I climbed to the peak of Mt. Baker (3,286 meters, or 5,085 feet) in the North Cascades. I was part of a group that attempted to climb to the peak of Mt. Rainier (4,392 meters, or 14,410 feet) to raise funds to try to end world hunger in the first "Hunger Project," but we were turned back near the peak of Mt. Rainier due to bad weather and ice falls.

I am motivated to try trail (non-ice) mountain hiking again, though only if I have a good support crew. With my leg brace and a cane or a walker, I think I could manage less steep climbs if there were no obstacles, ice, or water on the path.

4. **Driving.** I *could* drive, albeit with a bit of modifying in the car by installing handles for getting in and out easily. Driving requires mostly the use of the right leg/foot and the right hand/arm, and mine are strong. I feel that I am a skillful, confident, much-experienced driver, having driven since the age of sixteen, for some fifty years now, with no accidents and few tickets in two countries with different systems. I have experienced driving on snow and ice and on narrow roads. I would need to practice getting into and out of the car on my own. But I first need to convince others that I can do it, so I can renew my driver's license in Japan, which is very strict these days. I also need to practice driving and would prefer not to drive in bad weather or after dark. It is stereotypically said that right-brain hemispheric stroke survivors should have some "left-side neglect," so I might need to convince others that I have my left side in good view.

I have yet to try driving, and when I do it, I want to be a safe driver for myself and for others. Unfortunately, my doctor, the driver-licensing officer, my husband and my siblings are against my driving. Without their support, I really cannot drive, so I must work harder to prove my ability to drive safely. But I believed in myself enough to spend thousands of dollars to fix my car so I can drive, and I will keep trying, with independence as my goal.

5. **Dancing.** I have spent more than 10,000 hours doing various types of dancing. Whether ballroom dancing, folk dancing, Latin dancing, salsa/bachata dancing, belly dancing, or popular (Motown, hip-hop, swing and rock-music style) dancing, I must have spent thousands of hours on each. (I have passed the Japanese medal tests for rumba, cha-cha, swing, blues, waltz, tango, quickstep and others.) I am not sure if I could still dance now, as I have not

tried yet, but I want to try it with a good instructor. I have yet to meet a therapist who is also salsa crazy, but I hope to do so someday.

6. **Academic writing and getting published—articles, monographs, books.** I have probably spent over 10,000 hours in learning and practicing my skills in the genre of academic writing and publication. I have published numerous academic articles and have also done over fifty (mostly academic) oral conference presentations. In addition, I have done journalistic writing for the BSIG of JALT for over ten years as a volunteer writer (see bsig.org). I *can* and do write daily, but typing takes longer now.

In high school, I completed my 10,000 hours of writing practice before going to college as part of a special honors course I was enrolled in called "The Humanities Block." It was a block of three class periods every morning at Mercer Island High School, in Seattle, where we had to write weekly academic papers on difficult topics concerning Western philosophies. It helped my writing throughout school, including my Ph.D. thesis writing.

(By the way, Stanley Ann Dunham, who was the mother of Barack Obama, the 44th U.S. president, was in the same course in the same high school and the same honors program that I attended, nine years ahead of me, and we had some of the same teachers there.)

7. **Doing academic presentations.** I have conducted over fifty presentations at academic conferences, schools and such venues. I have also done presentations several times since leaving the stroke hospital in Japan. The challenge now is just getting from my home in northern Honshu, Japan, to venues that are often far from my home or overseas.

8. **Doing taichi.** I have spent over 10,000 hours doing taichi, a Chinese slow-moving martial art, including the hours spent in learning, practicing and teaching it. I am not sure if I can still do it now, as I have not yet tried it. Sitting in a wheelchair and trying to do taichi is possible, but that misses the essence of taichi movement, which I feel is the "stance" or the posture of having one's knees slightly bent, with stomach tucked in, and the center of balance over one's *tan tien* (an area a few inches below the navel). It might be possible to do taichi in a special room with handrails—like a ballet studio, I think. It would be very good rehabilitation practice, and I want to try it and to teach it to other stroke survivors.

9. **Swimming.** I must have put in over 10,000 hours in the

water as a child, with nearly my entire three-month-long summer vacation from school spent going to beaches and swimming, as I was raised on an island in a freshwater lake. I would like to try swimming with life vests and flotation belts on me, as well as a coach near me in a heated swimming pool. I would also like to try water skiing again with one or two skis on a clear lake.

10. **Studying Japanese.** Including classroom study, homework and consciously practicing language skills, my study of Japanese has amounted to well over 10,000 hours since 1975.

11. **Writing another book.** I know I can definitely do it again, but it takes much more than just 10,000 hours from start to finish, depending on genre, topic and editing. I have not only written a book but also published several academic/journalistic monographs on bilingualism (see bsig.org), along with chapters in several edited books. Since the stroke and my retirement, I have completed two 95,000-word manuscripts, including the one for this book.

12. **Typing with one finger.** I have been doing it for over seven years now, since 2013, including typing out this entire book. I am interested in learning how to type well and fast with just one hand.

13. **Walking with the leg brace on my weak leg.** I plan to continue walking with my AFO (ankle-foot orthosis) leg brace to complete over 10,000 hours of walking, even if it takes ten years in total. One of my 2017 New Year's resolutions was to walk a half-marathon (21,075 kilometers, or 13.194 miles), if possible, by circling inside of my house over one year. That is nearly two kilometers monthly.

I encourage my stroke survivor readers to also assemble a list of their mastered skills/abilities and to separate them into categories of "those they can no longer do," "those they can still do," and "those they aim to do from now on."

I think it might be a great challenge to aim to be an athlete for the Paralympics, although I do not think that I have any natural talent for it. It would surely take at least 10,000 hours of practice to even come close to being competitive in any sport or category. However, if asked by the U.S. Paralympic team to join in some category, I would have to accept. I encourage all stroke survivors to consider and pursue their sports talent.

Jill Bolte Taylor has written an excellent, best-selling memoir of her left-brain hemispheric stroke experience called *My Stroke of*

Insight (2008). But our stories are fundamentally different, as she had a left-brain-hemisphere stroke while mine was a right-brain-hemisphere stroke, causing very different problems and paths of recovery. I found it extremely helpful to learn as much as possible about my stroke, and I am continuing to research even more about strokes, recovery means and processes. Bolte Taylor wrote that it took her eight years to experience a total recovery, although she mostly had speech and cognitive damage, whereas I mostly have physical impairment to one side of my body. I am hoping that, like her, I might have a total recovery within eight years in total—perhaps by 2021.

I recommend that stroke survivors and their families research as much as possible about strokes. Using the Anat Baniel Method (see Appendix VIII), Bolte Taylor's mother helped to guide her smooth recovery in eight years' time. Might I just wake up one morning in 2021 totally recovered? Therapists and neurologists will all tell you that each stroke survivor's injuries and recovery times are different, depending on many things, such as the size and location in the brain of the injury, their age, and other factors.

My story is unique, as it includes comparisons between Japan and the United States regarding good and bad aspects of rehabilitation and hospital-like facilities for stroke rehabilitation. You will find highlights concerning positive aspects of both Japanese and American cultures, emphasizing how one can enjoy, accept, and transcend the difficult, often painful process of rehabilitation in the two contexts of mixed cultural expectations. As I spent the first half-year after the stroke in the United States before returning to Japan to be hospitalized for another half-year, I think I have a special perspective and outlook on these kinds of issues.

I have more questions than answers about my stroke recovery process: What can I do to speed up my recovery? Why have some people already healed while I am still left unable to walk and confined to a wheelchair? Will I experience a full recovery? And if so, how much longer will my recovery take? What kinds of rehabilitation have others done that helped them to recover use of their weak limbs?

It may sound odd to note above that I have "enjoyed" the process of stroke rehabilitation, as I have worked hard through much pain, agony and loss. I have lost a great deal of my physical prowess, perhaps permanently, as my left side became extremely weak (hemiparetic) due to a right-brain hemorrhagic stroke, and even after more than seven years of rehabilitation work, I still cannot walk well by myself. However, I have learned much through this process of pain, gain, *gambaru* (a Japanese concept from Zen Buddhism training that means to try beyond one's best, going it hard) and *gaman* (a Japanese Zen concept meaning to keep on going even when it gets tough) in two divergent societies over the past few years. I have learned how to (de)construct (in)sanity, how to endure or *gaman*, and about sharing love and expressing gratitude. I found that the people on the two sides of the Pacific Ocean have much to learn from each other. It is not only that the East should learn from the West (and vice versa) but also that we can take the best of both worlds and leave out the worst to come up with better models to improve our systems.

What made this journey "enjoyable" for me were the many awesome people who touched me spiritually as well as physically. I found myself loving both the men and the women near me—friends and family; my Seattle childhood family and my Japanese family; relatives and total strangers; paid helpers and volunteering (or roped-in) friends and family. So many people have made my journey significant through their contributions. Some were paid staff at hospitals and facilities doing their work professionally. Many were true friends when I needed them. Some were family who offered up their hearts and souls to nurture me back to good health. Many were people I met along the way, including other survivors who provided me with friendship and companionship through our similar struggles, including Mariam, Dane and Robyn in the United States. I met a wheelchair-bound high school boy in a hospital in the United States who was hit by a car while just hanging out with his friends, plus a woman in a wheelchair who said she was bitten by a tick that laid eggs which hatched into a hungry worm that feasted on her brain. I also advocate for other survivors and the families of those who were not able to survive.

In Japan, I have gained much from knowing Ms. Kumiko, Ms. Hidemi, and Ms. Eiko, among other fellow stroke survivors who attend the same day-care facility that I do. I express my gratitude as I also critique and reveal what I feel needs to change, to advocate for improvements for present and future survivors.

I have met many people and reconnected with others, including therapists, family, acquaintances and friends. They helped me or touched me in many ways when I was at my lowest point ever, very vulnerable and feeling worthless. Each person brought me the unique gift of their own spirit, and I have been greatly helped through actions, words and prayers. That is how I "enjoyed" the rehabilitation process.

CHAPTER 4

Types of Strokes

A stroke (also called "a brain attack") is defined as a lack of an essential oxygen-rich blood supply to the brain for an extended period of time, causing brain cells to die. There are said to be three main types of strokes (see www.stroke.org), which are as follows:

1. **Hemorrhagic stroke** is bleeding into the brain, usually caused by the swelling and bursting of a blood vessel (commonly termed an aneurysm). The flooding blood and spinal fluids cause brain cells to die and also lead to a rapid intracranial-pressure increase, causing an immediate life-threatening event. I survived a massive stroke of this type.

2. **Ischemic stroke** is caused by a blood clot or other types of blockages in a blood vessel leading into the brain, or in the brain itself, due to causes such as high cholesterol or atrial fibrillation (A-Fib). Ischemic strokes constitute the most common type of stroke. They often occur in the elderly.

3. **TIA (temporary or transient ischemic attack)**, or "a mini-stroke," is usually temporary (often lasting less than 24 hours) and is sometimes referred to as "a warning stroke," with others to follow.

How can I tell if I, or my spouse, or someone else around me, is having a stroke right now? There are several warning signs. A useful way to recall these signs is to remember the English word "FAST." In FAST, the F stands for "Face." Check to see if the person's face is drooping on one side (for example, ask them to smile). If worried about yourself, look in the mirror and observe whether your face is symmetrical or sagging on one side. Looking back at photos of me taken following the stroke, just before I was to travel back to Japan, I noticed my face drooping on the left (affected) side. (See the photo on page 25.) My sister later told me that my face drooped a lot after the stroke.

A is for "Arms." See if it is difficult to raise both arms. If one arm drops down, it is a possible sign of a stroke.

The S of FAST stands for "Speech." This is what I noticed about myself as I was talking with my sister when the stroke was first happening. I could hear myself having difficulty getting the words out. Talk with the person and try to determine if they have trouble speaking. I noticed my speech strangely slurring, even though my sister talking with me did not notice it.

The T of FAST stands for "Time." Time is very urgent. If at least one of the above prob-

Just before leaving the nursing home in Seattle to go to Japan. I flashed the peace sign as this is the typical photo pose still used in Japan before a photo is snapped (notice my face drooping on one side about a half year on from the stroke) (photograph by Edward Nudelman).

lems pertains (Face, Arms, Speech), then it is Time to act quickly. Call for an ambulance or get to a hospital right away. The quicker the person gets medical attention, the less damage may occur, and the better the chances are for survival.

If possible, please try to create your own way to remember these warning signs in your own language, if it is not English. For example, in Japanese, *ha-ya-i* might be a good word to recall, as it means "fast" or "speedy." The "ha" could stand for *hanashi*, or "talk." The "ya" in ha-**ya**-i could stand for *yabai*, which means "danger." Then the final "i" in ha-ya-**i** would stand for *igaku*, or "medical" (get medical attention immediately!). Otherwise, you could make your own acronym for an easy way to recall those essential warning signs.

CHAPTER 5

A Stroke of Endurance
Double Survivor

"Beware the Ides of March."
—*spoken by the Soothsayer in*
W. *Shakespeare's* Tragedy of Julius Caesar

In the quotation above, the Soothsayer in William Shakespeare's play *Julius Caesar* (1599) cries out, "Beware the Ides of March." (The Ides of March refers to mid–March or around March 15.) For me, this quote has special significance, for I experienced dangerous, life-threatening situations twice at around the ill-boding "Ides of March," two years apart, both of which I survived. Both events occurred without warning, and both caused various degrees of damage and needed a recovery period. Both could have been deadly, and both types of events commonly leave behind irreparable damage.

In a book of this nature, I thought it would be instructive, as well as enlightening, to provide a more detailed look at my first "Ides of March" experience, because I think it touches on the same necessity to struggle through hardship, which I underwent during my stroke. Perhaps this first event strengthened me in some way, or at least prepared me to battle through difficulty. Through the experience that I will now relate, I felt closer to the Japanese people, like never before, and I felt like I understood them better, having survived one of their many natural disasters. (Besides mega-quakes and tsunami, fires, volcanoes, wars, floods and so forth have been very frequent throughout Japanese history.)

In the mid-afternoon of March 11, 2011, I was in my office at Tohoku University in Sendai, Japan, working with Lily Noriko, my teaching assistant (hereafter, TA), who came in to help me prepare my classes for the coming week. I was on campus during the weekend, as I was on the Tohoku University entrance examination committee at the time and had helped write questions for the English examinations for the coming year. The final exam was scheduled for the next day. I needed to be around on exam days in case any problems should arise with my questions. My TA had brought me some very high-quality cakes, which we put in my office refrigerator to celebrate with upon completing our work. I looked forward to tasting them, but that had to wait until the next day, when I returned amid severe aftershocks to tidy up my office.

As Lily remained seated at my desk, working on my computer, I took a short break to use the restroom down the hallway, saying to her, "I will be right back." Then, about fifteen minutes later, just as I had returned, a very strong earthquake struck. I froze, expecting it to stop in seconds, as earthquakes usually did, but this time it did not stop right away, instead continuing for a heart-stopping *six minutes.* The quake became even fiercer with the next rattles and jolts. It made a tremendous amount of noise as the building shook, along with the clatter of my scores of bookshelves lining the walls of my office as they dumped my decades of work, papers and books knee-high into the center of the room. This was the infamous Tohoku earthquake and tsunami of 2011 (often referred to as the 3–11 Earthquake and Tsunami), and it was the fourth most powerful earthquake ever recorded, with over 16,000 dead and 228,000 people displaced.

I said to Lily, "This is really a big one!"

Lily's response made my heart drop into my stomach when she said what I already knew: "This is it! This is THE BIG ONE."

Lily is bright and savvy, and she knew what she was talking about. It caused me to feel very scared, almost in a panic. My heart started thumping. Lily was referring to "the BIG earthquake" that we in Japan were all expecting to occur at any time. Like a trailer for a Hollywood movie, "THE BIG ONE" was geared up to be really huge and disastrous. This earthquake did not disappoint—it was definitely **THE BIG ONE.** The mega-quake was so powerful that it actually shifted the Earth's axis and moved the islands of Japan by 2.4 meters (8 feet) farther out to sea, eastward.

Just then I saw my TA disappear under my desk. I felt that as the Japanese are well trained in what to do in earthquakes, she knew much more than I did. My natural instinct urged me to run down the stairs and get out of the building immediately, but instead I copied Lily, rushing over to join her under my desk. We hugged each other as the quake increased its ferocity, and the noise increased as my books jumped off the shelves. (Incidentally, another foreigner lecturer colleague of mine there from Korea, who did actually try to run out of his office to go out-side, fell down and suffered a severe leg injury, requiring a long hospi-talization, taking a year to heal.)

Just a few weeks earlier, there had been a strong earthquake in New Zealand that had brought down a building and killed many Jap-anese students there. It was still being reported in the news then, and I expected our building to collapse like that one in New Zealand, and also like the World Trade Center buildings of 9/11 (still fresh in our minds), starting with the top floor, where we were huddled under my desk. I tried to imagine how to minimize the damage and to assess the possi-bilities of survival and the pain we would have to endure in the process of our building collapsing. I could not believe that the building we were in could withstand such rattling and severe jolting, and I expected it to collapse at any second. But it held up amid lots of noise nearby of some-thing severely breaking in the room down the hall from my office, and I felt respect for Japanese architectural technology at that time when I realized our building had remained intact. It was not until much later that I learned that the women's toilet that I had just left minutes earlier had been compromised when the ceiling broke down on top of the toi-let. There was a so-called penthouse structure above the fifth-floor ceil-ing, which also held the elevator shaft, and that, too, seemed to have broken in the mega-quake. Surely I would have been killed sitting there on the toilet with my jeans down around my ankles. I most likely would have remained there after the first quakes, having remembered hear-ing that the toilets or baths are the safest rooms in a house during earth-quakes. But it was not so in this case.

I was also concerned about having a heart attack, as I was hyper-ventilating. I heard my voice quaver when I suggested to my TA (and to myself) to "calm down." Lying to her—and to myself, too—I said, "I'm all right!" Whew, whew, pant, pant. "How are you?" She answered in a similar lie. And we went several rounds with it, asking and answering in the same lie.

Finally the shaking ceased, and shortly after that a professor whose office was nearby, Professor Asakawa, knocked on my door, calling out to see if we were all right. We then emerged and, crunching my decades of work underfoot, went running out of there. We went down the back stairwell and assembled outside of the building with many others. Some 25 of us formed a circle, looking inward at each other's shocked faces as we stood shivering in the falling snow in the parking lot, donning white and orange helmets, bracing ourselves for the aftershocks, which

My office building, where I was at the time of the mega-quake in Sendai, Japan, on March 11, 2011. The second window from left is at the women's toilet that I had left just moments before the quake struck. The broken part is the "penthouse" over the fifth floor (author's photograph).

were frequent and fierce. Few had thought to grab their coats or their car keys, but my car keys were in the pocket of the down vest that I had been wearing all day. I had also grabbed my pouch, which is like a purse. My cell phone dangled from a case around my neck. We did not know what damage had occurred, and we tried to get news from the one person holding a battery-operated radio. It was difficult for me to understand what was going on in Japanese, as there was no official English information then. I just knew we were a part of history without knowing any details until much later.

I was in too much shock to pay attention to the news even though I wanted information. We learned that the earthquake had a magnitude of 9.1—the largest earthquake ever recorded in Japan, and about the fourth largest globally. We were far enough away from the ocean that we did not have to fear any tsunami (and apparently far enough away from the nuclear meltdown to not have to worry about radiation exposure just yet).

Many tried unsuccessfully to use their phones to call loved ones.

Just then my phone rang, and when I answered it, my (adult) son, calling from Hirosaki, Aomori, over 330 kilometers to the northeast of Sendai, said to me, "Mom, there was a huge earthquake here just now and the electricity went out." It was reassuring to hear that both he and my husband were safe. He did not know that where I was, in Sendai, was actually much closer to the epicenter of the quake (Sendai was rated at *Shindou* 6 [violent], which is nearly the highest on the Japanese ranking system of seismic intensity, from 0 to 6 plus; *shindou*—or intensity of the shaking—differs due to the distance from the quake's epicenter.)

Next, I offered to let Professor Asakawa warm up by sitting in my car with the engine on; he could also watch the news for a while on the navigation screen in my car. Finally, we all began to break up. Still not knowing the severity of the earthquake aftermath, I walked over to the entrance exam office nearby to clarify that the exam scheduled for the next morning was officially off and that I did not need to show up there early the next morning as scheduled. I then walked to my home nearby, still wearing the orange helmet I had borrowed, to check out the damage in my apartment. When I passed the police box, I peeked in and asked where we should go, and a policeman pointed out the *hinanjou* (refuge shelter) nearby.

When I walked up to the parking lot of my apartment complex, I saw a foreign woman from Indonesia named Ary, whom I knew to be the wife of Professor Koike, who lived in the same building as me. She did not speak any Japanese, and she looked very scared and anxious and was very shocked, as she had never experienced an earthquake before. When she said that she could not contact her husband, I spoke to her in English, saying that I would help her and that in the meantime she should go to the *hinanjou* just down the way. I helped her to practice how to say correctly in Japanese the word for refuge shelter to the police or passersby: "*Hinanjou wa doko desuka?*" ("Where is the refuge shelter?")

I ran up the steps to my fourth-floor apartment in an old building built in the early 1960s. It was strewn with broken glass from all of my dishes, which had jumped out of my Taisho-era (1920s) *cha-dansu* (tea chest), along with its glass doors, which were now also broken and lying on the floor. My toppled-over TV and microwave oven seemed to be all right at first, with no broken glass. (Later I found the microwave oven to be broken after all, and I had to replace it.) There was no water, electricity or gas available then. There was also no heat, as the heaters required electricity along with kerosene. Without water, I could not clean up, and the toilet also could not be used. The room stank of soy sauce, as the red-topped, easy-spill-out dispenser bottle had tumbled from the shelf and ricocheted onto the *fusuma* paper door, splattering my room with smelly black soy sauce here and there, eventually landing on and soaking the hand-made Tibetan carpet that I had purchased in Nepal decades earlier. I sighed and swept up the broken glass.

I threw a few things into my backpack, and then, donning the borrowed orange helmet again, I headed over to the nearby *hinanjou* where I had directed Ary to go. There, most of the people from my university-owned apartment building had already assembled. Ary beckoned me over to their corner, and I joined them, becoming part of a *kizuna* (bonded) group over the next several days as we spent our nights sleeping closely together. Even though we had barely ever spoken before, now we found our bodies intimately touching each other in the refuge center, head to foot like sardines where we slept together. We endured fierce aftershocks as we shared food there on the first night and got to know each other. Then, during the daytime, we managed to prepare two hot meals daily at Professor Koike's first-floor apartment until the electricity was restored some four days later.

The hardest part was not knowing how long we would have to continue like that without electricity, gasoline for the car, natural gas at home for baths and cooking, and proper food, water and other infrastructural things we had come to rely on in highly efficient Japan, such as trains, buses, telephone, cell phones and highways.

Among us were several experts in radiation, including Professor Koike. There were also a few geologists, one of whom informed me that my hometown, Seattle, should expect to be hit by a large earthquake and tsunami in the near future. I took comfort in being part of a group of such experts and kind people. Koike came to serve as the unofficial leader of our group after he invited us all (along with some of his colleagues and students from his lab) to gather in his first-floor apartment at 1:00 p.m. to make lunch together after we left the refuge center on the first morning after the earthquake. I was happy to have him as our leader and felt gratitude. It was also helpful that he spoke English, as he tried to keep Ary informed, since she did not understand Japanese at all, and they allowed me to listen in on what he said to her.

Koike suggested, "*yakuwari buntan*" ("Let's split up the tasks").

For my part, to begin with, I happened to have an old-model kerosene heater that did not require any electricity and that could heat up water or food, so we used that to cook meals, warm up the room, and heat water for cleaning. We brought down all of the foods from our defrosting refrigerators and other foods that we could contribute to making meals and items to be shared. I also offered to let people use my car for some errands. Those unable to contribute any food provided a bit of cash for extra supplies. Younger people went out by bicycle to wait in long lines for other supplies that we needed. I and a few others had extra kerosene tanks for the heater/stove. Someone produced a canister-fueled camping stove that we used as a second burner for cooking food. So, with all of our efforts and contributions, the seventeen of us (including Koike's colleagues and students) were able to live quite nicely over those four days at our apartments and four nights at the *hinanjou* shelter, where there was a generator to give us light, a bit of heat and the security of sleeping together.

It always feels better to be with others in times of crisis than to be alone, I strongly felt. That might be deep in our DNA, perhaps from the days of sleeping in a jungle around a communal fire, surrounded by dangerous hungry animals. In a group, I felt secure. Even if the roof were to collapse at the refuge center during an aftershock, I felt that it was better to die together than to have to die alone. In the end, I walked away from that calamity without even a scratch, even though more than 15,000 people near me were swept away in the tsunami and killed and over 2,500 are still missing. In addition, 230,000 homes were lost and many people had to live in temporary shelters. Others lost loved ones and property, and many more had to be evacuated due to contamination from a Level 7 nuclear core meltdown or having their homes damaged or swept away.

The morning after the mega-quake, I went back to my office to try to clean up a bit for a few hours amid very frequent, severe aftershocks, which unnerved me greatly. (See the photo on page 33.) I found the helmet and earthquake kit that had been issued to each of us a few months earlier in my office, under a large pile of books. The cakes that Lily had brought the day before were still fresh in my defrosted refrigerator. I ate one there and brought the rest back to Koike's apartment for others to enjoy. This time, we were celebrating life!

Just after the electricity was restored a few days later and we went home from the refuge shelter, I was contacted by some Kyoto colleagues who were sending a volunteer group up from Kyoto to Tohoku to prepare some cheering carnival-type foods for the survivors of the disaster. They brought nourishing soup and *takoyaki* (squid balls), hot coffee, popped rice made in a very traditional rice popper from around the

Back in my office the day after the mega-quake to tidy up amid severe aftershocks (author's photograph).

Taisho or Meiji Period, and other such foods. I joined them for a few days, making several stops in some of the worst-hit spots in Tohoku, and I helped them to administer foods, music and warmth to the locals there.

The sea-facing places had a heavy stench of rotting sea and human waste for weeks, even though everyone was scurrying to clean up the place and restore it to the way it was before. I went with a friend from Tokyo who came up to visit me to a restaurant in a resort area called Matsushima, in the middle of the tsunami-hit areas, and I got the seat of my pants soaked from sitting on one of their chairs a few weeks after the tsunami had washed into their restaurant. But the *tempura* lunch was delicious, and we went back there a year later, when my friend from Tokyo came to visit again. While I was doing the volunteer work in those places, I began to practice how to tell the story of *The Magic Fan* among children whom we had met there.

While in the refuge shelter, Koike told me of his colleague who worked at Microsoft in Seattle, my hometown. I hoped to stop in Seattle en route to present a conference paper in Chicago, but I would need to make my way to the airport within the next week, when I was scheduled to fly out. I had already officially applied for the days off from work for that and had paid for the entire trip, including the bullet train tickets to get to the airport, airfare, hotels and other things.

At Microsoft, there were many Japanese people and Japanese supporters on staff who wanted more information about what had happened in Tohoku, as they were unable to return to Japan just then. They had seen more poignant images of the tsunami damage on TV in the United States than we had yet seen, and I did not really know much about what had happened yet. It was arranged that a few days after my arrival in Seattle, I would contact Koike's friend and then go to Microsoft and make a presentation about what had happened in Japan from my viewpoint. With photos from others in our group, I put together a PowerPoint presentation to tell our story as best as I could. I doubted that I could get to Narita Airport, though, as all roads and trains were closed due to earthquake damage. Many people, especially foreigners, were scrambling to get tickets out of Japan, but I felt very reluctant to leave just then. I wanted to stay and help out as much as I could and be with my family there. But that would have to wait a few weeks until my return.

Amazingly, I just barely made it to the airport on time by taking a very roundabout bus and train trip, zigzagging across Japan and back, stopping along the way to stay a few nights at the house of the family of a colleague of mine in Yamagata, which I reached by bus after waiting several hours in a long line of people in Sendai. I was able to rest, get cleaned up and respond to emails there for a few days, while my colleague went around trying to get food and other necessities like a "hunter-and-gatherer." I spent another night in an expensive resort hotel facing the Seto Inland Sea, as it was the only hotel with a vacancy. I was not excited about having an ocean view then. Luckily, I was later able to get on a bullet train to Tokyo, where I made my way to the airport.

After becoming very sick with an infrequent fever while at the conference in Chicago, I realized just how stressed I had become through the ordeal. I was both reluctant to return to Japan and anxious to return quickly.

I have great respect for Microsoft technicians and felt privileged to be asked to go there. I also felt that I had a story that needed telling and was delighted to have an interested audience who wanted to hear about it. My presentation went off well there, and when I told them that I had started a volunteer project for survivors, they were eager to help.

The project had started with a little Japanese fifth-grade girl whose house had been washed away, whom my university student, Minako, had found in a refuge center while doing volunteer tutoring work of her own. I went with Minako to meet the girl and her family one evening after work. We promised the little girl that we would try to teach English to her and her friends at her school.

After finding out the name of her school, we contacted them about volunteering to conduct classes for fifth graders in their newly launched English program. The elementary school teachers did not really have good ideas of how to teach English in elementary school at that time, and the school was delighted to accommodate our request when we visited there. And so that is where we concentrated on the volunteer project. As all of Japan was just starting a new program of teaching English in the fifth and sixth grades of elementary schools, there was a lot of confusion among teachers tasked with the new job, and I was happy to offer the one skill I had that I thought might best help them. I made the lesson plans (sometimes with university students' help) and recruited volunteer students to conduct the classes. As I had previously worked at another college in the *Kodomo Eigo Gakka* (Department of Early English Education), I had a lot of ideas, materials, and experience for the project.

I recruited many foreign students who could already speak English well and who were interested in Japanese education and culture. I also recruited many Japanese students who were eager to volunteer in that region and who were very interested in English and connecting with foreign students. I had mistakenly assumed, in stereotypical thinking, that the best English teachers among them would be the attractive blonde-haired, blue-eyed Americans or Europeans, rather than the Asian English teachers. It turned out that the best teacher of English among us all, myself included, was a Vietnamese girl, whom we called Ti, who was a licensed, experienced English teacher. She had skills and intrinsic charisma as a teacher, with a true talent for engaging children. I called the volunteer girls "my girls." (See the photo on page 36.)

I had a children's picture book that I had bought decades earlier for my son, about a tsunami in Japan, titled *The Magic Fan* (1989), and I wanted to share the tsunami rebuilding story with the children of Tohoku. I felt it was a very lovely place to start, as it was a story set in Japan about a boy who experiences a tsunami and rebuilds his broken village with the help of a magic fan that he finds, which provides answers to him. The illustrations are of very high quality, and the story

Me with "my girls" in their national costumes—from left: Lily (Japanese); my
TA; a Chinese student; a Vietnamese student; Ti (Vietnamese); me (in center);
Nurani on my left (Bangladeshi); Valencia (Italian); Sulastri, my Ph.D. student
(Malaysian); Eri (Japanese), a student who later went to France to study for a
year or so (author's photograph).

is nicely told. The book was written and illustrated by a native Seattle-
ite from my hometown, named Keith Baker. When I emailed him and
asked him to make a contribution to our project, he agreed and contributed seventy books. Furthermore, he had his publisher (Houghton
Mifflin Harcourt) match that donation, so along with the help of the
Japanese staff at Microsoft (who also contributed many books and other
items), we were ready to begin. People at Microsoft also helped us to set
up a Facebook page for the project. We kept our operations very simple
by only receiving books (all sent to my university work address) and no
money at all, so we did not need to set up a bank account.

We called it "The Tohoku Tsunami Rehabilitation Project" (or "the
TTRP"). The Facebook page seems to still be accessible (and photos can
be viewed), but the project is closed now, and we are disbanded and
no longer seeking books or other donations. We conducted volunteer
English lessons and activities for over two years at the little girl's elementary school in Sendai. Many of the pupils and staff had lost loved
ones or their homes, their workplaces and other property, which had
been washed away by the tsunami. We started just after the earthquake
and continued for a few years.

Volunteer teaching a Halloween-themed English lesson at an elementary school in Miyagi after the mega-quake. My colleague, Joseph S. (American), is on the left; Ti (Vietnamese) is in the middle and Maya (Japanese) on the right (author's photograph).

In the spirit of learning English, I had given the school a list of popular American names for girls and boys upon their request. They prepared nametags with the American names in each class. Ms. Ti was the only one among us who actually used those names to call upon the children, and her natural teaching skills surprised not only us but also the school staff, including the teachers and the school principal who had taken the power name of "Apollo." Ti would look out at the class after we had taught a certain lesson and then point and say, for example, to a shy Japanese boy (with the nametag "Steven"), "OK, Steven, what do you want for Christmas?"

Ti would beckon the shy boy to answer with her arm movement while pointing to the cards we had made of various presents that children enjoy at Christmas. The boy would then stand up and answer in a clear, loud voice, saying, "I want *a video game* for Christmas," and so forth. We presented each child and their teachers with copies of the donated *Magic Fan* book as presents during the late December Christmas-themed lesson.

We also had a Halloween-themed lesson there (see the photo on page 37), two months earlier in October, when we gave each child a small bag of American candies to take home, among other fun lessons.

In addition, I gave each child a color copy of an unpublished children's book about Christmas that I had made myself, called *The Christmas Tree*. We tried to make learning English fun and memorable for them, and I think we succeeded in that. I often purchased materials for the lessons in the dollar/one-hundred-yen shop to keep costs down, but I was happy to pay out of pocket a bit for such materials or gifts for the pupils.

Sadly, I had to discontinue activities there after I became unable to return to my Sendai office, although I am planning to write a book about teaching schoolchildren in Japan and include some of those things.

Some of the best helpers in that project graduated and left Sendai, returning to their countries or hometowns, including Ti to Vietnam, Nurani to Bangladesh, Sulastri and LC to Malaysia, and so forth. In Japan, Minako, Eri, Lily, Shihori, Courtney and Kaji all graduated, and most of them left Sendai. I was sorry not to be able to say my last "good-bye" to most of my beloved students who left Sendai in my absence, but I wish them all very well on their life paths and look forward to the day when our paths might cross again.

We distributed all of the donated books, including some donated by the Association of Foreign Wives of Japanese (AFWJ). We gifted most of the books to pupils in their fifth-grade English classes over two years at the school originally selected. Other books went to local public libraries, school libraries or teachers in Tohoku. I hope that everyone seeing those books will feel happy and give thanks to the author, to the publisher, and to the Japanese people and supporters of Japanese people working in Seattle at Microsoft who contributed them, as I do.

I hope in relating this experience of extreme peril, readers will have a better understanding of a significant event in history, as well as how it might have prepared me for what was to follow in my life. I feel, having undergone this experience, that I have learned at least three kernels of truth regarding the Japanese psyche that I would like to share: the power of nature and the resolve to overcome; the vulnerability of mankind and how easily and swiftly things can go from bad to worse; and, finally, the brevity of life and our youth.

CHAPTER 6

A Stroke of Disruption

Near-Perfect Health Before the Stroke

Aside from high blood pressure that was being managed with medications, I feel my physical and mental health preceding the stroke was excellent. At the time of my stroke, I had been living in Japan for some three decades. I had married a Japanese man, and we had become a family of three. We ate mostly healthy *washoku*, or Japanese food. I thought of myself as being in "near-perfect health" then and, further, paid attention to staying fit and healthy, as did most Japanese. I had yearly extensive health checks through my place of employment along with my regular visits to my doctor, who monitored blood tests and the medications for high blood pressure and for my thyroid. I took my prescribed medications twice daily without fail. I went to the gym regularly, at least three or four times weekly, and more on weekends, on holidays or during long vacations. I was careful about what I ate and about keeping my body weight under moderate control.

I was very mentally stable, and always had been. I was as "regular" as a clock until after the stroke, when I was not able to exercise much. I ate high-fiber, low-fat, and low-sugar foods. I tried to limit my salt intake. I seldom had desserts or sweets, except fruits. I ate small quantities of high-quality foods for every meal, and I seldom snacked, like most Japanese. I seldom ate red meat but often had fish, seafood, and sometimes chicken. I did not smoke tobacco or linger in smoky environments, and I seldom drank alcohol (and then always in moderation). At age 62, I felt young and healthy. I felt that I looked much younger than my peers and was constantly told so by others. I also dressed youthfully and listened to youthful music. My thoughts and preferences were young. I was surrounded by university students, mostly in their twenties. I was physically strong, in good shape, and otherwise very healthy.

I think my stress levels must have been quite high at that time, but it had become "the new normal" for me, along with my high blood pressure. I did not seem to notice my blood pressure getting overly high very often, and I came to live with the condition, feeling energized all of the time and mentally driven to keep going at full speed. Most of my forays were overseas to academic conferences, where I would present papers. I had entered a graduate Ph.D. program in England, where I went as often as was possible for intensive teaching programs. Sometimes, through my university job, I was charged with taking students overseas, which was more stressful than going on my own. My out-of-control blood pressure was later thought to be one of the main causes of the stroke, even while taking medication. It is counterintuitive that this deadly high blood pressure is what some people imagine might provide extra energy to keep on going when others have long since tired out. However, this was not the case, and high blood pressure (termed the silent killer) has no effect on behavior, mood or energy levels.

I had also recently been invited to give academic presentations of my research work at several international conferences, some of them held locally in Japan and some overseas. I always accepted such requests when asked. I felt that I was "on a roll" then, but I was not resting enough between my overseas and local travels to conferences.

Even though I was very busy at the time, I felt compelled to continue the volunteer project after the 2011 triple disaster in Tohoku, along with the recruited students (see Chapter 5). At the same time, I tried to encourage all of those students to present papers at local international conferences held in Japan. I knew that it would be good for them to have on their resumes. I was willing to spend extra time to help them prepare their presentations, as a way to give back to them for the work they did for me by being my teaching assistants or helping with my volunteer project after the earthquake and tsunami.

Some of my students at Tohoku University seemed unable to keep up with me. When I tried to encourage them to attend conferences with me and present papers at a particular local event for girls or women, called WELL (Women Educators and Language Learners), many declined. I was on the executive board, and we tried to make it very student-friendly. I was willing to check their work for them beforehand, and to conduct practice sessions with them too, but many of them were too busy with other schoolwork, part-time work and job hunting. Several of "my girls" happily took up the challenge, while others felt pressured and believed that they could not keep up with my pace. Some of them—starting with Meng, a bright student from China—came to refer to me as "Superwoman." I, in turn, referred to them as "my girls," and I came to love many of them as if they were my own daughters.

Some of "my girls" introduced several boys who were also interested in doing volunteer work teaching English following the mega-quake. Some of the boys asked me to introduce them to other conferences of English teaching that were also open to boys, and one savvy Japanese student in particular, whom we called "Kaji-kun," took up the challenge.

I introduced Kaji-kun to a local professional event. I helped him to prepare his proposal, which was accepted. Then we worked to fire up his PowerPoint presentation. At the event, his presentation was very good. He was the only student presenter among university professors and native English-speaker presenters. He did a superb job speaking in English, and he fielded many questions from his large audience of mostly English-speaking foreigners. I think it helped him later when he applied to and was accepted into a graduate school at the University of Hawai'i.

Unlike stroke memoirist Jill Bolte Taylor, who was a brain anatomist, I write this memoir from the viewpoint of a stroke survivor or as a resident/user of facilities. I was not a stroke or brain professional, a respected person in the medical field, but one who was at the bottom of the ranking. I had no prior knowledge of my condition and felt extremely vulnerable, fragile and needy on a day-to-day basis. In my own field, I was at the pinnacle of my career after completing my doctorate a few years earlier and then having written a book based on the dissertation thesis, titled *Hybrid Identities and Adolescent Girls: Being "Half" in Japan* (2010). This book was awarded a prize from the International Gender and Language Association, which judged it to be the "best book on gender and language" for 2010–2011.

I have tried to ascertain what caused my stroke. I was told by my sister, who heard it from my doctor in the United States, that the main cause of my stroke was "high blood pressure that had gotten out of control." I had been taking two different types of blood-pressure-reducing medicines twice daily at the time of the stroke. That dosage had to be later increased to three times daily.

Prior to my stroke, I had carefully prepared a large packet of medicines in Japan to take with me on my trip to the United States, costing me some 20,000 Japanese yen. I was careful to take them as prescribed twice daily. After my stroke, entering the U.S. nursing facility, I was horrified when my medicines were all dumped in the garbage bin upon arrival there, to be replaced by a whole new regimen of other, costly U.S.-made medicines. Then those medicines that I purchased in the United States were again dumped in the garbage bin in the hospital back in Japan months later and there replaced by similar costly Japanese medications. Thus began the East/West battle.

Besides my out-of-control high blood pressure, I had had minor foot surgery (in December 2012), which took place just three months prior to the stroke. For the anesthesia, I had an epidural (also called "a spinal" or "a saddle block"), which is often used with birthing and C-sections or other surgeries below the waist, including hip and knee replacements and leg fractures. Any anesthetic drugs can be dangerous, but epidurals are considered safer than many types of general anesthesia. I have often wondered if the anesthesia or the surgery may have contributed to my stroke, although I cannot say for sure.

For other people, other causes of strokes may include smoking, heavy drinking, high cholesterol, metabolic syndrome, obesity, diabetes, A-Fib, hypertension or stress. The biggest lesson to learn here that I would like to pass on to others is to "keep your blood pressure under good control." At one point I think my doctor in Japan may have suggested increasing my blood-pressure medications, with me wanting to hold back, having been told that my liver was showing signs of being affected by overmedication. If I could go back in time, I would agree to increase my medications!

Also, through my Internet searches, I discovered that there is a correlation (but not necessarily a causal link) between people having migraine headaches, especially with auras, and then later having a stroke. I used to have regular monthly migraine headaches (often on the right side of my head) corresponding with my menstrual cycle. They had stopped at menopause, a few years before the stroke in my right brain-hemisphere. People with migraine headaches may want to consult their doctor about this issue.

Finally, genetic predisposition is no doubt a strong determinant, and in my case, my paternal grandfather died prematurely of a stroke when I was only five years old. I'm not sure if that stroke was hemorrhagic or a clot, but the possibility exists that I had a natural weakening of a vessel in my brain.

CHAPTER 7

A Stroke of Wonder

The Day I Went into a Coma, Entering a Parallel World

On the day that I went into a coma for several weeks, I did not have any warning, nor did I feel unwell. I had no headache, no dizziness, no faint feeling, as I had occasionally felt over a few years, especially after long, stressful flights. I felt perfectly fine that morning and was anxious to get on with the day, as my precious time in Seattle was limited and there were many things I had wanted to do in my week or so there before moving on to the real purpose of my trip, which was to go on to Los Angeles for a conference, where I had been asked to present a paper on my recent research about hybridity, or the identities of mixed races— specifically of Japanese and Caucasian Americans. In Japan, *haafu* is the current word referring to mixed-ethnic, mixed-race children who are half–Japanese and half-white. They are called *happa* in Hawaii (where the term originated) and in other parts of the United States. I was very much looking forward to the conference/festival and had prepared my paper well for it. Later, my speech therapist in the nursing facility in the United States asked me to do an oral presentation of the paper for him to test my cognition after the stroke. So I practiced it for that too, and felt I could deliver it well, but it was quite impossible for me to travel to Los Angeles. In addition, my brother had already wisely cancelled my attendance, which was best, as I might have tried to go there—I was that determined.

Early on in the rehabilitation ward of the nursing home I was admitted to in north Seattle, I struggled to make much progress. I could hardly get myself out of bed, even with help from an aide, or to the toilet at that time. I could not stand up unaided. I was in no shape to travel and had not acquired or worked out yet how to use a cane, nor did I have a leg brace. I could not walk at all then. Even if I had had a nurse or a relative go with me to Los Angeles (which I had not arranged), it would have been nearly impossible—or very difficult at the least. I would have to embark on lots of hard work in rehabilitation training for more than a year before travel might be an option, and then only under the best of conditions.

Before my stroke, while in Seattle, I had planned to go shopping, visiting and partying with friends and relatives and to do the kinds of things that I seldom was able to enjoy in Japan. My sister had been driving around with me since the day before, and we were looking for a house for sale in north Seattle that I could purchase and that she would live in and manage while paying me a small amount of rent. So both of us had a stake in the house, but I was limited by the small amount of what I could afford. We both wanted a "good deal," as did the hundreds of others searching for homes at the same time and place. I found house hunting to be very competitive and tiring. The housing market in Seattle was extremely hot at that time, and the available homes were "sad," as they all offered very poor value for the money being asked for them. Many were moldy, dark and in very poor condition. I was still quite a bit jet-lagged from my flight over from Japan, having arrived just a few days prior, with little sleep or rest. But we were nearly finished for the day and about ready to return home for dinner. I recall talking to my sister as she was driving. I noticed my speech seemed almost to be slurred and remembered recently hearing on television that slurred speech was one of several signs of a stroke. I asked my sister if she, too, had noticed my speech changing; she said that she did not, but said I certainly seemed tired.

We arrived back at my sister's house, and I rallied to help get dinner prepared. I was not hungry but felt a responsibility to make a suitable dinner for my son, who had accompanied me on my trip. It was very hard to prepare a healthy dinner that he could eat, as he had many severe food allergies and was a fussy eater, but finally I did it with the help of my sister, and I ate something light myself. That was to be my last regular meal before entering a coma for several weeks. I never felt any particular pain in my head as the stroke was occurring. Pain might have helped to give it more urgency.

Over a year later, my sister told me that my son and I had an argument after dinner, exchanging bad words. I was continuing to feel unwell, and I recall the nagging notion that "time was important." I went upstairs to talk with my sister about it. She seemed to know much about medical/health issues. I told her that I did not feel well. She moved over and invited me to get up on the bed and rest. That is my last memory before losing consciousness. She later told me that soon afterward, I slid off the bed onto the floor, making a loud thump. She called 911 for an ambulance, but I was already out cold and have no memory of anything. My sister told me that she had my son wait at the door to let the emergency crew in, as she was afraid to leave me, and she also called my brother for backup help. My son rode in the ambulance with me to the hospital, according to what my sister told me later. It seems that I was first taken to the University of Washington Medical Center and then transferred to Harborview Medical Center (HMC), which has superior facilities and centers, including a comprehensive stroke center, a neurosciences institute and a comprehensive acute rehabilitation and reconstruction center, among others.

I had fallen into a coma, and then I was put into a medically induced coma to stabilize my brain from that time onward and placed in the ICU. The next memory I have is finding myself newly married to the fifth son of a wealthy Chinese family of pig and goat ranchers in nineteenth-century rural China, named Gotama. I seemed to have warped into another world. I heard in my mind the name "Gotama," which I think is actually the Japanese pronunciation of a move in taichi, which my teacher in Japan would call out while doing the movements. I heard it as "Go-tama" and interpreted the "go" as meaning "five" in Japanese—thus the fifth son of the family. (The name is also similar to the name of the prophet Gaotama Buddha, or "Siddhartha Gaotama Buddha.") As for the goat and pig farming, I think I had a drawing in a taichi book somewhere that looks like a goat head on a man doing taichi, although I cannot locate the drawing. But this image seems to have come out of taichi, which I started practicing around 1975 in Tokyo and then later in Hong Kong, Taiwan and Osaka. I also taught taichi for some time in and around Seattle, from around 1978 to 1982. At the time of the stroke I was not doing taichi regularly, but for some reason that name remained in my memory and added to the formation of this dream or illusion. I felt very agitated in the dream-world.

In this dream-world, I suddenly find myself walking down a dusty unpaved road fringed by a lush green forest of pine and cedar trees and other greenery. I am carrying heavy things in cloth bags.

My mother-in-law steps forward and welcomes me into my new home and shows me my room, which is heaped high with lots of new bedding and furniture, much of it wrapped in red paper, before she starts trying to explain things to me. I drop my bags there in that room. My new husband is nowhere in sight, and I feel quite uneasy, as my knowledge of Chinese is very limited, but fortunately I have already been well informed of what my first task is to be.

I am supposed to make a huge vat of delicious soup that will feed our entire village for a summer festival coming up very soon, perhaps later that same day. I have had no chance to rest and need to get down to work immediately. I had met Mamma already several times before, so our faces are familiar to each other. Then Mamma wraps her arms around me to secure an apron around my waist so I can begin my work. Our family sponsors this event every year in appreciation for all of the help the villagers have contributed by working for us at low wages. The soup was made by the wife of the fourth son last year, as I looked on, and I feel pressure to make this year's soup better than last year's. I must make the soup fill the large vat, which sits before my eyes. I am informed that it should feed around 100 people this year, most of whom will be adults. It will be an insult to all if the soup does not meet the highest standards.

I begin by chopping the vegetables and cutting the meats while waiting for the water to boil. I am getting hot, and the smell is wafting all around me. I feel the walls creaking from the heat. I find three large cans of cut tomatoes, wash the lids, open them and pour the contents into the vat of soup-water, which I have set over the fire to boil. I am relieved that someone has already done the necessary shopping for the soup and prepared the fire and brought the water in to the large pot.

I find a large wok and fry up the two types of meat together first— half pork and half goat meat, over three kilos in total—along with some garlic, which I chop up well. I drain off as much extra fat as I can, pouring the boiling fat into an emptied tomato can. Then I begin looking for other vegetables to put in the soup. There is no refrigerator, but, directed by my mother-in-law, I find a cool pantry. In there, I find some vegetables. I wash, peel and chop up carrots, potatoes of two different types, a *daikon* (a Japanese giant white radish) and burdock root and put them all in the soup. Then I proceed to wash, chop and add two types of fresh Chinese mushrooms and two other local root vegetables.

Continuing with my task, I chop up onions and fry them in some of the grease left in the pan from the meat. It's starting to smell even better now. I add the onions to the soup and stir it and then add both Japanese and Chinese miso. Then I wash and cut up an entire Chinese cabbage and add it to the huge pot. Next, I add some clear rice noodles and some Chinese wheat noodles that have already been boiled, but, upon another tasting, I feel that the flavor is not quite right; it needs something else. I add a small amount of fish sauce from Vietnam and Thai hot sauce, which I locate in an upper cupboard. Then I add dried Japanese *shiitake* mushrooms, broken up into small pieces. I also spot some fresh tofu, which I cut up into bite-sized pieces and add to the pot. Finally, I squirt in some Japanese *tonkatsu* sauce to sweeten it up and some Japanese soy sauce to give it a saltier flavor as well. Luckily, they have a well-stocked kitchen with flavorings from all over Asia.

I stir the soup and taste the broth again. It seems to be almost complete. I wait for the soup to come to a boil again. Then I call it complete after another taste to test if all the vegetables have been cooked enough. I wipe my brow of perspiration and sit down for a moment to rest from the exhaustion I now feel. I decide to add about a cup or so of Japanese rice wine and also about two liters of extra water after tasting the soup again. I then add plenty of black pepper. The vegetables are soft, and I feel the taste to be deep and complex. I skim off some of the brine that has risen to the top of the pot and throw it out. Next, I take a clean saucer and scoop out some broth, a few vegetables, some goat meat and also some pork meat, and I ask Mamma to taste it. She slurps it loudly and mumbles that it is good, using one of the few Chinese words that I know from practicing taichi in Osaka, Japan, years before with a teacher from Beijing: "*Dui, dui*" ("good, good").

I know that Mamma approves of the flavor. So the soup is finished, and I slide the heavy pot off the fire along the railing for that purpose. I have passed my first test as the new wife of the fifth son there, and I have gotten along well with my new mother-in-law, I think, but I feel exhausted and tense. I just want to leave and go back home.

"How can I get out of here?" I remember thinking. "This place is stressful, and I want to go home as soon as possible."

It is also very hot, and people begin lining up, increasing my stress. I think that it was shortly after the completion of the soup that I awoke from the coma.

CHAPTER 8

A Stroke of Grace

Waking Up After an "Out-of-Body Experience"

"Laurel, wake up. Wake up, Laurel."

I heard a reverberating sound in my ears/mind/heart. My brother was urgently calling out to me, "Laurel, wake up. Wake up, Laurel. Open your eyes."

My sister's voice also reverberated in my mind. My mother and Susie, my sister-in-law, likewise called out to me. But it was my son Jonah-Iori's voice that echoed the most, with his plaintive voice merely saying in a loud, nasal, somewhat whiney tone, "Mommy, Mommy, Moo-oomy, Maa-aa-my. Mommy, Mommy, Mommy, Mo-oomy, Maa-aa-my."

That voice has always had so much control over me; even into his adulthood, it got me to react. It was as if he had said to me, "Mommy, do not leave me alone here. I need you. Come back. Mommy, I feel lonely. Come here now! Mommy, come back right now. Come back here and answer me. Pay attention to me, now! Can't you hear all of us calling you? Wake up now!"

I think that I must have woken up rather soon after that.

I had thought that perhaps my doctor had called in all of my family due to some drastic change in my condition. Either I was about to die or I was showing signs of starting to wake up. They were there either to say "Good-bye!" or to try to awaken me before it might be too late. Either way, I felt it must have been some turning point. It was like I had wanted to say to them, "Hey, what are you all looking at? I want to see too. Please let me join you all."

Many people watched over me while I was in the ICU (see the photos on page 51).

I felt like I was in a movie, and I wanted to be a part of the audience (not the show) and see what they were seeing, so I must have willed my spirit to rise up in an "out-of-body experience," and then I turned over to look downward at my helpless body lying on the bed and those around me, calling out to me. Being the proactive person that I am, and since all of these professionals and loved ones around me still had not been able to help me, I would have to take matters into my own hands, I felt. So I tried to think of how I could help myself. I concentrated very hard until it became clear to me: "I need to reunite my spirit with my body in order to survive

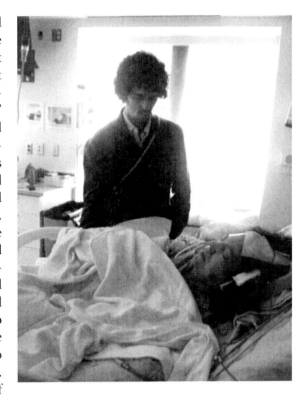

"Wake up, Mommy, Mommy, Mommy, Mommy, wake up now." When I had an "out-of-body experience," I rose up, turned over and looked down, and this is what I saw: my son, Jonah-Iori, looking down at me on the bed calling out, "Mommy" (notice all of the tubes coming from my brain to drain out excess fluids) (photograph by Edward Nudelman).

this moment," before my spirit drifted too far away. So that is what I did with urgency, as I lowered my spirit back down and reconnected it with my body. But I must not have reunited the left side well enough, as it is still very weak today, as I write this seven years later.

Later, I pondered how I could have control over my spirit like that. Was my spirit under the control of my will? Why am I not able to control my spirit like that at other times? Do our spirits need our bodies to be functional? Do spirits move around without our bodies? If so, there must be millions of such spirits. Do "parallel worlds" really exist alongside the world as we know it?

I know of another person who survived a stroke many years before

me who said she also had an "out-of-body experience" (OOBE) following her stroke. Her stroke was much lighter than mine, and she has
totally recovered now. I myself also had an OOBE some forty years earlier when I nearly died of dehydration or food poisoning after consum-
ing some bad food or water from a food stall in the open *souk* market
of Marrakesh, Morocco, shortly after my 21st birthday. In Morocco, the
OOBE came after days of severe dehydration from nausea, vomiting and
diarrhea. I had just received some life-saving medicine and clean water,
but I could have easily died, I felt. But I was only 21 years young then,
and I had lots more that I wanted to do. I was not ready to leave yet.

I feel that everyone is given a choice to continue struggling
to live more or to succumb to death and go to the next world at cru-
cial junctures like that. We all might be given the chance to decide
if we want to pass on to the next world or to work harder to stay in
this world awhile longer. Both times that I had an OOBE, I chose
to remain in this world, as I still had things to do. There are people here still for me to love and for me to be loved by. There were also several things for me to finish, such as writing and other projects that I had wanted to complete. Some people who are suffering too much grief, physical pain or loneliness, or those who do not have things to complete or who do not have people to love or be loved by, might choose to go on to the next world, I believe. Or their bodies may become too damaged for them to want to reconnect with it and do all of the neces-

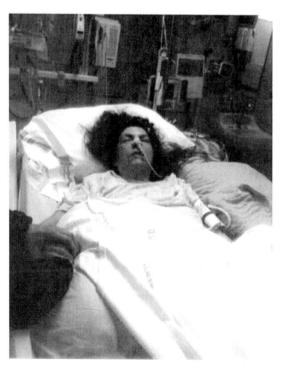

Still in the coma, about a week after the stroke. I am being comforted. You can see several tubes drain-ing fluid from my brain (photograph by Edward Nudelman).

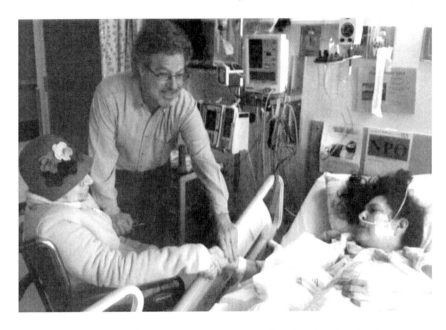

My brother, Eddie, and Mom comforting me in the ICU shortly after I came out of my coma (photograph by Edward Nudelman).

My mother's hand calms me in the ICU as I am fed through a nose tube (photograph by Edward Nudelman).

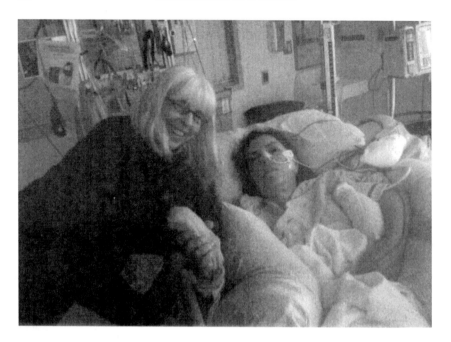

My sister-in-law, Susie, holding my hand in the ICU (notice the brain drainage tube) (photograph by Edward Nudelman).

sary hard work. A time may come for me later to choose to pass on, but that moment is not yet. That is still in an abstract, faraway future.

I have often wondered if I had sensed a stroke in my destiny unconsciously for quite a while, as I had carefully cleaned and tidied up both my apartment and my university office before leaving town in Sendai, Japan, thinking in the back of my mind that the next person to enter my rooms might be someone other than me. It was all to happen that way, fatefully, when my husband and son went into my apartment while I was still in the hospital in Japan. Also, I had purchased travel insurance in the airport before leaving Japan this time, which I seldom had done in recent years. Furthermore, I paid attention when there was talk on TV about strokes, knowing that my blood pressure had been high of late.

After waking out of the coma, I was moved around a lot. Even though I usually do not like to let others make decisions on my behalf, I passively gave in to the help of my siblings, who had carefully thought things out for me and had decided that I should be transferred first to a specialized rehabilitation nursing home. I would work to build up my strength to later return to HMC for an intensive program after letting my brain settle down and heal a bit first.

CHAPTER 9

A Stroke of Discordance
Challenges Regarding Institutional Meals

"Food is for eating, and good food is to be enjoyed.... I think food is, actually, very beautiful in itself."
—*Delia Smith*

"Eating good food is my favorite thing in the whole world. Nothing is more blissful."
—*Justine Larbalestier*

I feel like I have been on an extended diet of sorts since I was about thirteen years old. For as long as I can remember, I have been conscious of what I ate and the number of calories in food consumed. Also, since my maternal grandfather and my father had both suffered from diabetes, I have been careful about the content of the foods I consumed, including my sugar intake and how it might affect my blood sugar. I was very determined *not* to contract Type II diabetes due to lifestyle and consumption choices. I was also concerned about the amount of sodium in my food. Furthermore, I have long been paying attention to the amount of cholesterol in food. So the food served at the nursing homes and hospitals where I stayed in the United States seemed to me to be very unhealthy and high in calories.

While in the several-weeks-long coma in the ICU, I was nourished through a tube going through my nose down into my stomach, known as a nasogastric tube. I came to dislike the tube as soon as I became aware of it, even while still unconscious or semiconscious in the coma. Thus I took it upon myself to remove the tube by pulling it out as often as possible even though I knew I was not supposed to remove it. Even after starting to regain my consciousness, I had to continue with the tube feeding for some time, while the nursing staff and the speech therapist determined whether I could properly swallow food and liquids without aspirating. After I woke up, I began to realize that I was being fed through my nose, and I felt that the "food" passing through my nasal passages and going into my stomach was not fit for human consumption. While I am probably mistaken, I just had "a gut feeling" (no pun intended) that the pH level of the "food" might have been either too acidic or too basic. Perhaps that constant feeling may have contributed to my strange dreams about cooking.

Even though I was constantly scolded for pulling out the nose tube, I continued to remove the tube, even at risk of dire consequences. It must have been dangerous putting it back in, as well as pulling it out. I had to also suffer the strict scolding and clear frustration of the nurses who were tasked with the job of reinserting the tube as I choked and gagged, gasping for air, while they fed it through my nose, down my throat and into my stomach. My sister later reminded me of what I already knew—that the nose feeding had kept me alive and I should appreciate it. But by nature, I have a strong independent identity that wants to keep control over my own body, and I had learned "critical discourse analysis" while doing my Ph.D. studies a few years prior. While I was out cold in the coma, I was not aware of all of the other procedures that were performed upon my body, as it was totally out of my control. I understand and appreciate that most were life-saving procedures, but I later felt a basic, strong need to know of everything that my body underwent. I am certain that my siblings were notified, but I was not in

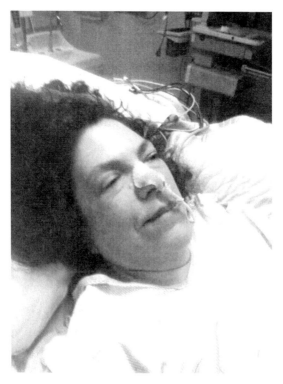

Not long after coming out of my coma, still in the ICU—managing a smile for my brother Eddie (photograph by Edward Nudelman).

the room. Irrespective of correctness, importance and medical necessity, it would have been nice to have procedures like nose feeding fully explained, especially in the context of alternatives (and even discussing possible alternate treatments).

Several years later, when I was residing in a short-stay facility in Japan, I saw an elderly Japanese woman being fed by a nose tube. She seemed "unhappy" about it, and she started to cry and then sob. The sobs soon turned into loud, plaintive wails. My heart went out to her, recalling how much I also disliked the nose tube. I tried to ask her if she was in pain; when she did not answer, I had a woman on staff ask her, but she still could not answer. It broke my heart and made me start to cry, too. I assumed that she must have been unable to swallow properly, and her speech may have also been affected, perhaps due to both age and having had a stroke. Unlike my ability to remove the nose tube at my own discretion, she may have felt restrained by Japanese societal rules, which relegated her to the passivity of acceptance as *riyousha* (user) and as a woman. In her frustration, her only recourse was to wail helplessly like an infant. When I asked the staff why she was wailing, the explanation was the "sick discourse" construction, simply indicating that "she was unwell," which was all the sadder for her, I felt.

I recall waking up on some mornings in the nursing home in the United States to find my only usable hand—the right one—bound in a mitt, making it impossible to use either hand, as my left hand had become incapacitated by the stroke. I wondered why they would bind my right hand, as it was not explained to me. I thought perhaps they worried about me getting violent or something like that. Perhaps other residents had punched staff members after coming out of their comas. However, I felt it to be against my human rights to bind me like that. I would tear the mitt off, using my teeth or asking others to help remove it and whatever else to then exercise my human right to remove the nose-feeding tube again. I felt that it was my right to decide if I wanted the nose tube, and I did not want it, even unconsciously (literally). Whether that emotion was right or wrong, that was what I felt.

Long after I had become very fed up with the nose-feeding tube, one day after having been transferred to a Seattle nursing home, I was wheeled into the dining room and parked in front of a large tray of food and drinks by the speech therapist. My eyes must have sparkled as they came to focus on the three glasses of juices, a glass of milk, and a banana, among other foods on the tray. Having not eaten solid foods for a few weeks, I felt hungry. I wanted to eat the banana and drink the juices and the milk, but my speech therapist (ST), sitting next to me, was asking me difficult questions to test my cognition, and I needed to concentrate to be able to answer, but I managed to get a couple of questions in first. I asked, "Is this food for me?" and "May I eat it?"

He said "yes" and "yes." He then had me count back from 100, subtracting sevens. I later realized that he was there to monitor my ability to eat and to swallow.

I immediately finished off all three glasses of juice and the milk. While I was drinking the juices and eating, the ST said to me, "Take a small bite. Chew it up well. Swallow it. Take another small bite or a drink slowly. Swallow it and continue slowly."

The voice of my speech therapist was authoritative, loud and clear, unlike my own, making me feel that I needed to obey him precisely. I still remember those words today, and I keep those cautions in mind when eating, so that I do not choke on food, as many in the dining room are often heard doing. We all tend to eat too fast. I recall how wonderful that food and those drinks tasted then, such as the milk and fruit juice. It was refreshing and delicious, and my body yearned for such real food.

I ravenously ate the banana like a starving monkey as the speech therapist had me next "name at least twenty vegetables." I was able to answer his entire set of questions well, and my short-term memory seemed fine, too, when he tested me recalling sequences of numbers. After I had taken my last bite of the banana, he said, "Now I am going to upgrade you to being able to eat anything."

At that time, I mistakenly thought I was being upgraded because I had answered his questions correctly. I later realized that as I ate unconsciously, the ST was observing me eating well, with no swallowing problems, and I had not choked on the food. Being upgraded to eating all foods had nothing to do with my cognitive prowess. I do not know of other parameters he may have used to check my ability to swallow, but his observation was correct. I was ready to eat everything. I no longer needed to use the nose tube after that.

I think I must have lost a bit of weight during the coma, being fed through my nose, and I felt that they were trying to fatten me up with so much food, but soon I realized that "one meal portion size fits all" there.

As shown in the two quotations at the beginning of this chapter, eating good foods is thought of by Delia Smith and Justine Larbalestier as being very "enjoyable" and "blissful." The question we may ask is: What is "good" food? It seems to differ from person to person, depending on personal tastes. There were several large men who resided with me in the nursing home in the United States whose body mass must have been double or triple my own (I only weighed around 120 pounds, or about 54 kilograms, then), but our meal portions seemed to be identical. Those large men liked to eat hot oatmeal cereal with their breakfast, which accounted, I gathered, for why I also had it served to me, just to refuse it and send it back daily, wasted. After living for more than half of my life (over three decades) in Japan, and having gotten used to preparing and being served much smaller meal portions, the huge meal portions in the United States seemed grotesque to me. But I made it a practice and priority to try at least one or more bites of each type of food on my plate in order to get proper nutrients that the nutritionist had carefully calculated.

Upon checking into hospitals and nursing homes in the United States, I was given orientations and shown where to find a kitchen for residents' use, with a well-stocked (and frequently restocked) refrigerator filled with cold drinks, sandwiches and other foods for us to consume at any time of the day or night. There were also dry cereals and other snack-like foods available. In the hospitals and nursing homes in the United States, coffee and teas were provided throughout the day, with sugar and milk or cream to add to them, as we liked. I was told, "Help yourself to any of this food or these beverages at any time of the day or night."

I did not consume any of those foods or drinks, though sometimes I had a cup of coffee in the mornings when offered by a staff member. I usually just had plain hot *ocha*, which is Japanese green tea with nothing added. I was the only one there who preferred green tea. I found the green tea (made from tea bags) available in the hospitals and nursing homes in the U.S. facilities to be more delicious than the lower-quality *hojicha* tea that is regularly served in Japanese hospitals. *Hojicha* tea is made from the stems of the tea plant and is inferior tasting. I purchased plain green tea in PET bottles instead in Japan or brought my own from home.

Desserts of cakes and other sweets were served with lunch and dinner in hospitals and nursing homes in the United States. Also, a "goodies" cart would sometimes circulate in the evenings after I was in bed, with treats such as ice cream or strawberry shortcake, which I always refused at that strange night hour—I had already brushed my teeth and settled down for sleep! Weekly movies in the evenings were shown in the U.S. facilities, along with popcorn and ice cream, adding to our caloric intake, but it was fun, and it simulated the smell and the feeling of having actually gone out to see a movie. There were no such movies shown at hospitals in Japan, although I wished there had been some, even without any treats.

Beyond the contents of the foods, the worst food problem for me in the United States was the large portions. For example, breakfast included cereals with added sugar and milk. It also usually included toast with butter, margarine and jams to spread on it, or sometimes French toast, eggs Benedict, pancakes, or waffles with toppings of butter and syrup to drench it with. In addition, there were often eggs cooked in various ways and bacon, ham, sausage or other meats. We were expected to eat all of the food on our plates and were checked for it and given a score based on the percentage we ate, as if we were children. I felt over-full after eating less than 25 percent of it. So I would shovel the food around on the plate to make it look like I had eaten more than I had.

The "eat-all-of-your-food police" would circulate through the dining room in the nursing home in the United States where I resided and spoon-feed some residents to make them eat more. I was determined not to be one of them, as I found it personally highly unpleasant. It was difficult to watch spoon-fed residents let the food dribble back out of their mouths, only to have it re-fed to them. I would actually hide food under my plate's rim, to give the appearance that I was eating more. After eating some 40 percent, I managed an average score of 75 percent. But, ever the high achiever in school, I disliked receiving scores under 90 percent.

In spite of leaving much uneaten, I still gained weight (over 30 pounds) during the five months I spent in the nursing home. I hated gaining weight, as it made it difficult for me to move and to work out in rehabilitation, not to mention the worsening of how I looked and the inability to fit into my clothing. I understood it would not be advisable to be underweight, but I couldn't understand how allowing someone to get overweight would help in any way to promote recovery and mobility. It was more difficult for the staff and my therapists to help transfer me. Sometimes I had to remove my trousers at night when my stomach swelled up painfully due to medications. I thought it strange to gain weight in hospital-like facilities. Still, I was one of the smaller among the residents, and many people there might have benefited by losing weight.

I found the food served in both the U.S. and the Japanese hospital-like facilities to be of low quality, along with their low-quality toilet paper, soap and shampoo. Much of the food was simple to prepare—

instant, dried, or canned in Japan, or frozen or canned in the United States, rather than fresh. I felt annoyed being served cheap canned fruits from the United States in Japan during the autumn, when local fruits come into season and prices fall in grocery stores. I wondered if I was getting a necessary nutritional and balanced diet. Also in the United States, in Seattle, where I was residing, summer fruits such as peaches, melons, apricots, plums, berries, watermelon, cantaloupe, and so on become affordable, abundant and delicious. Nevertheless, we seemed to only be served cheap canned or frozen fruits.

I arrived back in Japan in August 2014 and went into a hospital there right away. I soon lost all of the weight that I had gained in the U.S. hospital and nursing facilities. I was very glad to say *sayonara* to that weight, and I was relieved to eat much healthier Japanese food, which had fewer calories and fat, but I often felt hungry there and felt their rules were too austere, inflexible, and strict. After all, I was an adult, over sixty years young, and had been making eating choices on my own for my entire adult life. I felt that I had a right to snack as I pleased, but I was watched very closely by a "Sherlock Holmes Wannabe" nurse, who seemed to have been assigned to me. We were also not permitted to drink coffee (except for black, canned, wicked-tasting stuff), as coffee had the added calories of the milk, cream and sugar that we often put in it. Nor were we even permitted to eat the treats gifted to us by our guests. For example, my best friend, Akko, had thoughtfully brought me my favorite bread from an upscale bakery in central Tokyo when she came up to visit me in the hospital. I sometimes craved it, as a kind of "comfort food," but was not allowed to eat it. Before the stroke, I had become accustomed to having my daily morning cup of delicious coffee with soy milk and plain toast of rye bread and currants. Often after a meal, I felt hungry in the stroke rehabilitation hospital in Japan.

In Japan, my dear husband broke the hospital rule for me, which was totally out of character for him. He often sneaked my favorite fruits into the hospital, such as *kaki* (crisp Japanese persimmons) and fresh, local Fuji-brand apples, which he would peel and cut up for me to eat easily. We had received a box of *kaki* from my husband's colleague, and I was the main one in our family who loved them. I needed the extra fruit fiber to help my gut function, as the hospital meals included very little high-fiber foods. It also helped me to eat something sweet to counteract the bitterness left in my mouth after taking my evening medications of some fourteen tablets, most of which were neither encapsulated nor coated.

Japanese food flavoring mostly consists of salty soy or sweet sugary flavorings placed over very plain food. They seldom use herbs or hot, spicy flavoring, which I prefer. Most meals consist of a bowl of rice, salty miso soup, some salty pickles or a vinegar-based salad, a steamed dish of vegetables, and a main dish of vegetables with small amounts of fish, seafood, or meat.

I found the food served to us at U.S. hospitals and nursing homes to be heavy, greasy, and low in fiber, but high in salt, sugar and fats. I found Japanese hospital food a bit lighter than the food in the United States, with much less quantity, though it, too, was high in salt and sugar and low in fiber. I prefer smaller portions of lighter foods in Japan, with occasional fruit. While I lost thirty pounds (about thirteen kilograms) of body weight in the five or six months that I was hospitalized in Japan, I quickly regained most of that, having built up food cravings. My weight was 52.8 kilograms (about 116 pounds) when I left the hospital in Japan in mid–January 2015. At 155 centimeters (5 feet, 5 inches) in height, my BMI became low, but my weight later rebounded to over 66 kilograms.

I had favorite meals in the facilities I stayed at in the United States and Japan. In the United States, I liked the meal that they called "Asian fusion." It consisted of a Chinese fortune cookie, rice (usually fried rice), fish or seafood, and sometimes soup or noodles. My favorite meals in the Japanese hospital facilities were also their versions of foreign foods, such as (Indian) curry rice, Chinese food, and (American) chicken stews or sandwiches, although I am not very fond of the unhealthy Japanese bread called *shoku-pan*, which is made of 100 percent bleached white flour and is very light and spongy.

One day, during a lunch of sandwiches and chicken stew in Japan, the cook stopped by my room to chat with me to see how I was enjoying the "American lunch." Embarrassingly, it could be seen on my plate that I had left much of the sandwiches uneaten, including nearly all of the bread and some of the fillings.

I wanted to tell the cook in the Japanese hospital my true thoughts, but I held back. I lied miserably, saying, "It was delicious." But I wanted to tell her, "The key to a good sandwich is the bread, such as healthy and heavy German types of bread with whole wheat flour or high percentages of rye flour in it, or other types of grains, currants and nuts in it, flavorful sourdough American types of bread, or crispy types of French bread." I held back because such kinds of bread are very hard to find in Japan, and they generally cost much more. Although all are called *pan*,

My dear brother and his wife, Susie, included me in on family parties at his house and elsewhere quite often. This was taken at their house (photograph by Edward Nudelman).

meaning "bread," I feel that they should have different names, as they are totally different concepts.

Likewise, I wanted to say to the cooks in the U.S. facilities, "The key to a good French dip sandwich is the use of good French bread, such as a crispy baguette, not an American hot-dog or hamburger bun." I could not bring myself to consume those buns. Of course, the higher-quality breads cost more than the cheapest kinds in both places. I wish they would improve the quality of hospital food a bit while reducing the quantity in hospital-like facilities in the United States.

Taking hospital "leave" in Japan and eating out was an uncommon treat. We "users" of the hospital where I resided in Japan were permitted to temporarily leave the hospital if we had a person to take us out and back safely, if we applied over a week ahead of time, and, finally, if it was approved by the doctor.

There were only two types of outings allowed. One was called *gaihatsu*, which means "a day outing." We were permitted to go out for the day, returning that same day, preferably by dinnertime. The other type of outing was called a *gaihaku*, which means "an overnight outing." It included a single night and two days out. I greatly needed the *kibun*

With my family, shortly before going back to Japan, at a Japanese restaurant in Seattle across the street from the nursing home where I resided (clockwise from left: Sarah, my niece; James, Katie's husband; Sammy and Maddie, Katie's kids; me; Katie, my niece, holding Oliver; Eddie, my brother; Mom; Asher, my great-nephew, Sarah's son) (photograph by Edward Nudelman).

tenkan, which means "a change in spirit or mood by a change in the environment" or "an airing of the spirit," as I had felt stifled by many problems concerning traveling back to Japan from the United States (see Chapter 15). My husband kindly took me out and then back.

The first time out of the hospital in Japan for me was a "day outing," which included dinner out in a restaurant. I ordered *tempura*, a deep-fried seafood and vegetable dish, which was never served in the hospital. I also had an ice cream cone and coffee with cream and sugar while out. My next outing, on our wedding anniversary, was a *gaihaku* (overnight) outing. We went out to a French restaurant. My set-meal came with a salad, appetizers, soup, a main dish of steak and several desserts, French bread and coffee. I also had a glass of red wine. The hospital had no say over what I consumed while out of there. In spite of having consumed delicious special foods, I was relieved to return to the hospital after the *gaihaku*, as we had not yet completed the refurbishing work on our home to become barrier-free, making it very difficult to

At a Japanese restaurant in the United States near my nursing home (clock-wise from me: Mom; my brother, Eddie; my niece, Sarah; my sister-in-law, Susie [Eddie's wife]; two kids under the table) (photograph by Edward Nudelman).

use. My wheelchair barely fit through the hallways and doorways. I also did not have a bed yet and had to sleep on a futon mattress on the tatami straw-mat flooring.

In contrast to the two outings I had while in the Japanese hospital, while I was recovering in the United States, my brother, Edward, ensured that I was included on most family events. He would sometimes suddenly appear at the nursing home where I resided and shuffle me out the door, saying that he was taking me to the Starbucks corner of the "grocery store" across the street. At first it did not sound so exotic, but it surprised me how much these outings helped to raise my spirits. It meant so much to me to make that short trip across the street into a grocery store adjacent to the Starbucks corner. Just being in the presence of my brother is in itself entertaining and fun, as he has a great sense of humor and is loving, intelligent, generous and charismatic, and we have always been close.

Signing out on the spot in facilities in the United States was required, but we did not have to apply ahead of time to leave the nursing

My brother took me to a party at his house shortly before I returned to Japan. I am jokingly posing with the peace sign because it is still even today typically used as a photo pose in Japan (photograph by Edward Nudelman).

homes and hospitals there. Usually it was sufficient to sign out on a sheet of paper beside the clerk sitting by the door on the way out. My brother would just wheel me out as I was, sitting in my wheelchair, across the large parking lot, up a steep hill, and then across a crosswalk over a busy street to the grocery store. In addition to our coffee or a great iced-tea cooler beverage on hot days, my brother would select some pastries from the grocery-store deli. Along with his wife, Susie, and my mom, my brother treated us there several times while I was recuperating. Sometimes he also brought along some of his children and their families.

My brother also took me/us out several times to a Japanese restaurant that was conveniently located next to the grocery store. But the best outings of all were the several family parties that he took me to attend. On one occasion, at a joint birthday party for both Ed and Susie at Susie's brother's home, I hired a nurse for the evening, so I would not have to ask others for help. The nurse helped me to use the toilet there and wheeled me around. It was so much fun to be with my family and Susie's

At Eddie and Susie's garden party, I am flanked by Aaron and his beautiful wife Emily, with their son (my great-nephew), Ethan, behind them (photograph by Edward Nudelman).

family, who are very loveable, like my own family. Finally, my Aunt Shirley and Uncle Shelly had another party to which I was also taken. All of those events really made me feel so happy, and it greatly relieved the tension, pain and boredom of remaining in the nursing home for such a long time. I appreciated being included, in spite of the extra efforts it caused them all. I highly recommend that families or friends try to do the same for their stroke-survivor relatives or friends if possible, keeping in mind that even the simplest ordinary outing, whether next door, across the street or down the road, can be incredibly thrilling for anyone residing in hospitals or nursing homes for a long time, as it was for me. Using a wheelchair-taxi to get around is another option.

Hospital-sponsored outings were welcome events. A few times, I also joined nursing home– or hospital-sponsored excursions for residents in the U.S. facilities. It was fun, and we were sometimes given ice cream treats. In Japan, the day-service facilities that I used for baths also sometimes had seasonal outings, such as visits to the castle park when the cherry trees came into full bloom in spring or out to malls for short shopping stints, viewing crop art in fall, out to eat sushi or other events.

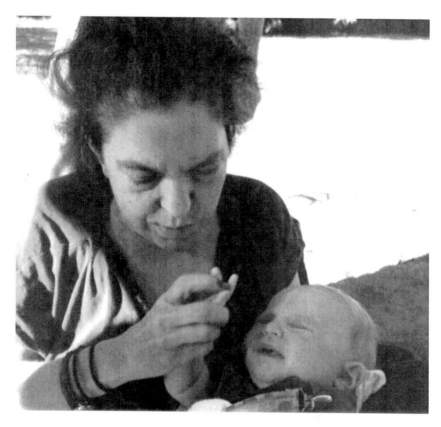

With my newborn great-nephew, Canaan, Eddie's grandchild, born to Sarah, my niece (photograph by Edward Nudelman).

Misunderstandings about weight gain were very troublesome. The new fat me, who was considered "obese" by Japanese standards and whose pants no longer fit, was judged by the doctor at the nursing home in the United States "to not have an appetite." That was so obviously off. However, it was wrongly concluded that the "loss of appetite" indicated that "she must be suffering from depression"—a stereotypical diagnosis for many stroke survivors. Thus I was put on antidepressant medications, even though I strongly contested that assessment. My appetite was actually very robust, and I was not depressed at all. I have never been depressed. I have a very stable mental constitution. Also, there is no history of mental illness, mental instability or depression on either side of my family. I was not in suicidal mode. "I was in survival mode!" I had never felt suicidal in my life. I was just a bit unhappy at being forced to eat so much, like an animal.

In conclusion, the situations surrounding my different experiences in U.S. and Japanese eating cultures—and specifically the method, amounts and types of meals served to me in hospitals, nursing homes and elsewhere—were varied and somewhat bewildering. I was forced to eat too much while in the United States and then deprived of eating as I liked in Japan.

CHAPTER 10

A Stroke of Cognizance
*Differing Practices and
Beliefs of Wellness and Healing*

This chapter looks at differing practices and philosophies of wellness and healing that I observed in the two cultures, along with awareness patterns exhibited by medical health professionals, as well as others who support them. My sister jokingly referred to us stroke survivors and others recuperating in the nursing home in the United States as "inmates," a term that I felt was appropriate, as we had little freedom to do as we liked and were more or less confined to our rooms for most of the day, like being incarcerated. I felt that we were often not treated with much respect and our human rights and freedoms were not respected very much.

Soon after coming out of the coma, during the time when I was still made to use adult diapers (which they euphemistically called "briefs" instead of "diapers"), I recall a stressed-out aid worker often pulling the covers off my body in the rain-dampened, chilly Seattle morning and shouting out in a very loud, high-pitched shrill voice, "Oh my Gawwwdd!!"

I felt that I was not even human to her; instead, I was "constructed" as a filthy, worthless, incapacitated being that had purposely made a big mess for her to have to deal with. I felt glad not be one of her children, whom I felt sorry for. What kind of parent would someone like that be?

Not only was nursing home or hospital life often boring, but it felt intimidating, and we had to endure insults to our self-esteem daily. We seldom had chances to escape from there and to go outside freely, except on a few special excursions. But I later realized that we had much more freedom than our counterparts in Japan.

I felt that the facilities in Japan were better staffed in terms of quan-

68

tity of nursing staff and aides, and the ratio of staff to users was higher in Japan, in my limited experiences. But the nurses and aides, especially in Japan, often donned rubber gloves whenever they needed to touch us in any way, even to shampoo or to fix my hair right after a bath. They also often covered their faces with masks, making our interaction even more impersonal and making me feel contagious in some way.

Once I told a story to one of my therapists in Japan about when I had contracted the norovirus several years earlier. After hearing the story, he left the room, returning a few minutes later with his face covered in a thick mask. I wanted to ask him why he had donned the mask, but I held back, and I missed the chance to find out his response. Paranoia about contracting communicable disease? Japan is a small country with many people, and they have a valid fear of disease. But there is a tendency to want to distance from someone who tries to communicate through a mask. I was surprised to have to implore my Japanese university students to remove their masks when giving their final oral reports in front of the class before 2013 and before the coronavirus pandemic. I asked one such masked student if he had a cold, fever or flu. "No, no and no." He also did not have hay fever or allergies. So I asked, "Why the mask, then?" His answer was that he did not shave that morning. Masks seem to have become an accepted way to hide one's identity.

In the two cultures, chronically infirm people are seen and treated somewhat differently. In the United States, stroke survivors and others who reside in hospitals or nursing homes for a long time are referred to as "residents." This term implies that the people will be living there indefinitely. The philosophy within those facilities is that "the residents should be safe and happy there, just as they should be at their homes." A philosophy of life in the United States is "After all, life is short, so we should try to enjoy it at every possible chance."

We residents in hospital-like facilities in the United States were encouraged to go on outings, participate in activities, enjoy eating delicious foods and watching weekly movies, and so forth. I particularly liked the weekly manicures, free of charge to us residents, provided by volunteers coming in from outside, as well as the morning newspaper readings with freshly brewed coffee and exercises with a professional full-time activities coordinator on staff at the nursing home. We also had volunteer musicians often coming in for mini-concerts or sing-alongs, which I liked to some extent, except the sing-along songs were geared for an older audience, before my time, with music from the 1920s and 1930s. In addition, there were sessions of "trivia questions" where we could use intellect or knowledge, but since most residents there suffered from dementia, it was not usually provided.

In contrast to "residents" in the United States, such infirm or hospitalized people in Japan are referred to as *riyousha*, which means "user." "User" has a much different nuance to it. It suggests that such people are just temporarily using the facility, like customers in a store.

The practice in Japan seems to imply and demand that the users of specialized nursing homes and similar facilities should be passive, still and quiet. I felt controlled, monitored and watched in Japan. There are many severe rules in place that add to the already strict societal rules imposed by Japanese society. Pain should be endured stoically, and users should accept without question decisions made by doctors, nurses or other staff.

However, in Japan there was one event that they arranged at a day-service facility that I often used. It was a sports competition. I placed first in a wheelchair race there.

In the facilities mainly designed for the aged in Japan, where I often was sent for short-term stays when my husband had business out of town, most of the more permanent users there seemed to suffer from Alzheimer's disease and other forms of dementia. A smaller percentage of them were physically impaired as the result of stroke, like myself. I was often the youngest person in such facilities, in my early 60s, whereas their ages represented an older generation.

It appeared to me that in Japan, the less mentally competent a patient was, the more the staff preferred to work with him or her, being easier to control, like a small child. The more independent the individual was (like myself), the more troublesome we were to staff, as we had our self-will and knew what we wanted, making critical judgments. Unlike the model that I had learned in school, the more docile and dependent users, with little or no self-will, and unable to express themselves, were the most loved and coddled in Japan. I came to wonder if this model corresponded with the "passiveness model" they were taught in school in Japan, in contrast to the more assertive, "independence model" encouraged in U.S. schools.

In Japan, I often saw the staff touching the heads of certain passive individuals with affection and showing an understanding of their problems, which might be good for them. There was one such individual at a day-service facility that I frequently attended who often seemed to be mumbling to himself or laughing while snorting in air and enjoying himself alone. He seemed to often get teased and patted or touched like a pet by many staff members there, especially women aides, seemingly so they could hear his joyful laughter. He had a puppy-like demeanor about him. In contrast, the staff seemed to ignore me or put me last for baths, rehabilitation or other things that we had to wait our turns for. It seemed that an independent person like me did not evoke or draw out nurturing and kindness in others. This is something all humans in distress need and crave.

Within Japanese racial discourses, some staff members were interested in me as a *gaijin* (foreigner or outsider) because I was the only Caucasian there and I looked different due to having whiter skin, different facial features and a much fuller body shape than Japanese people. Also, some staff members were hoping to learn a bit of English from me, which I was happy to comply with if they were really serious about learning more English. I was happy to answer their questions, chat with them in English, and so forth.

The director at one facility that I often attended for day service or for short-term stays used to greet me regularly in a loud voice speaking in English, saying, "It's fine day today, isn't it?" I would laugh when I saw him, expecting him to say that. If I said to him first in English, "By the way, how is the weather today?" his face would draw a blank expression until I said that in Japanese. Then he would answer as if on cue, "It's fine day today, isn't it?"

My therapist and I would often laugh and wonder what he might say on a rainy or snowy day. What he said is an expression, almost grammatically correct, but it is not normally used by native speakers of English. It would be more natural to say, "It's a beautiful day today, isn't it?" or "The weather is really nice today, isn't it?"

He did have a nice loud voice (so I'd give him a B+), and I could picture him as a small child in a kindergarten English class proudly standing up straight with his feet together and arms straight down, like a soldier, speaking loudly for his teacher, who would praise him.

When I would tell him that it was not a fine day today, but it was snowing out, he learned on his own to say, "How cold is it today!"

Occasionally, I ran into inappropriate behavior and conversation, which could be very trying. One such example was when a young male aide at a facility that I often used in Japan for short-term stays brought in an English phrasebook. He showed me a chapter in the book about conversations that may arise and would be helpful to remember for men trying to hit on and pick up a girl in a bar or similar place while overseas in English-speaking countries. The sample conversations between the two of them would continue into a bedroom or a hotel room. I found it to be very salacious and demeaning, but it was also quite humorous in that it is not language we usually hear or use, and not the sort of English that I had been teaching to my elite university students. I recommended that he not use those phrases, as in reality most girls would be insulted and certainly would not respond as shown in the examples in his book.

Activities or recreation in Japanese hospitals are a mixed bag. When I first arrived at the hospital in Japan, I asked a nurse if they had any organized activities for the patients there. I was met with a confused look, as if to say, "Are you crazy? Of course not; there is no such thing here. This is a hospital, after all." They then explained that the purpose of this institution was for users to just get on with the business of healing and then move back home.

The best way to heal, in this thinking, is to "passively lie still." Leave everything up to the staff to deal with for you. Just wait patiently for your turn. Eat your light food, take your bitter medicines, and submit to various periodic tests and probes stoically, quietly and bravely if they should be painful or uncomfortable. Be patient, passive and quiet, and all will be well. Spend as much time as possible sleeping or watching television.

It is not in my nature at all to be passive, being the proactive type. I try to make improvements as much as I can through my own efforts, rather than waiting for others to do that for me. Seeing how little opportunity patients had in my hospital in Japan to improve our minds, or be socially interactive, seemed counterproductive. They provided good physical care but were lacking in care for mental-emotional needs.

There was little opportunity to study, work or read while recovering in Japan. We were encouraged *not* to try to do any work or study and to limit reading newspapers. Even talking and laughing was restrained. Using the Internet was totally out of the question. Cell phones were not permitted usually, and signs were posted around saying so. Having a Wi-Fi for our use was also totally out of the question.

In contrast, all hospitals and nursing homes where I resided in the United States had Wi-Fi. Harborview Medical Center (HMC) even had a few computer terminals for the use of residents who did not bring their own laptop computers with them. In Japan, at one facility where I went for a short stay, I was charged a bit of extra money daily just for the use of electricity; if I brought my laptop, I seldom used it anyway, as there was no available Wi-Fi there.

Although some hospital systems in Japan have much catching up to do, they have come a long way in certain practices. Not that long ago, bathing and washing one's hair was discouraged, due to the belief that it would make the patient more vulnerable to catching colds. I recall that when I went to visit my sister in a small clinic after she had given birth by C-section in 1989 (also in rural northern Japan), she was not permitted to bathe or wash her hair. She asked me to help her to wash her greasy, dirty hair in the small sink in her room, which was against the rules there. Just as we were getting started, the doctor walked in, and we paused and said a few words of greeting to him. He reappeared just as we had finished the shampooing, but, fortunately, her hair looked almost the same dripping wet as it did before we washed it, and he did not seem to realize that her hair was wet now from water and not from grease. My sister felt tremendously better after that, and she did not catch a cold. That small rural hospital did not offer bathing facilities, as it was very old (as was the doctor). Not only that, but she was hospitalized there for an entire month for a C-section when the usual time for that was a mere week or less in most places in the United States at that time. It was midsummer and very tropically humid and hot, in a room without any air-conditioning, and my sister had gone through a fruitless labor followed by surgery. So she really needed to have some bathing arrangements. If the doctor had indeed noticed our justifiable infraction with the forbidden hair washing, he turned a blind eye, because we were never scolded.

One unexpected and pleasant feature at the Hirosaki Stroke Rehabilitation Center Hospital, where I resided for half a year in rural, northern Japan, was an *onsen* (a hot spring for bathing), which I enjoyed tremendously. In a large bath, as opposed to a shower, we found ourselves in an environment that took weight off our stressed limbs, relieving pain tremendously, like "floating therapy." We were given baths there, up to our necks, twice weekly in naturally salty hot-springs water, which was very relaxing. In my experience, being given baths in Japan was far superior to the showers I was given in facilities in the United States, where I slipped and fell down a few times. Fortunately, I was not injured in those falls.

I will say that HMC in Seattle had a state-of-the-art rehabilitation program that would be a good model for other such facilities anywhere to easily and cheaply emulate and incorporate. I wish that HMC or other top-class facilities in the United States would provide training for staff and directors of facilities in places such as Japan, China and elsewhere.

One of the things that made the program at HMC so fantastic to me was the integration of the team of people who worked with me on my individualized program there. The main drawback to the program was its high cost and my inability to access my Japanese insurance to help defray costs there (except for a small amount of travel insurance, which was mainly used up for my ICU care before coming out of the coma). Thus, this program may be difficult to replicate in places where it would be most needed, unless they could defray costs locally. I was able to choose the amount of time that I would participate in the program at HMC.

Please get travel insurance when you travel overseas, especially after a stroke or other disabling injuries. I highly recommend that people purchase travel insurance before leaving to go overseas, for one's entire family, regardless of the cost, particularly when going to the United States. Even with that coverage, I still had to pay out of my savings, which I fortunately had accumulated to a small degree in a Seattle account (since I had lived there three decades earlier) and which I had hoped to use to buy some property there. I was only able to afford three weeks of the HMC intensive rehabilitation program, at about $10,000 weekly, totally paid out of pocket, without any help from insurance. I would have liked to continue the program longer if I had been able to afford more of it. My brother had advised me to "spend my savings lavishly on myself now," saying to me, "You cannot take it with you when you leave." I had also planned to "die broke" after reading a book of that title, written by an economist (1998). But upon arrival in Japan, I was delighted to enter another fantastic hospital that was more covered by my insurance (see below).

In the United States, after coming out of the coma and leaving the ICU at HMC, I was sent to a more affordable specialized nursing facility in Seattle with rehabilitation therapy for a half-year while my brain continued to heal and in order to get the most out of the intensive HMC program later. When I arrived back at HMC for my rehabilitation program in early July 2014, I was very much ready for it. My family had given me lots of support. My Aunt Shirley and Uncle Shelly had bought me new workout clothing. My siblings had gotten me mentally in shape for the program. My physical therapist tried to get me physically in shape for it. I was so excited about what I could achieve in those three weeks. I arrived there in top shape.

Many features of the rehabilitation program at HMC in the United States are ones that I feel could be easily accomplished anywhere at a relatively low cost. One of the most important aspects of the program at HMC, which I felt to be excellent, was the practice of regular weekly meetings with my entire team, my family, and me to discuss my (and their) goals, achievements, problems, and shortcomings and then determine where to place the next goals.

I often found myself left out of meetings later in Japan. In the Japanese hospital, they always insisted that meetings be attended by *Otousan* (which literally means "your father," but in this case it referred to my husband). Nobody there ever invited me or even let me know of the time and place for the various meetings concerning me, including a visit from the local narcotics agent and police coming to take a deposition on me. (I had innocently brought my prescribed oxycodone into Japan upon returning there after my hospital stays in the United States. It turns out that it is illegal to bring oxycodone into Japan.)

The people at the Japanese hospital mistakenly assumed that *Otousan* was footing the bill for everything, when I actually paid for all of my own care. They also mistakenly thought that *Otousan* was translating everything for me into English, but he never did, as his English level was very low and we always spoke to each other in Japanese. Being that *Otousan* was my main caregiver, everything had to be OK'd by him first. I was never allowed to make my own decisions. It felt like I had to tag along behind *Otousan*, my husband, in order to attend meetings that should have been meant for me in Japan.

Being the feminist that I am, I felt that men and women were not treated equally in terms of expectations for recovering their independence, especially in Japan. It seemed to me that men were given more chances to recover than women, and they were encouraged to walk and drive earlier, whereas there was much less expected of women in terms of going back to work. Working means also being able to drive in order to get oneself to work. I had heard of several men who had gotten back into the driver's seat, but no women doing so. Thus I had no role models to help me reach that goal in Japan, although I think that in Western countries, it is much more equal in terms of a consciousness of gender equality in society. Even in subtle realms like this, I feel that Japan is quite late and backward. I often felt frustrated by that discrepancy, as I wanted to regain my independence. I wanted to walk, drive and go back to work more than anything, but I have failed to reach those goals due to poor support from others around me. I hope that this problem changes in Japan soon.

Later, after living at my home in Japan, my therapist at a day-service facility arranged seasonal, helpful meetings (at intervals of three months) for me with my various day-center staff, my home helpers, my husband (or *Otousan*), my care manager, and my home rehabilitation therapist.

Conference-call attendance is an important aspect of communication. While I was in the United States, people of importance to me who could not physically be at the meetings arranged at HMC were included in a conference-call setup. The first time, while most of us sat around speakers in a large conference room with tables, my brother joined us by telephone from his house, as he was busy then. At another meeting, my brother again joined from his cell phone, while my husband joined from Japan. At the same time, a professional Japanese/English interpreter was also asked to be in on the call, so that my husband could be totally included and I did not have to be tasked with the job of interpreting; I could just relax and listen or talk using my first language, English. I thought that it was very generous and high-tech, and I greatly appreciated the extra efforts for that service.

Later, after I had returned to Japan, when my brother suggested that we call him from my hospital in Japan on a conference call like that to work out a few snags, I had to decline, assuming that so-called high-tech Japan would not be able to easily do such a thing. It was not something that I dared to request in Japan. Japan makes high-tech products to sell, but Japanese society is relatively low-tech and late in its actual usage of the products it makes in comparison with the United States, where the usage of technology is common and well diffused throughout society, especially in certain cities (such as Seattle). Such arrangements in Japan would also be more costly than in the United States—another reason to hold back from making such requests there.

Staff introductions and blackboards in the patients' rooms are very helpful. This simple practice was excellent and user-friendly in the United States at HMC and could be achieved at a low cost anywhere at similar facilities. During the first few days of the rehabilitation program at HMC, each member of my team came into my room, one by one, and introduced themselves to me in a very friendly manner, telling me their role and asking me what I expected from the program and what I wanted to achieve, helping me to stay focused on my goals and purpose. They then wrote their name and their role in my program on a large blackboard displayed in my room and clearly visible from my bed. Also on the blackboard, they wrote my weekly schedule, including time and place of the activity for each event and other information. For example, for my physical therapy and my physical therapist (PT), it was as follows: "PT: Josh: 10:00 a.m. and 2:00 p.m.; Gym," along with other necessary details (e.g., "Take along the AFO foot brace"). That simple bit of user-friendly input was very helpful to me, as it was good to know and to remember the people and my schedule, which was very intense.

Having recently come out of a several-weeks-long coma, it was nice to have the reminders clearly visible at all times, and it helped me each morning to know what to expect for that day. Sometimes someone would come in at night or in the early morning to make slight changes to my schedule for the day on the blackboard. Usually, if I just waited in my room, someone would come to fetch me for the next planned activity. But for some, I was asked to make my way to a room, like school, where several of us gathered together. Some sessions "required" us to work together with other residents as part of the therapy. The nursing home in Seattle also used blackboards in the resident's room, but in a more simplified way. My speech therapist there would often come in and leave me notes of encouragement and techniques for speaking better. I felt that the Hirosaki Stroke Rehabilitation Center Hospital and other hospitals in Japan could easily use blackboards like that to make their programs better.

In Japan, at most hospital facilities I have resided in/used, while most staff members wore nametags around their necks, they never introduced themselves to me unless I asked their names first. It leaves a person feeling isolated and insignificant, and it doesn't need to be that way. In addition, the staff names were difficult to read, even though I can read most Japanese writing, and thus I couldn't call anyone by their name. It further served to separate staff from users.

"Bedside manner," or communication between doctors, nurses or other staff and patients/users/residents after or before a procedure or surgery, is quite poor in Japan in my experience, as doctors seldom introduce themselves and usually seem to explain things only when they are specifically asked.

I had suffered several miscarriages in Japan and thus spent much time in hospitals. Not only are miscarriages very painful physically, but they are also very painful emotionally and psychologically, and I was almost never asked how I felt in terms of my feelings of loss and my grief. I was never offered any mental/spiritual support. In contrast, in the United States, special staff are usually available at most larger hospitals to deal with the psychological and spiritual needs of patients and their families. (Religious counseling of various types is also usually available.)

I do, however, recall decades ago, after my first miscarriage in Japan, being asked by one nurse how I felt as I was left to recover while sharing a room with several healthy expectant mothers, which I found horrible in itself. The excited happiness of those still-pregnant mothers-to-be made me feel all the more grief; having lost my (much-anticipated) baby-fetus, I felt alienated and lonely there, as I was not able to share their excitement. I just felt grief in that room. The nurse was referring to my physical state when she asked me, "How are you feeling?" but I recall that I burst out crying, and the only words I had were "*Hidoi; totemo warui*" ("Terrible; very bad"). But she was too young to understand the strong emotions of grief and did not know what to say to me or how to console me. Poor bedside manner in Japan is unfortunate, I feel.

In the nursing home in the United States where I resided, all of the staff members (many of them immigrants from places like Pakistan, the Philippines, Africa and India) wore nametags around their necks. But even this practice occasionally led to confusion, since sometimes the staff member chose to use their given name, and other times an Americanized name. As for us residents, like most people, we all had two names—a given name and a family name (I was "Laurel Kamada")—but too often we would overhear someone referring to us by our room numbers (I was "#3"). I disliked that practice very much; not only was it very impersonal, but I also was often mistaken for another person, which I realized later upon reading a report written about me. We shared no similarities. She was some decades my senior. I wondered if I had taken over her room after she had left or changed rooms.

Institutionalized gossip should not be allowed. At the nursing home in the United States where I resided for a half-year, the doctor in charge compiled a very detailed report about me that was sent on to the next hospital where I was sent, HMC. From there, it was sent to other institutions overseas in Japan, where it was translated into Japanese and passed on around the country. In that report, I was unhappy about several mistakes and what I have come to refer to as "institutionalized gossip."

For example, I had been a *tanshin funin*, which is a Japanese word-concept that we do not have in English. It is a person who has a job transfer, which takes a parent away from the family for an extended period of time. This is a common social practice in Japan, where parents or husbands and wives have to live separately when one parent/spouse moves due to their job. Usually it is the father or husband who assumes this role. In Japan, the family is very child-centered. So, instead of uprooting a child who has worked hard, and also often at great cost, to include tutors and afterschool cram-schools in order to gain entry into a particular junior or senior high school (and who may be enjoying club or sports extracurricular activities with friends), one parent (usually the mother) stays with the child (or children) at home. The other parent, required to relocate for work, moves out of town and tries to return home on days off to be with the family.

The *tanshin funin* (live-away person) in our family was me, the mother. Being a feminist, I felt no compunctions about being the one to live apart, as, after all, I had sacrificed most of my career to quit my jobs several times and move where my husband had work. My husband initially accepted the arrangement, as I had gotten a good job at a high-ranked university out of town, in his home prefecture, and he wanted to support my career move. He kept his job near our house and lived at home with our son, who was already nearly over the official age of adulthood in Japan as a junior in high school. It would have been extremely difficult or impossible to place my son in a high school in Sendai, although I would have preferred to take him with me, as I had done several years earlier when I spent one year working in Kyoto (at that time, he was still in the lower grades of elementary school).

As a *tanshin funin* in Sendai, I could spend the latter (longer) half of the week at home with my family. It was a tremendously hard schedule, which included three or four hours of driving each way each week after three fully packed days of working hard, and often driving at night and during blizzards or snowy weather conditions. I would then, while at home, go grocery shopping at several different stores, prepare meals, do laundry, clean up the house, and run errands for my son and so forth in those few days at home, leaving no time for rest or relaxation. Sometimes I did homework of writing articles or preparing classes and grading papers. I would then also try to prepare enough meals while at home to hold over my son and husband for the next several days. I would plan to start the drive back to Sendai early on Sunday morning, so that when I arrived at my office in the early afternoon, I would have time to prepare all of my nine (sometimes more) classes for the coming week or to prepare materials for the volunteer work of teaching English in an elementary school and practice it with the volunteers at least once. Sometimes I also would arrange to meet students in my office, including my graduate student.

This commonsense work arrangement is often misunderstood in the United States, whereas it is understood and accepted in Japan. It is very hard to explain in Western societies, where families are adult-centered, so when a parent needs to relocate out of town, the whole family generally moves with him (or her). I believe that after talking privately (I had assumed) to an aide in the nursing home about me living for half of the week in another town in Japan for work, separate from where my husband resided, it ended up in the doctor's report that my husband and I were "estranged." When I found that word in the report, I was very surprised, as I have never used it, and I dislike the other nuance that it conjures up, such as the idea of some kind of infidelity in the relationship, as is often seen in TV dramas. Not only that, but I refuted it. My husband and I were not "estranged" at all. Instead, we were like best friends, and we trusted each other very much, but that was no one's business except our own. It is very personal and private. I wonder how it was translated back into Japanese, but it is not likely to have been as *tanshin funin*. Such information has no place in a medical report to be sent from one institution to another.

The doctor at the nursing home in the United States who wrote up the report never tried to confirm its validity by asking me about it, making it "mere gossip" that he had heard from the aide whom I had talked to, trying to explain the concept of *tanshin funin*, and he perhaps came up with the word "estranged" through his own imagination. Since that report moved between institutions, it can be thought of as "institutionalized gossip." It having then been sent on to Japan, and to several institutions I was affiliated with in Japan, it became "trans-national institutionalized gossip" by that point. "Estranged" may as well have been tattooed on my forehead, I felt. That report may still be circulating around in Japan, for all I know.

There is no exact English translation for the term *tanshin funin* (but it is certainly *not* "estranged"), as it is culturally not generally practiced in the West. First of all, in the United States, school entry is not decided by examinations, but rather by proximity of home to school, so there is no need for entrance examinations and the practice of *tanshin funin*. It is routine for pupils/students to change schools and to enter a new public school easily without exams, and the local schools are legally bound to admit them.

When I first arrived at HMC, I pointed out the mistakes in the report when each person stopped by to introduce themselves. The doctor in charge kindly promised (but seems not to have remembered) to correct the report. I also contested the "construction" of me as "depressed," as I was not. The tone in the report tried to illustrate a state of depression by repeatedly referring to my "lack of appetite." I was never directly asked if I felt depressed, even though I was prescribed antidepressant medicines.

What was depressing was being falsely constructed as depressed. As I stated earlier, I was accustomed to eating small meals in Japan, and I struggled with the huge meal portions served at the facilities in the United States. The doctor who wrote the report had falsely assumed that I did not have an appetite. Since the loss of appetite is thought to correlate with (or to be causally related to) depression, I was labeled as depressed. But they had it all wrong. If anything, I was concerned about my diet, my weight and the quality of the food that I ate. I had worked hard to maintain a lower weight and felt unhappy being forced to eat more after I had become full, and "the hospital-food police" made me unhappy there, if anything. But it did not warrant my being put on antidepressants (which were later discontinued when it was revealed that overmedication was causing liver damage). I also rejected being put into stereotypical categories of this or that of what is often or typically seen to occur among stroke survivors within medical discourses of (in)sanity and (un)wellness. I had read the literature too, and I knew where they were coming from, but I rejected being stereotyped as a typical stroke survivor and automatically put on antidepressant medications just because some survivors may become depressed.

Frustrations mounted in not being able to walk. I was not happy to find myself unable to walk or use my left hand. I also felt a lot of pain in my body daily and nightly, which was exhausting in itself. But I have always been a mentally determined person with a positive life outlook, and I rejected being constructed as depressed. I refused to accept that false assessment of my mental state. I never shed a tear over the calamity and the poor condition in which I found myself. I have never been suicidal and was far from it at that time too. It was not pleasant that suddenly I found myself spending most of my time in the presence of people who could not communicate or talk with me at all, who were a generation or more older than me. Many had dementia, whereas before the stroke I had been interacting with young and savvy university students or graduate students.

The comparison of youth versus aging in stroke is complicated and influenced by long hospital stays. I had perceived myself as being youthful until the stroke, when I seemed to have suddenly aged to my actual age, in the low sixties. Even though it never came about, I felt confident that I would be able to return to my office and my work. Unfortunately,

I did not have support from my husband, who believed it would be too hard for me to live in another city, far away, by myself. I felt it would be very possible if I could find a barrier-free apartment and then make it user-friendly. As an American, I tend to have a positive attitude that if I keep on trying hard enough, I can do it and make things happen as I envision them. In contrast, it seems to me that Japanese people in general (including my husband and my doctor) tend to have more negative views of things and see the world as being "fixed and immutable." Matters might not always be so simple, but I felt it was certainly possible for me to live by myself and continue to work. I simply was not able to find a barrier-free apartment before reaching the retirement age of 65, and that time limit kept me out after my last fall term of 2015 ended. It badly hit my identity and also my goal to recover and to see my students and friends again. Instead, I began writing.

For the first time ever, while in the nursing home for that long time, I felt that I had come to look my actual age. I felt like the main character in the Japanese fairytale of *"Ura-shima-Tarou."* It tells the story of a boy who goes into a magical world under the sea, where young maidens attend to him, and when he returns a year or so later, he finds himself an old man. It is similar in some respects to the fable of Rip Van Winkle, who suddenly awakens to find himself an old man with a long white beard. Even though I was not playing and enjoying myself like Ura-shima-Tarou, I had identified as much younger than I was, and, indeed, everyone said I looked young. Then, suddenly, my real age seemed to catch up with me after the stroke and hospital life of over a year, and I began to see myself as appearing over sixty and not in my thirties anymore. I have had to adjust to that new image of myself, with hospital hair, in a wheelchair with a blanket over my pajama-covered legs.

While the antidepressant medicines were discontinued in the United States before I left, I was later put back on them in Japan when I made a sarcastic joke while counting. Sarcasm and ironic humor are often taken at face value in Japan. The Japanese word for "four" is generally pronounced "shi," which is also a synonym for "death," and any reference to death is considered a warning sign of depression. When asked to count to ten for exercises, to relieve the monotony, I devised a numbering system with a variation for fun, as Japanese numbers can be read in a number of different ways. In addition to "shi," four (4) can be read as "yon," but I sarcastically used the "shi" reading and was thought to be making a reference to death. I was thus considered depressed and put back on the antidepressant medications.

Personal notebooks are a must. Another good practice in the United States at HMC, and one that could be easily and cheaply incorporated into similar facilities anywhere, was "information arranged in notebooks." I was given two large binder notebooks at HMC that contained information, along with pages to fill in myself. Those empty pages were where I got started on writing this book. I later asked my siblings to bring me many notebooks and pens. I found writing to be helpful in reducing my stress and boredom and helping me to organize my thoughts and ideas. Any such facilities could easily and at low cost, with a large positive effect, provide that benefit to stroke survivors or others residing there. The notebooks had information about strokes and also about my own program, including photos and details about the staff who would work with me. I later added information that I downloaded from the Internet and printed out with staff help.

CHAPTER 11

Physical Therapy
in the United States

Pain Is Gain (A Stroke of Awe)

"Walking is falling forward. Each step we take is an arrested
plunge, a collapse averted, a disaster braked. In this way,
to walk becomes an act of faith. We perform it daily: a
two-beat miracle—an iambic teetering, a holding on and
letting go."

—*P. Salopek, from* National Geographic, *2013*

The quotation seen above epitomizes the complexity of walking.
The author, Paul Salopek, walked continually for 21,000 miles (33,796.2
kilometers) over seven years, experiencing the essence of walking on
two sturdy legs. In my case, I had to relearn how to walk as a heavy,
full-grown adult. Certainly, learning to walk for the second time, as an
adult, is as difficult as (if not more difficult than) trying to learn to speak
a second language. (For a living, I taught English as a second language.)

The first time we learn to walk, usually between the ages of one
and two, we are light in weight, and falling is not a major liability. Also,
we often learn that skill by holding on tightly to the hands of two parents who love us dearly and ensure our safety and cheer us on with our
every attempt, better than even the world's best physical therapists. We
have been crawling around for months, building up leg and arm muscles for the task. We have practiced standing up from a sitting position
on the floor before attempting to take our first steps alone. My son, as a
baby and as a toddler, used to have a very cool baby walker in which he
transported himself quickly all around the house. (I would like to have
an adult slim version of that for walking to the store near my house.) It
is thrilling to share a young child's exhilaration as they take their first

steps and then run with joy. It was also a very exhilarating experience for me to walk again when I took my first clumsy steps with my therapist and family members watching over me, cheering me on (though I have yet to try running, swimming, bicycling, dancing, skiing, and so forth). The relationship between a stroke survivor and their therapist is thus very intimate.

My first physical therapist (hereafter PT), named Aaron Scheidies, a Paralympics athlete in triathlon, who was assigned to me almost immediately after I came out of the coma in May 2013, was excellent. His vision is impaired, making him legally blind; he has only around 15 percent of his vision due to a condition known as "juvenile macular degeneration." I did not know that fact until one of our last sessions together, and I also did not know until very late that he was a top-ranked paratriathlon athlete. Aaron personally worked out very hard and took part in local paratriathlons while tethered to a seeing athlete. Aaron, along with his visually unimpaired partner/trainer, Colin Riley, took first place in a local triathlon while he was working with me. That is fantastic, and I am very proud of my therapist for that. I had hoped that they would place at the top in the Paralympics in Rio de Janeiro, Brazil, in 2016, but Aaron's category was unfortunately dropped from the Rio schedule, so he could not compete there as originally planned, to the great dismay of us all. Then I wanted to cheer him on at the Tokyo games in 2020, where I had hoped to serve as a volunteer interpreter. I later had to give up the idea of volunteering when I realized that they mostly wanted able-bodied young people living in or near Tokyo.

One very important thing that Aaron taught me was to trust him. At first it seemed so incongruous to me to put all of my weight onto my injured, bad leg and to force that weak, painful leg to walk for me. After all, even dogs and horses do not put their weight onto a lame foot. They limp, using their other good legs instead, and hold up the bad foot. At first, I would try to hold up my bad leg, and I found it very difficult (not to mention painful) to, first, unbend that left knee and, second, place that weak (nearly paralyzed) leg down on the floor, and then, third, shift my weight onto it, and finally make it balance and walk for me without falling down. Falling was very taboo at the facilities where I resided in the United States and also later in Japan, and the staff did their part to try to make sure that we never fell, as broken limbs or injured joints can greatly hamper recovery time and can be very painful and terrible.

But Aaron, holding on to me tightly, would pull me far to my weak (left) side, with me resisting and him saying, "Trust me, Laurel. I am not going to let you fall. I've got you. Trust me. I will not let you get hurt. I have got you good. Trust me."

It was when I finally learned to trust him, as well as my other future therapists, that I was able to start building up the necessary new muscles in my legs. It took a lot of training, but Aaron was the perfect trainer for that. He also must have been told that same phrase by his seeing trainer, who would try to encourage Aaron to run, swim and bicycle faster in near-total darkness: "Trust me, Aaron, I am not going to let you fall [drown, crash, etc.]."

Another of my main problems is that I have always been an over-achiever. Even at that time, I wanted to walk from the start. I felt envious of some of the other women whom I had seen walking into the dining room at the nursing home with lightweight walkers. I thought that if they could walk, then so could I. They were far older than I and frailer and much less motivated than I was. I was in relatively good shape, as I had often worked out in a gym or ridden my bicycle around, and I had tried hard to keep in good shape before having the stroke. Aside from the stroke, I was also in relatively good health. But Aaron insisted that I needed to go slowly, step by step. I was overly enthusiastic to climb those steps in leaps and bounds. He taught me to sit up in bed, to roll over in bed, to put on my shoes from the bed, to transfer from the bed to the wheelchair and back, and from the wheelchair to the toilet and back, and so forth. We went slowly, step by step, with Aaron making sure that I had totally mastered each task in its order, one after the next. Aaron would remind me often, "Trust me, Laurel. I am not going to let you fall. I've got you good. Trust me."

An occupational therapist (OT) simultaneously worked with me to do many things "one-handedly," such as change my clothes, brush my teeth, wash my face, and so on. Sometimes Aaron just had me working out on a machine to build up the proper muscles necessary for walking again. I became skillful at transferring, and my legs became very strong. I learned coordination and balance with Aaron's guidance. I kept asking Aaron to get me up and walking again, but it never happened at that time.

The amount of time that a PT or an OT at such facilities could allot to each resident was quite limited, it seemed. But physical therapy was the only thing I wanted to be doing all of the time, if possible. Unfortunately, it was not possible to have more than a few minutes of rehabilitation practice on most days while in the rehabilitation facility in the United States.

One day Aaron had me enter the parallel bars and stand up to walk. I tried very hard to walk, but my first steps walking were heavy, as I held on tightly to a handrail in the parallel bars on my right side with my good hand. I did not yet have a brace for my weak leg. I first slid my right hand forward. (Later, in Japan, I learned to use a cane that clacked forward first.) Next, I stepped forward heavily, with my right foot clomping loudly, as Aaron helped to support me, with the rest of my weight being supported by my weak left leg. Then I used the momentum and my hip to swing my left foot forward. So it was "Slide my hand, CLOMP [right, good leg placed forward while being held up by the left, bad leg], SWOOSH [left, bad leg forward]. Slide good right hand [or the CLACK of the cane], CLOMP [right, good leg forward again, while balancing and putting weight onto the weak leg], SWOOSH [left, bad leg], slide hand, CLOMP [right, good leg], and SWOOSH [left, bad leg]. SLIDE/ CLACK, CLOMP, SWOOSH, and so on." (I have recently been trying to get my left leg to bear more of the weight, making the "clomp" sound of my right foot stepping forward less prominent than before.)

The most difficult part of the process was putting weight onto my weak leg; as another PT used to tell me, "Load that left leg." That was important, so that I could better step forward with my right leg. Stepping forward with the good right foot is the most difficult and sometimes painful part while relying on my bad left leg/foot to support my weight. Also, my left foot often becomes swollen or edemic if overly stressed, and then it becomes very painful. At that time, while working out with Aaron, I had yet to have a leg brace made. Without wearing a leg brace, much pressure and stress is put on the weak leg.

Later, I found it difficult to continue walking naturally without using a leg brace and holding a cane on my right side. I found it difficult to balance on my bad left leg well enough to step forward with the good right leg. It took muscles that were not well enough developed to raise the left leg to continue walking. The use of the cane helped to take some of the weight off the legs to propel my next step forward. Now (over seven years later) I am working on trying to continue pacing forward without needing to use the cane, but I am finding that very difficult to do so far.

So, for me, walking is indeed "falling forward" to get started after I stand up. I put the cane forward first for balance and to break the fall; then I load the weak left leg with most of my body weight painfully; then I clomp forward with the good foot and quickly follow through with the left foot while balancing my body weight on the good leg and the cane in my good right hand, and so forth until I reach my goal or find a resting place.

When I step forward with my left/weak leg, I particularly feel the quad muscles tense up above the knee on the left leg. Next, stepping forward with the right leg, I feel muscles tense in the right calf and the right buttocks. Several other muscles are at work in the complex process of walking. I also have different muscles that come into play if I almost lose my balance and nearly fall (I call them my "whoops" muscles). Those same muscles are ones I use when trying to navigate narrow or obstacle courses, which my home therapist sometimes purposely created for me to practice. I could work up a sweat rather quickly, walking just 100 meters or so, even in winter. It was good exercise to get myself warmed up when my body became tense from the cold and I needed to generate more internal heat and energy, but I usually do not dare to practice walking alone without a therapist or a helper near me. When stepping downstairs, which is required when leaving my house, I must use my bad left leg first. This puts pressure on my right knee, which I need to be careful of, as knees are very delicate and important for walking, transferring, and other movement. If injured, knees take a long time to heal.

One day while working with Aaron in the United States, he suddenly decided that I should try "Electrical Stimulation Therapy." There are various names for this treatment: NMES, TENS, FES, SES and so forth. I later came to refer to it as "the Russian electrical shock-torture therapy."

Like everything else, I had never heard of it and felt scared at the idea, but Eddie, Susie, and Mom were called in to be there when I first tried it. Also, I trusted Aaron, so it was no problem for me then. It was just another adventure to experience and to hopefully benefit from at the same time.

There were various settings on the machine. Aaron always set it to the "Russian" mode, which I assumed was a higher amperage. Then he attached several electrode pads to my left leg over strategic muscles and ramped up the electricity quite high. I felt a twinge of pain. It was a sharp, very annoying pain, but it was bearable. After all, I trusted Aaron totally.

With my audience around me, while I was sitting in my wheelchair, Aaron instructed me to kick out my (good) right leg. I did so with no problem. Then he said, "OK, Laurel, now kick out your left leg."

Even by cheating a bit, using my stomach and hips, I could not get my left leg to budge much at all.

Next, Aaron repositioned the electrodes over strategic muscles on my left leg and amped up the electricity. Just at the peak of the electric amp and the strongest pain, Aaron said loudly, "Kick out your left leg now, Laurel."

I did as instructed, and I tried my best to kick his leg, but each time I missed making contact with him, as he pulled himself back to avert my advance. I found it easy to move my kicking muscles at the peak of the electrical amp, and doing so relieved the pain a bit, so it was kind of a natural movement process.

Aaron repeated the treatment several times. When I had about taken all I could stand, Aaron removed all of the electrodes from my leg and instructed my brother to start the video now, if ever. Then, with my family watching, Aaron shouted out, "Kick out your left leg, Laurel!"

For the first time since the stroke, I could move my weak leg unaided, on my own. My brother was elated, as if he had just witnessed his own firstborn child walking for the first time, and he cheered and praised me lavishly. Susie and Mom joined in the cheering as well. Aaron beamed, too, and soaked up much of the praise. We had accomplished it together, but I felt that Aaron was the one who deserved 99 percent of the praise. Even today, as I write this, some seven years later, I can still kick out my left leg unaided, probably well enough to kick Aaron now if he were seated near me as before. However, being able to kick did not seem to help me to walk much better. But it was difficult for me to assess myself.

Even though I referred to that therapy as the "Russian electrical shock-torture therapy," I actually found myself requesting it later for my hand, but few therapists in Japan were as well trained in the usage of the machine as Aaron was. As I felt it had worked successfully for my leg, I wanted to also use it on my hand and even more places on my leg. I was able to find one occupational therapist in Japan who used it on my weak left hand a few times. When used on my hand, it helped my clenched fist to open. I later realized that any kind of stimulus, such as pain in the limb, was sending a signal to the brain, helping to re-energize the pathways. As my brother said to me then in the United States, "Pain is gain," or "No pain, no gain," so I still endure pain for the gain.

Unfortunately, during the half-year that I worked out with Aaron, I was never able to walk on my own like those older ladies who came into the dining room on walkers, whose brain injuries were far less serious than my own. I still remember Aaron hugging me and saying "Good-bye" the last time I saw him, bringing tears to my eyes. I was going off to Harborview Medical Center for my three-week intensive program, and Aaron was leaving the nursing home at the same time, as his contract through another agency had ended at the nursing home. I hoped that when I returned, he would be back (even though he had explained to me that he would not be there), and I was very disappointed to hear that they had lost Aaron, as he was exceptional in every way. I missed him dearly after that and have thought of him a lot. I have not been able to contact him since then.

I was psychologically ready for the event of re-walking by the time I entered the three-week intensive program at HMC. It is good that Aaron had gotten me along as far as he had, as the program at HMC was very expensive and I felt I could not afford more than three weeks of it. I entered for the first three weeks of July 2014, and I worked very hard. I was assigned several therapists and had a large team of some twenty specialists working with me during that time.

My second major physical therapist was named Josh. He had me up and walking during my first week at HMC, after having my foot fitted for a specially made leg brace, called an ankle-foot orthosis (AFO). I found that wearing the brace made a huge difference in my ability to walk, and I wished that I had had one made earlier with Aaron.

My American-made AFO was very different from the sturdy Japanese-made ones that I later used and came to prefer, although I have seen the cheaper-style ones being used in Japan, too. My first AFO, made in the United States, was made almost entirely of plastic, and it covered and braced the back part of my left leg along the calf, ankle and bottom of my foot, leaving the front side open except for two straps. Josh also provided me with some very nice donated Asics sports shoes (made in Japan) to wear with it, as the brace required a pair of sturdy shoes to be worn with it. In contrast, the AFO that I later had made in Japan (called a *sougu* in Japanese) is made of very sturdy leather that covers all of the foot and most of the leg up to just below the knee. It looks like a sturdy boot with a metal brace coming up to the top of the calf, where it is strapped tightly around. There is another strap around the ankle and two more around the toe area. A matching leather shoe is worn on the good foot. There are several kinds of leg braces available in Japan. My PT in Japan selected the best kind for me to purchase.

I later realized that I was not able to walk at all without wearing the leg brace and using a cane. Although I came to prefer the sturdy Japanese-made leg brace over the U.S.-made one, my first Japanese *sougu* was very tight and difficult to put on by myself. I later had it remade to better fit my foot, as the swelling caused by wearing it was very painful and would not allow me to comfortably use it for more than a few days consecutively. The later-made leg brace was not covered much by insurance and was very costly. I had had surgery in December 2012 in Japan, on both feet, to take out bone spurs over the joints of my big toes, but it was not very successful, as the bones are still enlarged and painful in tight shoes. This is also the case with wearing the *sougu*, even though it is supposed to be form-fitted to my foot. It is still too tight around the big-toe joint, causing me to feel nauseous and causing my foot to swell after walking too much with it. Also, like my fingers on my left hand, my left toes are very tightly curled, and sometimes that causes pain and swelling if my foot is not properly placed into the boot before walking. It is important that I can put on my leg brace myself quickly, in an emergency, but it is difficult to put on myself.

I do not like the idea of being dependent on a piece of (uncomfortable) equipment in order to walk or to run to escape in emergencies, if necessary. As natural disasters are extremely common in Japan, everyone is cautioned to keep a pack handy in case they suddenly have to evacuate and run to safety. I often try to think of what I would do in the various situations around Japan, far from where we live, that I regularly see on the television news, including floods, landslides, typhoons, volcanic eruptions, earthquakes, train fires, tsunami and so forth. My husband promises to come and get me in such an impending disaster, and I trust him. As we live very close to a river, sometimes after heavy rains during the snow-melting season, I worry about our river overflowing its banks and coming into our house. Having been in Tohoku, Sendai, during the triple mega-disaster there on March 11, 2011, almost exactly two years prior to the stroke (see Chapter 5), I may have a bit of PTSD (post-traumatic stress disorder) when I think of the power of natural disasters and the stress of staying in a refuge shelter for several days and trying to find enough food and water daily, not to mention problems of privacy and personal hygiene.

I always wear the *sougu* while traveling by airplane, train or car. Given the need to wear the *sougu* when going out, I realized that I would no longer have the need (or the joy) of shopping for shoes, and I would never again be able to enjoy wearing my favorite red shoes. As it is, I sometimes wear different types of shoes on each foot. In fact, if I were just to remain sitting in the wheelchair, I could possibly wear high-heeled shoes again, but I might not be able to use a toilet without wearing the AFO. I have found it troublesome to visit others, as I cannot walk after removing the AFO (wearing shoes indoors in Japan is not permitted), nor would I be able to visit clinics and hospitals without removing it. As it is, either the wheels of my wheelchair or my *sougu* and shoe must be cleaned before entering a clinic, grocery, restaurant or other such house or most public spaces. Thus I seldom go out.

I have wondered if I could ever return to doing Latin dancing of salsa and bachata and how it would go at dance studios and clubs, with me using my AFO and a cane while other women wear their high-heeled shoes. I would also probably need to keep my wheelchair nearby, as I cannot imagine leaving my chair for very long (currently, my stamina is limited to just a few minutes or walking about 300 meters by myself, at the maximum, with a cane and preferably with a therapist nearby, too). It has been my dream and long-term goal to one day return to doing Latin dancing. It remains one of my top goals, but I would need to be careful. I have yet to meet a PT who is also salsa crazy (or a salsa instructor who is also a therapist), nor do I expect that I ever will.

At the intensive program at HMC, my new PT, Josh, had me up and walking almost right from the start there. I walked while holding on to a handrail with my right hand as he scooted along behind me on a low-to-the-floor wheeled chair, helping to keep my left knee from buckling as I walked. We did that twice daily for one-hour sessions each time. I often went to bed feeling pain in my newly developing muscles or swelling in my left foot, but it was a good pain to me. I took mild pain medicine (acetaminophen) for that, but, again, I would recall my brother's words: "No pain, no gain."

So as long as the pain was moving me closer to my goal of regaining my ability to walk, I could *gaman* (or hold out and persist). At HMC, I also often had to wear a painful boot on my affected foot in bed during the night to try to prevent foot-drop. I never had the problem of foot-drop, but it was very painful being bound up and unable to move in the bed. Also, my severely curled-up hand was often put in a splint at night to keep it opened. That was also very painful, and sometimes I would have to call an aide to remove those two things so I could sleep.

Jill Bolte Taylor (2004) has stated that individuals with brain injuries have heightened sensitivity to the energy of others who come near them (via Betty Grondin-Jose on Jill's website). I have felt very much the same way she did in terms of both good energy– and bad energy–giving people. I have always felt good energy from all of my therapists, especially those with whom I spent a lot of time. The process of physical recovery is very much a team effort between the trainer/therapist and the recipient/stroke survivor. I felt very strong, positive feelings toward my first therapist, Aaron, which went both ways. I also felt strong gratitude and love for some of the other people whom I felt respected me, especially my therapists and at least one or two nursing assistants. However, I also felt mistrust and fear of some others around me in the nursing home in the United States, or later in the hospital in Japan, who treated me neither very kindly nor respectfully, as Bolte Taylor also mentioned.

I confided in my therapist, Aaron, whom I came to trust in many ways, asking, "I wonder if I will ever be able to walk again."

Aaron did not give me any false hope. He told me, "Each person's recovery schedule is different, and many variables determine recovery and improvement, such as severity of injury, type and location in the brain of the injury, and the age and strength of the survivor."

Aaron more or less left it at that. I am still consulting experts on that question, but I have come to accept the notion that I may never be like I was before. What matters is that "we learn to do what we need to do, and we are able to do so safely." And the key here is "safely." We need to "challenge ourselves to stretch our capabilities within our means, without having any accidents or injuries." That was strongly drilled into me early on in the nursing home in the United States, and I still am very careful not to get injured. If we need to perform a certain task often, we will naturally get better in time, such as transferring to the toilet, using it and transferring back to the wheelchair, standing up to reach the sink, climbing a few stairs to enter or exit one's house, and so on.

CHAPTER 12

Physical Therapy in Japan

"The most wasted of all days is one without laughter."
—*Nicolas Chamfort*

Warau kado ni wa, fuku ga kitaru. ("Luck will come to the house where there is laughter.")
—*ancient Japanese proverb*

I started my rehabilitation in Japan almost immediately upon entering the Hirosaki Stroke Rehabilitation Center Hospital once back in Japan, soon after my return in August 2014. I met my Japanese physical therapist (Mr. M) and my occupational therapist (Ms. Yoko) when I first arrived there, but my doctor had inaccurately diagnosed the swelling in my left leg as "economy-class syndrome" (or deep-vein thrombosis). Thus, during that first week of my hospitalization and therapy in Japan, my designated therapists both stayed away from that leg and did not have me do any walking, even though I was eager to get up and walk, hoping the new environment would have a positive effect.

By my second week back in Japan, after having wasted a whole week without therapy, my physical therapist (PT) came into my room early in one morning, while I was still in bed sleeping. My husband had come in even earlier that morning to deliver my English newspaper and my clean, folded laundry to me on his way to his office at the nearby university, where he worked as a geologist and professor. He was sitting in a chair off to my left-hand side, slouched over and sleeping in a dark corner.

My PT came over to the left side of the bed and leaned over the bed railing to begin massaging my weak leg, trying to release the tension from the muscles on the left side of my body. But it was hard for him to reach me well, so he pulled up the metal bed railing on my left side, which gave way with a very loud squeaking sound. Then my new

PT, with my husband sitting nearby, kicked off his shoes and proceeded to crawl into my bed and continued the massage, but I remained very tensed up. At last he finished on the left side and crawled out of the bed, replacing his shoes. He then replaced the rail with another loud squeak. Next, he scuttled around to the other side of the bed and pulled up the railing there with another loud squeak. He knocked off his shoes and again crawled into my bed on my right-hand side, this time mumbling, "*Gomen, ne*" (which means "Excuse me, OK?").

I mumbled back, "*Daijyobu desu*" ("It's all right").

He worked for a while, trying to remove the tension on my right side now, but it seemed to take some time. Just then my husband stood up and left the room without a word, to return to his office, as his work was calling him away. My PT paused for a few seconds and then continued with the massage for another ten minutes or so. Finally he spoke, saying something like "Your body finally let go of that tension."

Then my new physical therapist crawled out of my bed again, slipped on his shoes, replaced the squeaky railing, and said, "*Otsukare-sama-deshita. Matta ashita, ne.*" This is a common Japanese greeting that we do not use in English, but it translates directly as something like "I am sorry to have made you tired. See you again tomorrow."

I called out after him, "*Otsukare-sama-deshita. Arigatou-gozai-mashita. Matta ashita, ne.*" ("Thank you very much, but sorry, I have made you tired. OK, see you tomorrow then.")

That is how my physical therapy started in the Hirosaki Stroke Rehabilitation Center Hospital in Japan, where I resided for a half-year. I continued to have PT and OT sessions there daily, for an hour each session. Those therapists worked hard to massage away my tension and stretch out my muscles before having me walk or move daily. On my PT's and OT's days off, I was assigned substitute therapists. Sometimes other therapists also suggested doing the massage session in my bed so as to save time going up and down the elevator to the workout space on the first floor and to allow more time for therapy. Beginning the therapy in bed while lying down is the safest position for a therapist to begin working with a new stroke survivor in order to safely test how well she/he is able to move. Aaron, my first therapist in the United States, started out the same way with me, and it was a regular pattern that I noticed of starting with the basics and slowly working through the various steps. I usually declined to have the session in my bed, in order instead to go downstairs to get much-needed *kibun tenkan* (a change of mood in a different atmosphere).

I had another regular occupational therapist (OT) there, Ms. Yoko, for hour-long sessions daily, who also worked hard to massage the tension out of my body before having me stand up and move around. We got along very well together.

Very early in our relationship, we established that "a daily laugh is very good for one's health, especially their mental health." I felt it to be very important, especially for us users/residents/survivors who have to spend long periods of time in hospitals or other such institutions. However, there is one caveat here: the laugh cannot be enjoyed alone (or such a person may be taken as crazy); the laughs must be shared with another person or persons. So Yoko and I decided that we would find ways to make each other laugh so we could share our daily laughs. But we quickly learned that we were both poor at remembering jokes and that retold incidents from our lives were not that funny either—at least not in a laughing-out-loud manner. Instead, Yoko and I would laugh at ourselves or others there. Mostly we laughed at me and my shortcomings. I felt embarrassment when I was found to have done something out of rule. For example, Yoko often pulled encrusted pieces of rice off my clothing from a few meals earlier, which had found themselves stuck to my front for all to see. I laughed out of embarrassment, but Yoko, always kindly and without scorn or reproach, shared the laugh with me.

There was another thing that made us laugh. The story goes like this: Often when we got into the elevator on the second floor, to take us down to the workout space on the first floor, there were already people in the elevator coming down from the third or fourth floors. One such person was a young man, a therapist, whom I will call Mr. I. He was very kind and friendly and always greeted us both where few others did there. I perceived him as handsome and thought he might be a good match for Yoko. I felt that they were both single, and I noticed that he also greeted her daily with a wide smile. In my opinion, he was a very attractive young man with his naturally curly hair. He reminded me of my younger brother's best friend as a child, whom I knew very well, as we more or less grew up together. Thus Mr. I seemed very familiar to me.

I wanted to ask Yoko if she found him attractive too. I was searching for the current Japanese slang word meaning "good-looking man," which was *ikemen*. (The word *ikemen* is a portmanteau, which is a blend or a combination of parts of word sounds from two languages, combined into a single new word. In this case, it was a combination of the English word "men," meaning "man/men" or "guy/guys; dude/dudes," and the Japanese word *ikeru*, meaning "can go/can pass," as in "He is a passable man/dude" or "He will do.") However, I could not quite recall the word, so instead I created my own portmanteau, which does not actually exist: "*motte-man*." This word is derived from the Japanese slang word used about one generation earlier to refer to a "cool-looking guy." It was constructed from the Japanese word *motteiru* (shortened to *moteru*), a verb meaning "to have" (meaning "He has it"), but it somehow did not sound quite right to me when I said "*motte-man*." I knew the word ended in "men," but I wanted to use a singular form such as Superman, Spiderman, or Anpanman, so I asked Yoko if she found Mr. I to be a "*motte-man*." Immediately, I realized how ridiculous that word sounded. We both broke out in laughter upon me saying that. Yoko knew what I meant and corrected me by saying, "*Ikemen?*" to which I said, "Yes, that is the word I was searching for. *Ikemen!*"

By this time we were both in the midst of enjoying our daily health-ensuring hearty laugh shared together. From then on, whenever we saw Mr. I in the elevator or elsewhere, we would always enjoy our daily laugh together then and there. I made her promise not to tell that story to Mr. I, a promise that she sincerely kept, but one day I had a substitute OT when Yoko was off for the day. I had to explain to her why I laughed upon seeing Mr. I and told her the story. I asked her not to tell it to him, but she soon told him, and he became Mr. M or Mr. MM after that for "*Motte-Man*," and I was all the more embarrassed about it in front of him. The substitute OT told me that she had found another therapist there (whom I will refer to as Mr. S) to be more attractive, so our group of friends expanded to include Mr. S too. As Yoko had known Mr. I in college, she also thought that the other therapist, Mr. S, was more attractive.

We all greeted each other there, even early in the morning when most people seemed to wear unfriendly frowns on their faces. I considered them all my friends as well as my regular therapists there. Later, when my sister came to visit me in Japan, we planned a party at our friend's shop for live blues music, food and drink. I invited them all. They all accepted and showed up at the event, to my great joy that day, to help me celebrate my "I am back" party.

So that is how Yoko and I came to share daily laughs together. She was a very professional therapist, and I enjoyed working out with her daily, along with my PT. I felt all of the therapists at the Hirosaki Stroke Rehabilitation Center Hospital were very professional.

Like the quotation from Nicolas Chamfort and the ancient Japanese saying at the beginning of this chapter, I strongly believed in the importance of laughter as a positive contributor to a speedier healing process.

Along with the great hour-long therapy sessions twice daily and the hot-springs bath twice weekly, I found the Hirosaki Stroke Rehabilitation Center Hospital cutting edge in terms of helping us to feel relaxed as we worked on our rehabilitation. The hot, salty baths there helped to relax my tense, swollen body and to temporarily reduce my body weight when suspended in the hot waters. Even for a short time, hot baths had a great effect on mind and body. Also, in cold northern Honshu, Japan, a very hot bath in winter keeps the body warmed up throughout the freezing nights. I wish I had been able to make even more progress in walking while hospitalized in Japan, but by the time I left the hospital, I had started walking using a 4-pronged cane. I also had learned how to climb up and down stairs quite well, thanks to my therapists there.

In contrast to the hot-springs baths in Japan, in the facilities where I was recuperating in the United States, we were only given showers, which I feel are far inferior to even a regular hot bath. It is easy to slip and fall in the shower, which happened to me on a few occasions, and I came to fear being given a shower there. Instead of feeling relaxed, I often felt tense.

On one of the occasions when I fell while in the U.S. nursing home facility, I slipped in the soapy water run-off after having my hair washed. *Plop.* I was down on my rear end, wearing nothing at all except my birthday suit. I was stark naked with my legs spread open wide in an uncomfortable position, unable to move on my own, even though I was not injured. A rather big chaotic panic follows when a resident falls down in such facilities. Two of the three people helping me with the shower immediately ran out of the room to get more help. In the meantime, a thoughtful nurse's aide tried to help dry me off a bit and placed a nightgown over my head. It was on just seconds before a few very strong-looking young men rushed in to help.

Suddenly I noticed a very strong-looking open-palm hand in front of my face, beckoning for me to take hold, which I did most happily. Ronaldo, a kind Philippine aide, whom I had met once before that, had me on my feet in seconds. Luckily I did not pull him down on top of me, as he had the strength to pull me up, even at a very poor angle. Ronaldo was my hero for a long time after that. Immediately there were some five or six pairs of hands on me, getting me dry, clothed and back into my wheelchair and then into bed. Later a nurse came around to see if I had any serious injuries. I did not break any skin or bones and came away with just a small bruise on my bum. But after that, I came to dread having showers there.

In a different facility, we were stripped naked in our rooms and wheeled through the hall with nothing covering our shamed and vulnerable bodies (except for a towel over our private parts) to be taken to a shower room. I came to prefer being given showers by a male nurse's aide (NAC) there, Mr. D, not because he was a man, but rather because he was extremely professional, having worked in the business as an aide for some 28 years and certified as a NAC. He was very respectful and mature with women residents, unlike some of the other male nurse's aides and *kaigo fukushi* who cared for me later in Japan and who took me to have baths (see Chapter 19). I also trusted Mr. D the most because he was very strong and I felt sure that he would not let me fall, and I trusted him as I trusted my PT. The 28 years that Mr. D had been in the business showed in his professionalism.

I was seldom informed of my bathing schedule ahead of time and often requested information from a certain receptionist who teased me for asking who would be the person to give me a shower, knowing that I preferred Mr. D. Actually, it was in contrast to another aide who was often assigned to give me a shower but was much less professional. While being kind and helpful to me, she often arrived late and then rushed me through the shower, including a very poor combing out of my longish hair, so that I would lose a large handful of my hair each time. In contrast, Mr. D was very gentle and considerate, letting me know what he was about to do before doing it and often checking with me that it was all right. He never stepped outside of his professional boundaries, and he let me do what I was able to do by myself. Also, when I needed to transfer somewhere, his strength ensured that I would not be dropped. He knew how to safely transfer me so as not to cause further pain to my sublexed left shoulder that seemed to be slowly ripping out of its socket, especially when I was transferred by poorly trained aides who would grab hold of my arm and painfully jerk it upward or backward. Mr. D also allowed me to proceed at my own pace. For that, I greatly appreciated his professional, resident-friendly approach. Another resident there, Marian, used to always say, "I like Dean too." I later sometimes confided in Mr. D how some of the other aides there had mistreated me. He kindly listened and tried to solve some of the problems for me. When I moved to HMC for a short intensive stint, I missed Mr. D greatly; I never saw him again after that and have not been able to contact him either.

I actually sympathized with some of the poorly trained, stressed aides, as, decades earlier, I myself had worked as a nurse's aide as my first part-time job when I was just fifteen years old and in high school, with no training at all. I found the work extremely difficult, tiring and draining, and after three years of working after school and on weekends and holidays, I was very happy to quit that job. I worked for low wages, which were under the minimum wage at the time, and worked just as hard as other full-time staff, if not harder than some of the other staff who often exerted their power over me. I was paid a mere $1.25 per long hard hour (before taxes) as my starting rate. At the end of nearly three years, it was raised a mere ten cents to $1.35 per hour before taxes, but it was not enough to keep me there, and I went back to baby-sitting for just fifty cents per hour.

I was a very sought-after baby-sitter, with people booking me weeks or months in advance. I often baby-sat for one family near my house with an impaired daughter who had spastic muscles and was unable to walk at around age seven (perhaps due to cerebral palsy). I enjoyed helping her to learn to walk and to hold and use a spoon on her own. It is ironic that now I find my hand and leg as spastic and tight as hers were. I loved her and enjoyed taking care of her, and perhaps that "good karma" might be of help to me now. If I could go back in time, I would recommend that her parents try Project Walk (see Appendix VII) or the Anat Baniel Method (see Appendix VIII). I believe in karma and feel that loving people who are kind to others will also be treated kindly in their own sickness or old age. Sometimes when I observe my aides at the facility in Japan laughing and bantering together as they help me with my bath, I remind them that in the time it takes to snap one's fingers, they will suddenly be sitting on the bath chair instead of me and a young girl or boy will be washing them. Then I snap my fingers to illustrate how soon they will find themselves in my position.

Having had experience in the job as a nurse's aide, I really respected any aides who helped me in any way in both the United States and in Japan, although some of them were not as kind and respectful of me as others were. As Jill Bolte Taylor (2008) also expressed. I would feel unsafe in the hands of those less professional aides but respected by other, more professional people.

It seemed that a majority of the staff working in the nursing home in the United States where I resided were untrained immigrant foreigners. Many seemed almost underage (and possibly underpaid as well). Many had emigrated from Pakistan, India, the Philippines and various parts of Africa, and many spoke their own languages together with each other, rather than English. Some had their whole family working there part-time or full-time with them. I did not appreciate being cared for by some of the younger men, perhaps in their late teens, but I realized that those facilities have to make ends meet and that immigrants and teens are often forced to accept low-paying jobs. I am against such practices and advocate for better working conditions for those immigrants and all staff in these facilities.

There were several times in the United States when our aides worked more than one consecutive shift, sometimes sleeping there and then working the first shift the next day or such, perhaps due to being understaffed. Working several consecutive shifts was very bad for the aides, but I felt that it was us residents who suffered the most for that practice and policy, and I wished that those aides would go home and get rested before working their next shift.

CHAPTER 13

Some Specific Aids in
Walking for Paralyzed Limbs

"In recent years, a wave of studies has documented some incredible emotional and physical health benefits that come from touch. This research is suggesting that touch is truly fundamental to human communication, bonding, and health."

— *D. Keltner, 2010 (accessed online, June 2015)*

Touch as Healing

Touch by itself, not to mention professional specialized massage, is, I feel, a very effective healing therapy, especially when administered by a professional therapist performing massage who is trained in how muscles and tendons are affected by stroke weakness.

If touch alone can be very healing, what can be said of the massage and stretching administered by a professional, well-trained and experienced therapist?

Self-Stretching

I am also interested in learning more about self-massage or self-stretching, but it can be quite difficult to try to do self-therapy. Thus I highly respect all of my therapists and appreciate their skills and their healing touch; this group includes students in training in Japan, who have carefully worked on my body for their practice and also to my benefit. Many of my therapists have in mind long-term goals for me or consider my needs.

It is no wonder that my rehabilitation sessions have always been my favorite times of the week or day. Even though it can also be quite painful at times, I highly recommend that all stroke survivors attend their rehabilitation therapy with enthusiasm, as it is very important to keep our bodies flexible and soft, rather than tight and tensed up, as I often am. In the United States, when my muscles and tendons were the tightest, just after coming out of the coma, I sometimes took mild pain relievers before my physical therapy sessions, anticipating pain.

Although I did not feel tired after deeply sleeping in a stroke-induced coma for a long time, many stroke survivors say they felt very tired and lethargic after having survived a stroke and experiencing a coma. It seems that my earlier massage and stretching sessions, which occurred shortly after regaining consciousness while still in the United States, were the most painful for me, as my muscles and tendons were the tightest then. At one point I asked my doctor in the United States if there was any medication to help alleviate the tense spasticity of my muscles. To my surprise, there was such a medicine, called baclofen in the United States, which had a very positive effect on my body. After I started taking that drug, my muscles did not feel quite as tight. When I got to Japan, instead of baclofen, which was not available, my doctor prescribed a made-in-Japan medicine that seemed to me not quite as good, but it helped too. While the anti-spasmodic medicines seemed to help me a lot, Project Walk (see Appendix VII) does not recommend their use in its rehabilitation training. The people behind Project Walk feel they can release the tension in the limbs through massage and body manipulation, instead of by using drugs. I also feel that it is better to not have to use drugs, if possible, as they can damage organs, such as the liver.

Different practices in physical therapy between the two countries taught me that the Japanese way of gently massaging out the built-up tension in the muscles before putting weight onto a weakened leg is an excellent way forward. But in the United States, I also realized that learning to bear pain is sometimes necessary for moving forward and that "pain is gain."

I also learned that physical therapists can and do get very physical sometimes, and one's relationship with therapists is very valuable and includes some of my best and happiest memories in the healing process over the first year or so of my rehabilitation.

Walking with a Cane

Walking for me continues to be "an act of faith," as Salopek expressed in the epigraph at the beginning of Chapter 11. For me, each step is very much a collapse that I try to avert, and a disaster that I try to break, by stepping forward with my weak left leg or with my strong right leg as I put my weight and balance on my weak left leg. Using my cane, it becomes a "three-beat rhythm" as I step forward with the cane and then stomp with my good leg while I place my weight and balance on my weak leg/foot, and then swoosh with my weak leg.

Wearing the Gait Belt

In the United States, almost all therapists and nursing staff use "gait belts" to support the residents/users or stroke survivors when they need to transfer them or to catch them when they seem like they are about to fall. A "gait belt" is a rehabilitation tool in the form of a belt worn around the stroke survivor's waist to help support people with walking deficiencies. It looks like a karate belt except that it has a buckle at one end so it can be securely tightened around a user's/resident's waist. They are usually white in color. (See the photo on page 105.) All staff members in hospitals and nursing homes in the United States taking care of stroke survivors and other incapacitated residents wear them around their own waists while working so they can whip them off quickly and use them on residents whenever needed. At the same time, all residents have their own gait belts that they generally wear around their waists throughout the day. In contrast, I never saw a gait belt being used in Japan. I was surprised that even therapists at the new top-ranked stroke rehabilitation facility in Japan never used them.

Instead, in Japan, staff and other helpers often pull up users by the scruff of their pants—a far inferior practice, I felt, as it is very uncomfortable to the user having their pants wedge into the crack of their bum (although it was explained to me that as many elderly users in Japan use diapers, it does not actually go into their crack). My pants have ripped from being pulled up that way. I have also seen Japanese staff prodding a person forward in the vicinity of the user's bum to get them to move more quickly. I feel that this practice is even worse, as it is degrading and humiliating. I asked staff to refrain from doing that and other such methods with me. In August 2016, I was told that the practice of righting

Party at Eddie's house, in the backyard, shortly before leaving Seattle: me (notice the white gait belt around my waist), flanked by my brother, Eddie, and niece-in-law, Emily (photograph by Susan Nudelman).

users by the scruff of their pants was now being discouraged in Japan; instead, gripping the arm has been used and taught more recently, but I feel that this practice is also bad for those stroke survivors who (like me) have painful sublexed shoulders.

I personally feel that Japanese therapists, nursing staff and others concerned would be very wise to incorporate use of the gait belt, starting at the colleges, universities, and other schools that train nurses, *kaigo fukushi*, occupational and physical therapists and others. I would like to see gait belts used regularly in Japan, as I think they are very stabilizing and safe, certainly much more so than the practice of pulling up people by the scruff of their pants or by the arm of a (potentially) sublexed shoulder. I was originally warned to be careful of my sublexed shoulder while in U.S. nursing homes, as, even by its own weight, the arm can be ripped out of its socket just by walking or engaging in normal movement.

I always have my untrained home helpers use my gait belt on me for safety. I also prefer to use a sling on my weak arm when being aided by helpers, especially inexperienced ones, to protect my left shoulder from painfully slipping or dislocating out of its socket.

Self-Practice of Walking

When I have no therapist or helper around to spot me and I want to exercise by myself, first I put on my leg brace. Then I park my wheelchair near a right-hand-side handrail in my house, set the brake stoppers on my chair, and practice standing up and sitting down about ten times. Then, while holding on to the handrail, I walk forward to the end of the handrail and step backward and forward and backward, usually to a count of ten times or for a certain period of time.

The Weakened Hand

I recently learned from my home therapist some hand exercises, besides just trying to open up the fingers of my weak hand by stretching them open. This is how to do it: Get a cloth as if to polish a table. Use large motions to the count of ten to swoosh around in circles or just move forward and backward or diagonally up and back on a large table. Stretch out the shoulder, back, elbow, and wrist—all of the arm. Then try to lay the hand out flat, with the wrist down flat and fingers straight outward.

Summary

Above, I have made observations about physical and occupational therapy that I received in Japan and the United States. While there are some institutionalized and personal differences, physical and occupational therapies and therapists are quite similar in the two places, and both provided good experiences and memories for me.

*   *   *

I have wondered if my physical therapy to be able to walk well and to use my left hand might require me to go back and redo all of the things/actions that I put my legs/body through since birth, as if to recover my memory and the body-brain connections of all of my accumulated movements. If losing one's memory requires relearning language and re-experiencing a history of interactions with people in their world, does my body also need to relearn how to move by doing again all of the physical activities I had experienced in my life until the stroke? My therapists never told me that, but I have pondered it.

While growing up, our family lived on an island in the middle of a rather large freshwater lake, and much of my childhood play included water sports at the lake. If I need to redo all of my actions and body movements since birth, what follows are some major things that I would need to do again:

- **As a small child:** being walked as a small toddler, holding the hands of two adults simultaneously (often both parents, though I also had two very close grandmothers); balancing on my father's hands and playing other acrobatic games with my father; being lifted up to touch the ceiling by my father while keeping my body straight-reaching upward; being thrown up into the air and then caught before falling to the ground by my father or an uncle; being projected or thrown forward in a swimming pool, a lake or salty bay waters by my father, before swimming to the water's surface and then swimming to shore or safety; playing airplane with my parents as they elevated me with their feet on my stomach, with me balancing with my arms spread out wide as if flying like Superwoman (I also played this game with my siblings, and then, some forty years later, with my own son on my two feet while balancing my son as the airplane); pretending to be escaping some prison and crawling on my stomach through an underground tunnel through the dirt in the forest by our house, before climbing a tree many meters high; running barefoot over gravel roads and through forests; horseback riding; riding my tricycle and then a bicycle; climbing a very steep hill daily walking to and from school from kindergarten until the end of first grade; creative dancing; playing tag, Red Rover, and other games that required running fast with neighborhood kids; taking ballet and tap-dance lessons; taking swimming lessons in the cold lake waters.

- **During elementary school:** doing gymnastics at home; ice skating; climbing down into the steep gully on wooded trails near our house and then climbing back up; playing 4-Square and hopscotch and playing on the jungle gyms and the bars at school, swinging around on loops on the bars, flipping both forward and backward; climbing hand over hand on monkey bars; sledding; tobogganing; racing; playing tetherball; diving into lakes or swimming pools; playing volleyball and school PE sports and games; trekking up mountain paths and often running back down; attending summer camps with swimming and horseback riding; swimming in mountain lakes; climbing over tennis court fences; climbing trees; jumping off cliffs on Tarzan-like ropes into the lake; water skiing on one or two skis; snow skiing.

- **In middle/junior and high school:** taking ballroom dance lessons; dancing with my best friend to the music of Motown and soul music; bicycling; playing croquet or miniature golf; doing wheelbarrow races; dancing to pop and rock music bands at weekly local dances; doing gymnastics in our living room; playing American football with our rule of "two-handed touch-below-the-waist" with neighborhood children and youths; trying to play tennis and running after missed balls; walking on my hands; standing on my head from a prone position or making a triangle first with my elbows and then standing on my head; doing cartwheels and somersaults (both forward and backward); doing stretching exercises; bending over backward until my hands touched the floor behind me; doing sports and gymnastics in school PE class; pretending to do ballet or modern dance; throwing and catching baseballs and footballs.

- **After high school as an adult or during college:** bicycling; roller skating; ice skating; dancing to Motown, rock and popular music; skiing; mountain climbing wearing crampons while climbing up and down glaciers on high mountains, like Mt. Rainier and Mt. Baker; practice falling into a crevice and pulling someone else out who was roped to me; running; taking belly-dance lessons.

- **Various lessons:** dance; tennis; small-craft sailing; snow skiing; beach/yard volleyball; badminton; body surfing; scuba diving; snorkeling.

- **Taichi:** learning, practicing and teaching both the short and the long forms in several different schools of taichi—sword form, long pole form, saber form, and *ji-gong* (the internal energy form).

- **Dance lessons and practicing/dancing:** salsa and bachata, belly-dance lessons, and social (ballroom) dance lessons—waltz, rumba, tango, quickstep, blues, swing, modern and Latin dance styles, rock, Motown, jazz or disco.
- **Taking swimming lessons in maternity for expectant mothers.**
- **Playing with my son when he was little:** balancing on stepping blocks; running; climbing things such as ropes and steps; playing on swings and teeter-totters; pushing and jumping onto a merry-go-round; going up steps and then sliding down slides; jumping across a span using a Tarzan-like rope; bicycling; playing basketball; climbing into treehouses; playing Frisbee; swimming; walking.

CHAPTER 14

A Stroke of Disorientation
Post-Coma Illusionary
Ideations ... "I am not crazy!"

Tunisia

Softly she floats on a bed of dreams.
Outside the pear trees seem to over-bloom,
and the walkway is a brilliant grass rectangle.
She tells me she is in Tunisia or Turkey.
She explains everything quite logically,
from heated sands to hissing sidewinders.
The food is bad, but she keeps the leftovers
in a small plastic cup, a few grapes, some yogurt
with half a hard-boiled egg balanced on top.
She wants out of the desert, and she wills
this through a combination of familiar words
and relentless rivers of consciousness.
Outside, men and women come and go
with greetings and salutations. Inside, clouds
part over room three. Hot air rising over
cool air produces waves. So too, a mirage
and a pebble entering a calm blue lake.
—Edward Nudelman,
from *Out of Time, Running* (2014)

The poem above, "Tunisia," written by my brother, Edward Nudelman, aptly describes my early experience after coming out of the coma. Eddie was my one of my main advocates while I was in hospitals and specialized nursing facilities in Seattle, Washington, and he came to daily visit me, along with his wife, Susie, and my mother (and sometimes her dog, Lennie). Eddie wrote this poem while I was recuperating at the first long-term nursing facility in north Seattle. I had this strange lingering sensation (medically referred to as a "perseveration") that the nursing home, and all of us in it, were in North Africa, not north Seattle. Thus, I felt that I was in Tunisia or possibly Morocco (but not the Turkey that he mentions, actually). He is correct that I "wanted out of the desert."

I think that my perseveration about being in North Africa was connected to an actual experience that I had had some forty years prior, when I had just turned 21, while traveling in the North African country of Morocco for over one month. Although I enjoyed it there very much, I became very sick—I almost died, as I became very dehydrated due to severe diarrhea and vomiting over several days. (Perhaps I had contracted cholera.) It was there that I had my first "out-of-body experience" sometime after receiving some medicine and clean water.

While in the nursing home in Seattle, after coming out of a stroke-induced coma, my doctor indeed said that I was tending to "perseverate," a behavior not uncommon in early stroke survivors. In its verb form, "to perseverate" means to do or to say something repeatedly or to go the limit, to be stubborn. In its noun form, "perseveration" is a situation marked by repetitiveness, recurring actions or words.

As mentioned, one of my main perseverations at that time was that I firmly believed the nursing home was in North Africa—at the very least, we were not in north Seattle. I repeatedly asked my brother to confirm that.

Another major perseveration that I had in the early days of my recovery was feeling like I had three arms/hands and three legs/feet. I was constantly told by many people there, "No, Laurel, you have just two hands and two feet, just like all of us." It felt like a sort of phantom hand and foot that others could not see. I could not mentally will them to perform things for me as I could with my good right hand/arm and my right leg/foot. I felt that the phantom limbs were the "spirit" of my hand and foot that did not get properly re-melded back into my body when I regained consciousness following my out-of-body experience.

My brother once asked me to show him my third leg/foot. I said, "Here it is. Can you see it?" I said that as I rubbed my right leg against my left leg. My brother told me to look at what I was doing. I finally saw I was rubbing my good leg against my other leg, which was dull to feeling. It finally made sense, cognitively. Everyone was kind of laughing at me, and then suddenly my phantom middle leg/foot disappeared forever (although the phantom hand/arm continued to remain for a while). It did seem weird that there was no shoulder for the third arm and no buttock for the third leg.

I even went so far as to ask the manicurist in the nursing facility if she could do all three of my hands for the usual price of two hands, and she said it would be all right. She may have also been one of those there who told me that I had two hands just like everyone else. Otherwise, she just let that bit of craziness ride for the sake of communication and for business. I never followed through with the triple manicure. I wish I had and then had taken a selfie of it.

There were several other situations when I seemed to be having schizophrenic-like illusions rather than perseverations, per se, although I am not sure how it is actually termed. Several times, I thought I saw someone at the nursing home or hospital in the United States whom I had known in England. I had made many trips to a university in Lancaster to take short courses while working on my doctorate.

First of all, I thought I was seeing and talking with one of my mentors, named Lia, whom I had worked together with (over email) on a book project and whom I had recently met up with in Brazil at a conference. Perhaps the aide in the hospital just resembled her, and when I called out the name "Lia" and clung to her for help, she was not able to unlatch me and deny being Lia, so this illusion carried on every time that I saw her, which was quite often during that period.

This happened again with another aide there whom I thought was another person: Ms. C, a colleague of mine in the same Ph.D. program in Lancaster, England, with whom I had been quite close there. Like me, Ms. C is from Seattle but resides in Japan. I thought I had seen her at the nursing home. The same illusion carried on for a while every time I saw the person who resembled her. I wanted to ask her about her new, younger husband whom I had heard about from her at our last meeting, but instead, at the nursing home, I overheard a conversation that she was having with another aide about him. I thought that I heard her saying that she had split up with him.

When I mentioned this experience to my sister, she rejected it outright and explained to me, "No, Laurel, why would those people be working here in Seattle? You just dreamed it. It never happened. Just forget about it."

But such things cannot be easily forgotten. I felt let down that my closest supporter, my sister, did not try to understand my reality then. She seemed to have brushed off my illusion as "crazy" in a blanket fashion, which I was not willing to accept.

A few years after leaving Seattle, I wrote emails to both Ms. C and Lia asking them if they remembered seeing me in Seattle, but they both apologetically said that they did not see me there. So, my sister's claim, which I had not wanted to accept, was correct.

"No, Laurel, why would those people be working here in Seattle? You just dreamed it. It never happened. Just forget about it."

As you see, by reading what I have written here, I could not just forget about it. It *did* happen! However, when I happened to run into Ms. C a few years later at a conference in Japan, she denied it again. But, to me, it *did* happen, and it is imprinted on my memory as clear as day. My brother and Susie also kindly explained to me in Seattle that it was just the nature of my brain injury and that it did not mean I was crazy. It was an unavoidable byproduct of the disorganization of brain cells caused by the stroke, but their kind words did not rest well with me. I rejected being constructed as brain damaged and felt they were confusing my situation with mental illness or dementia of their other relatives (at the time, they were caring for my mother, who was afflicted by dementia). I was not willing to accept their explanation, which I took to be just the stereotypical prognosis of most stroke survivors that they had read about in the literature. I was not willing to be constructed as "the stereotypical brain-damaged stroke survivor."

Although I understand my family's desire to accurately portray my understanding of reality, I think it would have been better if they had listened to me and tried to understand my experiences and thoughts. There was no one else there whom I could talk to about this problem, and hospital (or nursing home) life easily becomes very alienating (even in my own country, but especially later in Japan, away from my better support people). Are there any books or papers written to assist health-care workers with regard to what to say to early stroke survivors in scenarios such as these, to defuse tension and anxiety? If there are, I don't think this literature is widely dispersed or discussed. I wish it had been for me, and I wish it now for others in the future. Hospital life can so easily become lonely, boring, and often painful. In addition, sometimes a patient has to deal with problems such as human relationships and situations of interpersonal exchange with those in charge of our daily needs as we struggle with our injuries and deficiencies. Hospital life is also tiresome, and it was hard sleeping, because lying on my left side was very painful. It took a long time to get used to the "community of practice" at hospitals, I felt. I had to relearn their procedures and practices and expectations of me every time I changed facilities, which happened numerous times and extended to two different countries. I did not sign up to join that group—I just landed there suddenly without any choice in it. So, all along the way, whatever can be done to calm a stroke patient and reassure them goes a long way toward helping them recover.

There was a similar incident when I had an illusionary experience while in the nursing home in the United States. There was a special event there—a Mother's Day party. As my son was in faraway Japan, I did not expect to see him. In the party room, people were gathered together and were eating and drinking a bit of light wine. Suddenly I saw my favorite nephew and his wife coming in: Aaron and Emily. My first thought was how sweet it was of Aaron and Emily to pay me a visit on Mother's Day, when I am just Aaron's aunt who lives far away in Japan, whom he seldom sees anyway. When Emily passed by me, I said to her, "I love you, Emily," as I often said to her, and I really loved her for coming to see me. As I expected her to, she answered, "I love you too." But then both of them went to sit with Lorraine, another resident at my facility. I just waited for them to realize that they had made a mistake and come over to my table, but when nothing happened for quite some time and I was getting anxious to have them join me, I asked an aide to have my nephew come over to my table with me. She went over to talk with them and then reported back to me that he was actually their nephew, and Lorraine, the woman over there, was his aunt, and they wanted to stay there. It might have helped if "Emily" had not played along by saying, "I love you too," but I understand she was probably just trying to be nice.

Finally, my "real nephew," Aaron, showed up with his father (my brother) and joined me at my table, but without Emily. I wondered if someone from the nursing home had called them and reported my sad story and that is what brought the real Aaron over after all. But my brother later said that Aaron is such a kind kid and he came on his own.

I pointed out to Aaron that his lookalike was sitting over there, but he did not think there was a resemblance. Later the real Aaron paid me another visit on the actual Mother's Day Sunday, and he brought flowers and chocolates.

"Thank you, dear Aaron. You will never know how much that meant to me."

My dear niece, Lena, made the same gesture on Mother's Day by paying me a visit and bringing chocolates too. I may have cried tears of happiness that day, as it is great to have such a loving family.

So, yes, the line between reality and alternate worlds can be fuzzy when you're talking about a brain injury. While I was in the hospital in Japan later, I continued to receive frequent cognitive tests asking me questions similar to the ones I had been asked in the U.S. facilities, such as asking me to count backward from 100, subtracting sevens. They next asked me to name vegetables. In Japan, I answered in my second language (Japanese), but I gave names of vegetables that are common in Japan, as well as those seldom seen in Japan, such as parsnips, turnips, red radishes, artichokes, Brussels sprouts, and rhubarb.

In Japan, the cognitive test also used a small, briefcase-like box with many gadget-like items placed in slotted beds similar to one used in the United States, and they asked me to remember some of the things. One aide pulled things out of her pockets, which I still recall: tissue paper, a ten-yen coin, a key, notepaper and a pen. To this day, I still remember most of the things in the briefcase, too, as I thought the case with perfect indentations was interesting and I thought about other things that I would have wanted to include in there which were missing: chopsticks, a stapler, scissors, tweezers, nail clippers, and so on. Although this occurred over seven years prior to this writing, I can still recall most of the items that were included in it: a key, a toothbrush, a spoon, a pen, a comb, a pencil, and a wristwatch. I also remember the three things I was asked to recall while we talked about other things as follows: a table, an apple and a one-yen coin. I usually was able to answer all of the questions correctly with 100 percent accuracy, which I enjoyed doing, as it was a boost to my self-esteem.

Along with these cognitive-type questions, I was, at other times, asked another set of questions to determine my mental level of depression or stability, such as the following: "Do you sometimes or often feel inferior to those around you?" In Japan, where self-deprecation and modesty are an important part of social interaction, I pulled off a severe *faux pas* by saying that I actually often feel *superior* to those around me, in my attempt to emphatically express that I was not depressed at all. I may have lost points for saying that, but I felt I should have gained points for having to answer using my second language. I wondered how Japanese people would fare if they had to use their second language (English) to answer these questions. Fortunately, all of the questions and answers were simple and well within my Japanese abilities.

Another thing I recall from my time in the United States, having just woken up from the coma, was how I would sometimes confuse reality with images on the TV and conversations going on around me. At the time that I came out of the coma in April 2013, the big news item was the Boston Marathon bombings. The police had caught the older brother or shot him dead, but the 19-year-old younger brother was a fugitive, still at large, and was being sought through a massive manhunt.

I began to feel a bit paranoid that I was going to be arrested along with my half–Japanese son, whom I thought resembled the suspect they were looking for, and I mistakenly thought that my son was also staying in the same nursing facility with me, as he rode in the ambulance with me there. Although I am American, having lived in Japan for decades as a *gaijin* (foreigner), perhaps I still felt a bit *gaijinized*, or marginalized as an outsider, even in my own native country. Many people in the nursing home knew of my strong affiliation to Japan. I already felt disliked by many of the nursing staff there for often pulling out my feeding tube, which they had to replace, and I was often scolded by them. So I had this fear/fantasy illusion of the police coming to the hospital asking "if they had seen any disruptive foreigners here," and they would say, "Yes, we have seen such a person like that," and then point me out. I feared being harassed and arrested. Then, when they saw my son, I feared that he would be arrested too. I worried and fantasized about this. Finally, the suspect was caught and it was widely reported on TV news, and my fantasy disappeared.

I perseverated like this for some time, but when I arrived back in Japan a half-year after regaining consciousness, my brain and the illusions had settled down, and those mind games also ceased. Fortunately, I was able to recover from that stage on my own without medication or any lingering bad effects. I realized how realistic those illusions had appeared to me, and I felt betrayed by my most trusted supporters, who could not seem to understand or sympathize with my fantasies. But at the same time, I question those people who played along, pretending to be someone else whom I had imagined them to be. It would have more helpful if the aide had said, "No, I am not Lia. You must have the wrong person. My name is XX." Perhaps they did say as much, but I just did not hear it, as I wanted to believe my fantasy, which was so strong. My "out-of-body experience" when I first came out of the coma (see Chapter 8) also felt very real. And, while in the coma, I found myself in what seemed like a parallel world (or perhaps it was a vivid dream).

When I first came out of the coma in the nursing home in the United States, everyone there spoke to me in English, but having, in the past, researched a bit about the recovery of the bilingual brains of survivors of brain trauma causing aphasia or the inability to speak, I wondered if my weaker second language—Japanese—had returned. I had learned that often the second or weaker language returns later or has more difficulty in returning, if at all. As my stroke was located in my right-brain hemisphere, I seemed to not have had any language problems, which are more likely to be affected by left-brain hemisphere strokes. Still, I searched the hospital for a Japanese person to speak with then. A nurse introduced me to one Japanese man there, but he mistakenly thought I wanted to speak with him in English instead of Japanese, and he felt too stressed to do that, so he refused the meeting. It is too bad, as I could have helped him to reduce his stress by using Japanese with him and helping to interpret for him to communicate with the staff.

Instead, I telephoned Japan and talked with my husband in Japanese. I realized that both of my two languages were very robust, and I had no trouble speaking or understanding in both my mother language and my later-acquired second language. I still felt a strong need to use Japanese and called Japan several times. It may be of some importance for medical professionals to query a stroke patient, especially early on, regarding whether they are multilingual. It could alleviate fear and uncertainty, and it would have been a welcome intervention on my behalf.

CHAPTER 15

A Stroke of Dread

Horrible Travel Back to Japan and Nearly Being Incarcerated

After finishing up my last week of intensive rehabilitation in Seattle, I was finally ready to travel back to my home in northern Japan—but not without a huge amount of trepidation, as well as sadness in saying good-bye to my sister, mother, brother, and other loved ones who so faithfully supported me during my recovery. I didn't know if I would ever see them again.

In retrospect, I made four major mistakes just before traveling by airplane back to Japan: (1) allowing others to pack my bags for me; (2) allowing both doctors and family to convince me to wear a catheter; (3) not taking responsibility for my own valuables and entrusting them to others; and (4) bringing into Japan the U.S. prescription medicine oxycodone (an opiate pain reliever).

Even though I realize that those who tried to help me prepare for the journey home had extremely good intentions, which I greatly appreciate, I let others take over too much of the decision making, which I usually set aside a week or more to complete in advance. It's a stressful time, as I tend to get very agitated before air travel. In traveling when physically impaired (and perhaps more so for those recovering from stroke), one needs to be mindful not to forget to take anything important that might be needed, while not making one's luggage too heavy, and then go through a checklist of important actions. For me, not attending closely to the list caused me much heartache and pain.

Do not let others make you wear a catheter, unless you want it or feel you absolutely need it. There was a lot of discussion before my departure as to how I would go to the toilet during the long ten-hour flight over the Pacific. My family, after discussions with a nurse and a doctor, believed that I should be catheterized. They felt it would be next to impossible for my husband to help me into the tiny airplane toilet. This idea did not sit well with me. I had thought that I would try to hobble my way over to the toilet with my husband's help during the flight. But when it was decided that it would put too much stress on him, I listened to other options.

I was against wearing a catheter from the start, remembering how hard it was when I was forced to wear one after having given birth by C-section years before. I began insisting, "This is my body, and I will make my own decisions about it. I am not going to wear it. Period! End of conversation. I will walk to the toilet with Ko's help."

But that was just the beginning. I started to weaken when they said, "You cannot burden Kotaro like that. He says he can't do it."

Next they brought in a staff member whom they knew I respected, who took their side with scientific and medical rationale that I could not refute. They also reminded me frequently that my sister-in-law is a retired RN, and I respected her greatly for her nurse training and trusted in her medical knowledge as well as good sense and loving concern. My husband, my son, and my brother also all sided with them, and I was left standing alone, outnumbered, with little defense left, except "No, thank you, I hate those things."

Being outnumbered and overpowered, I eventually allowed a nurse in Seattle to insert a catheter into my bladder shortly before leaving, which I greatly regretted later. I also put on a fresh diaper for adults. My brother, in the meantime, called one of my best friends and arranged for her friend's daughter, who is a fourth-year nursing student, to meet us on arrival at Narita Airport in Tokyo to remove the catheter. But we later scrapped that plan due to time constraints in transferring planes. Perhaps I should have been trained in catheter removal, to cover a worst-case scenario.

I realized early on in the Seattle airport even before we boarded the plane that "the unfortunate catheter" did not seem to be doing its job adequately, and I worried for the long flight. There was some leak somewhere, wetting my clothing and making me smell bad, and it felt clammy against my body. This caused my son to feel shame. My husband must have felt shame too, but, unlike my son, he kept his thoughts to himself. While the urine bag strapped to my left leg was filling up correctly, urine was also seeping out along the outside of the tube into the diaper, which quickly filled up and overflowed into my clothing and then into the seat of the airplane. The other major problem (along with the horrifying shame of wetting my pants in a public place as an adult) was that during the trip, the seepage was extremely painful. So, with the pain and the shame, each time a tear ran down my face. When my husband asked if I was all right, all I could say was "*kurushii-yo, totemo kurushi.*" That translates as something like "It is painful. It's very terrible," so, being the sensitive guy that he is, each time he shared the misery with me. Before we landed, he promised to take me to a hospital upon arrival in Japan to have the catheter removed. But it turned out to be much later—not until our arrival in northern Japan, in Aomori, after the plane transfer, the final hour-long flight from Tokyo to the North, and another hour-long car drive.

The second big mistake was "not packing my bags myself." I had allowed my family to pack all six of our bags (including three carry-on bags), so when I needed items from our carry-on luggage in a big hurry, it was futile. We needed to find a clean diaper after removing the wet one when we went into the airport toilet, needing to get on a flight soon. We did not have much time to search for one, not knowing if any had even been packed at all, so my husband, Kotaro, went out to buy some. Unfortunately, he returned with the wrong type, but it was the only type available.

In Seattle, I had been in pain and felt too tired to get out of bed and back into my wheelchair to contribute anything while my family was packing our stuff. In addition, my weak leg was swollen and painful, and the thought of having to stand on it was too much. I felt grateful having them take care of the task of packing for me, so I let them do it. Later, this led to me having to lie to the first immigration officer on my way out when I was asked, "Did you pack your luggage by yourself?"

I lied a bit and said, "Yes, but I had some help."

That was when I remembered that I had left a huge chunk of Parmesan cheese in my sister's refrigerator that I had been planning to take to Japan. I realized that it was just as well to have forgotten it, as, upon arrival in Japan, I would either have seen it discarded in the garbage bin or have had to risk the consequences of lying about it. I never for a minute thought about the prescription oxycodone that I was carrying until it was snatched out of my pouch in the stroke rehabilitation hospital a few days later (see below).

In setting out from Seattle, we had left the house on time and arrived at the Sea-Tac International Airport with enough time for us to search for and find the wheelchair toilet and for me to use it. Already the leg bag of the catheter was full, so we emptied it there for the first time. Later, on the airplane, when it was full again, my son asked me, "Why do you 'pee' so much?"

I had to think about that, as I had not intentionally "peed" at all, and had tried to drink less fluid than I usually did, but with the help of the diuretic blood-pressure-reducing medicines that I was taking, a lot of urine accumulated in my bladder to be released through the catheter or the leak.

The third mistake that I made was leaving my valuables with someone else. While in the nursing home in Seattle, I had left all of my valuables with my sister, to take to her house for safety, such as my two good watches and other things too. When it came time to leave Seattle, instead of returning those things to me, she had given them to my husband to pack, but he later said he had no clue where they were. I'm sure she considered that a safer proposition, but I would have loved to be in on the loop of that decision. Things like my passport, airplane ticket and money were accounted for, but some things had to be replaced later. (Six years later, I actually located one of the wristwatches in a small case while searching for something else.)

The final mistake that I made was carrying the pain reliever oxycodone into Japan, where it is an "illegal narcotic drug." I did not know that it was illegal in Japan, a country that fiercely monitors and prosecutes drug trafficking. I was never checked for the medication in the security line for passengers going into the airplane out of Seattle or at the immigration checkpoint when entering Japan.

However, the next day on my return, while in a Japanese hospital, my pouch (which I used in lieu of a purse) was slightly unzipped, and a nurse spotted the oxycodone bottle and plucked it out with her long fingernails. She seemed to gloat over her ability to "bust me," I thought, wondering what the next step would be. She quickly turned the contraband bottle of drugs over to the head doctor, who promptly contacted the police, the immigration office and a local narcotics agent after finding out what they were. I wished he had just discarded them and talked to me about why he did so, instead of contacting the police. My name was clearly written on the bottle, as it was a prescription medication from a U.S. pharmacy. A few days before our planned departure from Seattle, my sister had kindly filled my prescriptions for that medicine, along with over twenty other medications for me to bring back home to Japan, in case they were not available there. (I later heard, some years later when Julie Hamp, an executive of Toyota Company, was detained for a similar offence in Japan, that oxycodone is actually available in

Japan but is seldom prescribed.) I feared for several days that I would be indicted, put in a mugshot and sent to a Japanese prison in my already poor condition and jet-lagged state of exhaustion. That worry must have elevated my blood pressure more than it already was. My case was later dropped. (Julie Hamp's case was also dropped, but not before she had to resign from her executive post at Toyota.)

After I finally arrived in Japan, things got worse. While I thought that things could only begin to improve, I soon started feeling the ill effects of traveling. I was admitted to the hospital the next day. My doctor was concerned that the swelling in my weak foot/leg could be "economy-class syndrome" (or deep-vein thrombosis—that is, a clot). The worst part was that I had to wait several days for the sonography expert to show up at the rehabilitation hospital to confirm or deny it. In the meantime, an edema sock was put on that foot. I might have died in the meantime if it actually had been a blood clot that had dislodged and then traveled to my lungs, heart or brain. In such a case, you would not be reading this book now. Fortunately, a few days later, when the sonography specialist showed up, it was determined that it was not a blood clot or deep-vein thrombosis, but rather edema due to water buildup after a long trip with little or no movement.

A final disruption: The caper of the nurse plucking the so-called illegal narcotic drug out of my pouch, and then summoning the doctor to confiscate it, was not quite complete. I had tried to explain to them that it was one of about twenty other prescription drugs that my very reputable doctor from a reputable hospital had prescribed, which my sister had purchased for me at a reputable pharmacy a few days before my departure. They were not street drugs that I was planning to sell in Japan. I seldom took them, except when I was experiencing intense pain caused by spastic or tightened-up muscles. I had to anxiously wait over a week for the results of a formal review before being told that they had decided to drop the case against me.

The nurse was a great disappointment to me in what I expected a good nurse to be—supportive, kind, and helpful in relieving one's pain and stress. The doctor also was a big disappointment, as he did not support me after that when I needed his help. He wrote a letter to my university office where I worked, saying I was not well enough to return to work (although I disagreed with that). I lost my job in the end, though I had hoped to return to my office and to teach my last term before I was officially retired. In addition, that doctor did not support me when I needed to renew my driver's license.

After having tried so hard to resist the construction of me as "depressed," I think I finally slipped right into a depressed state at that time, as I felt extremely low and stressed, unable to escape the prejudices and lack of sensitivity that seemed to surround me.

Being very jet-lagged, stressed and sick, I arrived in Japan in very poor condition, so after the narcotics charge case was dropped, the only direction I could go from there would be up, I reasoned. Eventually, I did begin to readapt to life in Japan and began to enjoy the comfortable rehabilitation experience afforded in the hospital in my hometown, with two hour-long sessions daily with fantastic therapists, two hot-springs baths weekly, and three healthy meals each day. After I got used to life there, things began to improve. I also had guests visiting me nearly daily, which helped to raise my spirits, along with my husband's daily visits. I started to lose weight, which helped my condition improve as well. So, as I settled down, I eventually came to enjoy life again and enjoy being back in Japan.

But I want to say this about oxycodone and other such opium-based pain-relieving medicines: Stay away from them! Opioids are too smooth and nice as painkillers. I can understand how they could easily become addictive, especially for those of us with chronic pain secondary to a serious medical condition. If given a choice, opt for weaker, non-opioid-type painkillers such as Tylenol or generic types of acetaminophen, and try your best to resist ever trying opioids, even apart from the legal issues. Try "mindfulness" activities such as yoga, taichi, or simple meditation to control pain if it is serious and chronic. Fortunately, I do not have an addictive type of personality, and I seldom requested opioids and took them very infrequently; however, I deeply understand the torment of chronic pain, so the temptation is ever present.

CHAPTER 16

Rebirth

I'm Back Party

"Karma brings us ever back to rebirth, binds us to the wheel of births and deaths. Good Karma drags us back as relentlessly as bad, and the chain which is wrought out of our virtues holds as firmly and as closely as that forged from our vices."
—*Annie Besant*

"Each night, when I go to sleep, I die. And the next morning, when I wake up, I am reborn."
—*Mohandas Gandhi*

The quotation above from Mohandas Gandhi expresses the notion that "rebirth" is something that might occur many times in a person's life. In Gandhi's view, it occurs between each night and each new day. For me, it has only occurred once or twice in my life, over a span of more than six decades.

Shortly after my arrival back in Japan, my sister, Janice, came to visit me. I was still acclimating to a new lifestyle and trying to adapt to the many changes in my physical as well as emotional life. I had asked my sister to come visit back when I was near the end of rehab work in Seattle. It was my brother's idea, but I was happy to sponsor the trip, as my sister knows Japan and Hirosaki very well, having lived there for several years, and I knew she could help me from a spiritual and a psychological point of view. She came over and stayed with me for one month. We have always been very close since we were small and are said to look like identical twins. (See the photo on page 125.) Once, at the nursing home in Seattle, when she came to visit, a resident there who knew me called out to her, thinking it was me, "Praise the Lord. Laurel, you are walking." I wish it had been true and that the resident did see me walking, but it was my dear sister coming to visit me that morning.

Sisters in every way: a few years before the stroke, with some of my sister's wonderful paintings in the background (author's photograph).

During my sister's stay with me in Japan, she helped me to laugh and smile again—really for the first time since all of those bad experiences that had occurred on the difficult trip home. We planned many trips around town together during her stay, going out by special wheelchair taxi. We went out shopping and eating in restaurants for fun, and we went out to get my hair cut. She also came to one of my day-service places to experience it with me.

For me, it is always easier doing things and going places and planning parties when I have my sister's help, as she is very good at such things. She is also very social and has many friends and some ex-relatives living near me through her ex-husband's family. So besides our plans, other people she knew planned a few events that we attended together. She helped me to plan and pull off our "I am/we are back!" party at our friend's shop to celebrate my going home from hospitals and facilities after being incapacitated for a year and her own return (after a three-year hiatus) to Hirosaki, where she used to live and work.

The party came off very well, and I was so happy to welcome four of my favorite therapists from the Hirosaki Stroke Rehabilitation Center

"Family" day service in Japan. My sister came to visit me in Japan and stay at my house, and she also came to my family day service at my rehab center. Here we are with the staff (photograph by Edward Nudelman).

Hospital, who kindly attended the party. They surprised me with the gift of a beautiful giant bouquet of flowers from them and the rehabilitation hospital. It was the largest bouquet I have ever seen, let alone received. So I felt very thrilled, grateful and honored. The food and drink there, along with the blues music, was fantastic. In all, I had a great time, as it really represented my being back in the world of life and enjoying friends—the true joy of life to me. I think I had a smile on my face the whole time. To top off the evening, the owners of the shop surprised me by bringing out a cake to the tune of "Happy Birthday" played by the band. At first I wondered whose birthday it was. It turned out to be a cake for me, as Ms. Hiromi, one of the owners, whispered "Happy Re-birthday, Laurel" as she placed the cake in front of me. I wiped away a tear of happiness and then made a wish and blew out all of the candles in one breath. It was my first re-birthday party. I was reborn, and it was really the best birthday party I have ever had, almost like a surprise party and the perfect way to end the evening. The homemade lemon cake itself was delicious, too. We took it home and ate it when we arrived back at the house for a kind of after-party. I want to say "thank you" to the two owners of the shop, Hiromi and Emiko, and also to Hiromi's husband, Mr. Arata, and the others working there, and to all of my guests for giving me such a memorable party. Thanks also to the blues band who melted away my blues.

The idea of "rebirth" is connected with the Hindu concept of good karma. Perhaps my karma was good, helping me to be reborn within the same lifetime, rather than having to die and start all over again in another body with a new spirit and different persona (or perhaps as a different, nonhuman creature). I am grateful for being able to come back and complete my work in this lifetime.

My sister went back to the United States a few days after the party, and I missed her very much. When summer came around the next year, I really wished that we could afford for her to make yearly visits, as it is very hard for me to go to Seattle now. I had become used to making yearly trips home over my thirty-plus years of living in Japan, making living far from home bearable.

Another of my goals is to find a way to make overseas travel easier. For example, I thought perhaps I would try using a walker wheelchair that I discovered a fellow stroke survivor using at a short-stay facility. But my therapists told me that using a walker is much more difficult than it looks, and it is easy to be pulled forward and fall down, so I have had to put that idea away. Having tried using it, I would agree, but I still want to move on in my independence.

I also wanted to try out a "robotic suit" strapped to the left side of my body to assist my walking. It would be a dream come true for me if I could use it on a regular basis. That dream is third, after my first wish for world peace and my second dream of being cured and walking on my own, without any apparatus. (My wish to try out a robotic suit later materialized in Japan—see Appendix IX.)

CHAPTER 17

A Stroke of Gratitude

*Japan's Care Manager System
and My Recent Adjustments*

In Japan, there is a social system not only designed to help stroke survivors and other physically disabled people like myself but particularly designed for the aged, such as people suffering from Alzheimer's disease and other types of dementia. Through this system, they are able to access and administer special insurance funds. However, it is a bit complicated.

The first step is to get a *shogaisha tecchou*, which is a booklet issued from the City Hall in the city where one lives in Japan, certifying one as physically or mentally handicapped, disabled, sick or aged 65 and over (based on a doctor's assessment) and giving each person a ranking from 1 to 5, depending on the degree of their physical and cognitive ability to function independently. Since I am mostly wheelchair bound and cannot perform many ordinary physical tasks, I have a low ranking, enabling me to access a larger amount of the money covered by the government at less out-of-pocket cost to me for my care.

The next step is usually to find a "care manager," who is licensed to handle one's care, based on the amount of insurance money one is allotted monthly and the sorts of care one requires. The system is quite complex, so I was happy to have someone else work it out for me, but it is possible to be one's own care manager. Since I am not working any longer and usually have no regular appointments, the monthly schedule was originally based more on my husband's schedule, as he often had to go out of town and my plan was designed to meet his needs as much as my own. However, my husband takes over my care much of the time to save on costs a bit. My care manager prepares a monthly calendar for me of services I receive, places I am sent to, and costs I have to pay beyond insurance coverage. It needs to be checked at City Hall, and sometimes my hours of care have been reduced to save on public expenses.

Before he retired, when my husband had to go out of town for business for several days, he did not want to just leave me home for such a long time, and thus he enrolled me in what are called "short-term stay" facilities, usually for five to ten days at a time. These typically include meals, baths and sometimes rehabilitation and recreation or activities such as Japanese *shuuji* (calligraphy). There are only two such places in my vicinity for me to choose from. I prefer the one with a rehabilitation therapist available, but the other place has a great staff, who are very kind to me, and I have my own room and toilet. On occasions I have prepared special Western-style meals for everyone there in my small section group, including the users/residents and the staff. I have made spaghetti with meat sauce, eggplant lasagna and chocolate pudding for everyone, and they seemed to enjoy the change in menu. I am usually sent to that facility. Where I am sent also depends on their availability at the time that I require the service.

As we are not set up at home for me to use our home bath safely, I am taken out twice weekly for baths at day-service facilities, which also include lunch and usually rehabilitation therapy, as well as a snack with instant coffee in the mid-afternoon, and sometimes a game or recreation. I am picked up and brought home each time by van, where I am able to remain seated in my wheelchair while traveling.

My husband also takes me out about once every three months to see my doctor, where I have my blood, urine, and other things tested and I get my medicine prescriptions refilled. In addition, I often am taken by my husband to see a surgeon about my chronic ingrown toenail problem. Also, sometimes on weekdays that are not holidays, I have people coming to my house to help me, usually with meals or to get me ready to go out, or to help me back into the house after being out and assist with preparing dinner. It helps take the burden of work off my husband. At most, I might have a helper coming in three times daily for about one hour each time. If there is time during their short stints, sometimes they also help with cleaning or laundry or having me do walking exercise, organizing my things that I brought back from Sendai, and so forth.

I really appreciate the Japanese system, as it helps me and my family immensely. However, I often wish I had spent my working career in the United States and that I could draw my retirement wages there and have access to affordable American health insurance so I could be near my extended family there. But, having paid into the system in Japan, I am forced to remain here instead of being able to return to the United States, where I would prefer to live now. In recent years, the amount of care that I am allotted in Japan and the type of work that my helpers can offer me has been reduced and prescribed narrowly. Still, I appreciate it very much, as it is a great help to me.

My Daily Routine These Days

Usually I stay home all day by myself. My husband gets me out of bed in the early morning and prepares my very simple breakfast of just one slice of bread taken from the freezer and toasted with nothing on it. Sometimes I have one small *natto* (fermented soybeans) package. My husband also makes me a cup of coffee to my liking, with lots of soy milk in it. And then I take my morning medicines with yogurt and a small number of frozen blueberries. Sometimes I also have hot green tea. A helper used to come in the morning for just thirty minutes on days when I needed to go out. But that service was discontinued due to cutbacks in the system.

My "newly turned" adult son prefers to take his meals out with friends. The dishes that I often make are *tonjiru* (a pork and vegetable miso-based soup), spaghetti with meat sauce, curry rice, *niku-jyaga* (a Japanese beef stew), stir-fry, *gyoza* (Chinese-style potstickers), potato salad, lasagna, Japanese-style hamburgers, and other simple dishes, which I usually have along with a vegetable salad. My husband does the grocery shopping, so the menu depends on what he brings home.

My lunch is simple too. It is often an *obento* (boxed lunch) that my husband purchases or some frozen fried rice called *chowhan*. Otherwise, I may have a packet of instant curry poured over frozen or leftover rice or an instant rice packet, along with three pills for medicines. On weekends and holidays, my husband prepares simple dinners, usually *gyoza* soup, *natto* rice and other such instant, easy-to-prepare foods or leftovers with little variation.

My care manager (CM) is in close contact with my husband, rather than with me, as my schedule depends, first of all, on my husband's schedule, and she enjoys communicating with him in Japanese, even though I speak Japanese quite well. Other roles of my CM include negotiating with carpenters when I need home repairs or advocating for me at my facilities if problems arise. As for the cost of the various services received monthly, usually the insurance covers only a small amount of it, and I have to cover the remainder out of pocket. My share has recently doubled from 10 percent to 20 percent, plus other costs of using the facilities and expenses for van pickup, meals, rehabilitation and other services offered there. The insurance allotment is getting stricter, and the time I have with home helpers was recently reduced, to be taken up by my husband instead. So even if I am willing to pay out of pocket for certain services, it is often not permitted. My CM calculates the costs and benefits, and she usually drops by my house once monthly to deliver the new schedules. My CM conveniently runs her own company of carpenters, helpers and other staff and services of staff that take care of me.

Chapter 18

A Stroke of Relief
Back HOME After One Year

I had wanted to "go home" since my early days in hospitals and nursing homes in Seattle, but it was impossible then, because I had no "home" in Seattle and no hope of traveling back to my home in Japan before I could complete enough rehab to manage the long trip. It made me feel lonely and frustrated. I especially wanted to go home to eat as I liked, to use the Internet freely, to relax and do as I liked at my own pace, but no one could provide me with a "home" to go to as an option, even upon my recovery. My mother, who had developed dementia, had been moved out of her house to live with my brother and Susie several years earlier, and her house was being rented out. I had sold a small house in Seattle I owned long before that.

Before I left the hospital in Japan to return to my house, I agreed to undergo Botox treatments (not for beauty, but rather for stroke weakness in muscles). I think my doctor wanted to try it out, and he felt that I would be a good candidate for the procedure, which involved receiving many injections into my strategic muscles of the neurotoxin called Botox. I had the maximum quantity of it allowed safely and legally per time. The nurse prepared some twenty tiny syringes for each shot to be injected in various locations around my body. Most were injected into the hamstring muscles and tendons on the back side of my left knee; some went into my left hand. I was surprised to have a large audience around me to watch, as my care manager had invited all of the people who would be associated with me from then onward after leaving the hospital, many of whom I had not yet met. I wondered who they all were and felt my privacy to be intruded upon. I had to remove my pants and lie face down and did not appreciate the audience. My doctor would say, "OK, here goes," before injecting the Botox each time as I flinched, so it must have been a bit of a show for them. There was no applause at the end, as they were neither family nor friends. They were just strangers who were never properly introduced to me. My husband was busy then and could not attend. When I ran into some of them several months later, they told me they had met me before, but I did not recall ever seeing them, being preoccupied then.

I think my doctor may have incorrectly thought we were wealthy, as the Botox is very expensive and seems to not be covered very much by insurance. But he was correct that I was ready to try anything that might have helped me to improve. My doctor felt the treatment had been successful and that it would help me to walk better, but in the end, I could not feel enough benefit to warrant repeating it.

Finally, after just barely making it back to Japan, I could go back to my Japanese home, following another half-year of hospitalization. Going "home" was not something I could just ask a relative in Seattle to provide for me, as I often used to do when I went to the United States for short visits and would ask my sister to put me up for a week or so. I first would need to refurbish any such "home" to make it accessible for me. After it was decided that my husband and son would come to get me in the United States and bring me back home to Japan, I looked forward to going "home" to my repurposed house there. While in the hospital in Japan, during the half-year I spent there, I also felt a strong desire to leave the hospital and get back into my house and home.

So, it was "a stroke of relief" when I finally did move back into my reformed house in Japan a year after my stroke. It seemed to take forever to get my house repaired enough for me to actually go home. The "I am back" party had long been over, and the huge bouquet of flowers presented to me had wilted and had to be thrown away before I was discharged from the hospital and taken home to live there.

The first stage of work on the house involved taking out the *tatami* straw mats in the room that I was to use for sleeping, called the *shinshitsu* (sleeping room). We replaced the mats with wooden flooring so I could roll over it easily in my wheelchair. A portion of the cost was subsidized by my insurance, as the first phase of home reforms only. After the flooring was completed, a rented bed was set up in my bedroom. I also set up a table in there with my computer and printer on it. It was such a relief to get reconnected over the Internet with my world of friends who lived far from me, hundreds of good friends whom I had occasionally met up with at conferences, conventions and such.

The final phase of my return to life, after getting my house refurbished and made wheelchair-friendly and returning home, was establishing a weekly routine while my husband went out to work daily. It involved working out a schedule with my care manager.

After fixing the sleeping room, the toilet was also fixed in the first round of repairs by putting in a toilet seat that was higher than the original one. It had a bidet on it and a heated toilet seat, which helped a lot during the cold winter days and nights in northern Honshu. A handrail was also installed on the wall on the right side next to the toilet. Unfortunately, the first handrail had to be replaced, as it was nearly flat against the wall, making the toilet very difficult to use by myself, which defeated its purpose. My home therapist and I asked to have it replaced by a larger handrail that protruded over twenty centimeters from the wall, making it easier to use on my own. I could lean against the wall with my right shoulder and hip for balance, freeing up my good (right) hand to lower my pants and to sit on the toilet safely and then, when finished, to stand up, hold on to the rail and lean against the wall, use my good hand to raise my pants back up and then swivel-pivot back into my chair. Aside from those important basic changes, some step barriers were removed from entryways and wooden ramps installed, so I could safely use my wheelchair in our first-floor space. (I necessarily have stopped going upstairs in the house.)

The toilet and bedroom doors became easy-to-open sliding doors, making entryways larger so that my smaller rented wheelchair could pass through without too much damage to the walls and corners of the house. They had taken a lot of damage as helpers pushed my wheelchair or when I tried to maneuver through the narrow hallways that are typical in Japanese homes.

I hope that owners, planners and architects in Japan take into consideration the needs of more wheelchair-bound elders and other impaired people in their future construction plans. Rooms need to be made larger in private homes, and especially in hotel rooms and other public spaces, to become a world-class barrier-free society.

Lastly, the only input I was allowed on the initial home-reform work was to put in a handrail extending from my bedroom to the toilet. I usually use the wheelchair instead of walking, pulling myself forward by using the handrails. An intercom system was put on the outside, by the front door, so that when someone rings the front doorbell, I can see their face and talk with them on a screen. The main unit is in the living/dining room, and I also have a small portable unit in my bedroom.

As for entering and exiting from the house, at first we used two rented ramps to wheel me up the front outdoor steps and up the inner *genkan* (entryway) step, but it was difficult and dangerous, especially with snow piled up outside on the steps. (Prior to my stroke, I had served as the main snow shoveler in our family. My husband and son failed to take over that task for our family after I was retired from it, so there was/is usually snow piled up just outside our front door all during the long winter.) I had to rely on others to maneuver my wheelchair, and more than once I was toppled over in my wheelchair into the snowy bushes beside the steps.

The second-stage repairs (which included some changes that I insisted on, even though the insurance would not cover the improvements) were to put in handrails on both sides of the steps in the passageway going from the house to the garage, plus an extra concrete step. With that change, we no longer needed to enter from the front door using rented ramps over piled-up snow, which was very dangerous for my helpers and for me. The reformed entryway inside of the garage requires me to stand up and walk up or down several steps myself, but it has proven easier, safer and dryer than the previous way. I had practiced climbing stairs nearly daily with my PT (Mr. M) at the Hirosaki Stroke Rehabilitation Center Hospital, so I was confident that I could do it well. With a bit of practice, I have earned much praise for my ability to maneuver those entryway steps. I do wonder what would happen if I injured a leg/foot or a hand/arm and could no longer climb up those stairs, but I will cross that bridge if and when I come to it.

When going out, the first thing is to put my AFO leg brace on my weak left foot. Next is positioning my two wheelchairs. One is a very large chair made in the United States. It was quite expensive and is sturdy, heavy and well designed, so I call it "The Cadillac." As it is too large to fit through my narrow hallways, I have rented another small, narrow, lightweight Japanese-made wheelchair, which a friend has referred to as "The Daihatsu." I prefer to take my Cadillac with me when I go to most wide-halled, barrier-free facilities for day service or short stays, as it is more comfortable and easier to maneuver. It has a side wheel I can use to propel myself, whereas the narrower one does not. I ride in the narrow chair up to the exit door leading into the garage, open the door, and wait while helpers move my big chair through the front door around to the garage door. When it arrives, I can stand up (after I lock the brakes on my chair), put my feet down on the ground, raise the footrests and fold them back. Next, I stand up and take hold of the handrail with my right hand. Someone from the day service or my husband or my helper usually spots me as I climb down, so I do not slip or fall. (Actually, though, I think I am very stable compared to the very elderly people whom my assistants usually care for.)

When stepping down stairs, I step down first with the weak (left) leg, which is heavy now from the weight of the AFO foot brace. That puts pressure on my right knee, so I try to move fast to follow with my right foot as soon as possible, preserving the right knee. I usually first put a non-slip light glove on my right hand to give me a bit of traction. I continue until I have reached the bottom step. Then I sit down in my wheelchair, and it is loaded onto a ramp from the van, and I am lifted up and into the van or taxi or whatever. Alternatively, I can use my cane to walk from the bottom step of the exit door to the passenger seat of a car and get in it. A helper or the driver (or hopefully I, myself, later as driver) then will load my wheelchair.

Before leaving the facility or the vehicle, I must again put the leg brace on my weak foot. I am loaded in a vehicle and driven home, and then I am lifted out and wheeled over to the garage passageway door. When that door is opened, I can start climbing up the stairs. I take my feet off the footrests and fold them back, so I can get as close as possible to the steps. I lock my chair on both sides. Then I stand up and step up first with my right (good) leg, after balancing all of my weight on my weak (left) leg/foot, repeating until I am in the house and sitting in my lighter wheelchair.

There are still other house revisions needed. I would like to put another line of handrails on the stairs going up to our second floor, where I have been only once in over seven years. (Recently I climbed upstairs, but it was very difficult, as my right arm and leg are still quite weak.) I need handrails on both sides for going up and coming back down. Also, I would like up-and-down handrails on both sides going from our deck down to the lawn, so I can enjoy the garden once again. Lastly, there are some rooms on the first floor that still need the ramps, so that I can pass through easily. I recommend that stroke survivors do all their home repairs as early as possible to be able to use those improvements sooner.

Soon after arriving home, I was able to continue my physical therapy at a day-service facility, first for one time weekly and then later twice weekly, along with the baths. Finally, I increased my physical therapy rehabilitation to three times weekly at the day-service facility. I have appreciated the PT-OT in charge there, Mr. Kudou Kazutou. He devised a good plan for me that included endurance, strength and balance therapy. He had me walking long distances, which he sometimes timed, to try to increase my speed. He has continued helping me to practice climbing up and down stairs, and he incorporated techniques to stretch out my body (or what he called "body maintenance").

CHAPTER 19

A Stroke of Disempowerment

Through the Lens of Gender and Racism in Japan

"We are all different. Don't judge, understand."
—*Roy T. Bennett*

I have been *gaijinized* in Japan, or constructed as a foreigner, since I first came to Japan nearly forty years before the stroke, from 1975 to 1976, and then from 1982 onward. This is not just a problem of the rehabilitation facilities and *ryojin kensetsu* (public homes for the elderly in Japan) that I attend. More properly, it is endemic in Japanese society in general. There are many stereotypical notions about foreigners in Japan. Within "a discourse of homogeneity," many Japanese people consider Japan a homogeneous society of Japanese race, ethnicity, nationality and language. Within this context, anyone who was not born of two Japanese parents in Japan and who was not raised in Japan is considered a *gaijin*, which literally means a foreigner, or outsider. *Gaijin* are stereotypically expected not to understand Japanese customs, ways of thinking, or language. So what happens when you add "disability" to "foreigner" and view the world through the lens of "gender and racist marginalization" in Japan? Even though I have spent the latter part of my life (some forty years) in Japan, many Japanese people born after me still shout out at me, feigning amazement, when I say something simple and ordinary in Japanese like "thank you" or "please." Many people often respond with "You speak Japanese so well," or they ask annoying things, like "Can you use chopsticks?" and other quite uncomfortable and inappropriate comments.

R.A. Miller sarcastically asked in his 1982 book, *Japan's Modern Myth*, if Japanese mothers teach their children that whenever they see foreigners, they should ask them, "Can you use chopsticks?" and "Does your country have four seasons like we have here in Japan?" and other such ethnocentric and stereotypical ruses. Miller pondered why such comments are so widespread and uniform among the Japanese. I wonder the same things some forty years after him and have had to deal with *gaijinization* on a near-daily basis over the three-plus decades that I have lived in Japan, and I wrote my Ph.D. dissertation on the theme of looking at "othering" in Japan through the eyes of "hybrid" or mixed-ethnic/race Japanese-nationality teenage girls born and raised in Japan who are referred to as "half" there. These "halves" come from mixed-parentage families of one foreign-born parent and one Japanese parent. My son and my niece are among their number. It gets even more layered and oppressive for individuals who have already met with marginalization due to their ethnicity or mixed birth, or simply their race, to have to contend with the compounding difficulty of physical injury. I think in settings such as these, the results of a stroke can be particularly devastating and compound the loneliness and isolation felt by this sense of "other."

Being white skinned in Japanese society comes with many stereotypical notions of what we should be like. As a white *gaijin*, I am not expected to speak Japanese or use chopsticks, nor am I expected to like *sushi, sashimi, natto* and other such traditional Japanese foods.

I have previously written about marginalizing discourses in Japan in which I examined related issues of *gaijin* attractiveness versus *gaijin* grotesqueness.

There are other stereotypical notions that are formed in Japanese people whose knowledge is misinformed about Americans and other foreign women through the vision they construct via Hollywood movies, music, and sexually exploitative men's magazines such as *Playboy* or *Penthouse*.

I would have loved to continue teaching at a high level and further this critique on the unacceptable behavior toward *gaijin*, and perhaps I will someday. For now, this book will have to suffice, and this somewhat academically inclined chapter (along with some graphic examples from my own experience below) may help to explain what so many unfortunate people are facing in marginalization, not only in this country but around the world.

Within Japanese racial discourses of homogeneity, *gaijin* attractiveness, and *gaijin* grotesqueness, I have experienced sexual harassment or sexual abuse as a *gaijin*—a white foreigner—in Japan in the facilities where I am often taken for baths, day service and short stays. As a *gaijin* user there, sitting defenseless and exposed, naked in the bath chair, it is not just my *gaijin* face and lighter (or naturally curly) hair but also my whole body that is open to becoming a target of sexual harassment, which I have endured from both women and men in Japan. It is both unacceptable and unprofessional. When I see this unconscious behavior displayed by the aides or *kaigo fukushi* in Japan (who are like U.S. certified nursing assistants), I try to point it out to them. I would like to educate them about their unconscious positioning of foreigners, where we should normally expect professionalism.

It started with many young Japanese women/girl staffers at bathing service facilities in rural Japan who would strip me down while they were fully clothed, have me transfer to a wheeled bath chair, and then wheel me into the bath space to scrub down my body and shampoo my hair as I sat, unable to move or to cover my totally exposed body. I felt that it was as if those workers assumed that physically handicapped stroke survivors or mentally compromised elderly no longer feel any embarrassment or shame. That is often not the case. I have also witnessed poor, unprofessional treatment of elderly Japanese women, who I could tell felt shamed. I always felt so vulnerable, fragile and exposed under such situations. I often felt that my body was being seen as a "grotesque" foreign body, even though many girls expressed (false) envy within "a discourse of foreigner attractiveness." Admittedly, I am not small in terms of breast or bra size, but I am within the normal, average range for Western women. (In contrast, most Japanese women tend to have quite small breasts and often wear bras that are heavily padded to make them appear larger.) But they may as well have expressed envy of the large breasts of an overweight male sumo wrestler, I felt, as comments that came my way did not come across as genuine flattery to me. They made me feel oddly deformed or alien, excluded from typical Japanese people and their more "normal" bodies. Also being disabled, I was made to feel even more abnormal, particularly as an outsider.

What follows is the story of what happened often with several female staffers in Japan at a day-service facility for baths: The girls on staff there would gaze at my naked, exposed breasts while scrubbing me down in the bath, and of course they were not disabled at all, but young, healthy and fully clothed. They would look at my body and then shout out something like "*Sugoi, oppai ga ookii ne, dekai. Urayamashii desu. Watashi wa chiisai, nanimo nai desu.*" ("Oh my God, you are so huge.

Your breasts are huge. I envy you. Mine are so small. I do not have any breasts. I am flat chested.")

I would then ask those girls in Japanese, "Show me your breasts to prove it," in order to put us on a more equal footing. But they would say, "No, I cannot show you here."

I wanted to say to them, "I also cannot show you mine here, but you stole your look at me, and then you humiliated me with your crass comments."

Those girls evidently felt that self-deprecation made it all right for them to call out our racial differences, marginalizing and considering the *gaijin* as a disabled, vulnerable and elderly woman, naked on a wheelchair and unable to move, as "huge," or as "physically different." But it is *not* all right at all! I also wondered if they envied the large breasts of other Japanese women and verbally expressed it to them too, or if their flattery was reserved for foreigners (or for me alone, as I was the only foreigner at any of the places that I used).

Those girls felt they could humiliate me as an abnormal outsider. In addition, there were plenty of men/boy aides working in the woman's bath, who then turned to get a good look.

I informed the girls that their comments were equivalent to "sexual harassment," and also "unprofessional," although they did not seem to really understand what I meant. They knew the word "professional," as in Japan there is a TV program with that name, but they have never learned the word "unprofessional." Thus I hope that lessons in professionalism and diversity awareness will be taught in Japanese colleges and other schools that certify them and other nursing staff, as well as the schools certifying directors, owners and others who hire them.

Mostly I hope that individuals will gain more integrity and learn on their own how to be more respectful and professional in their treatment of vulnerable users. Both the male and the female certified nursing aides in Japan and elsewhere should be careful not to point out differences of body shape, color, or size to any gender: male, female, or other.

What I would like staff members at these facilities to understand is that, first of all, interactions of this nature are based on unequal power structures, as the user is stripped naked and the aide is fully clothed. Not only that, but the user is also physically or mentally handicapped/disabled (or both), while the aide is able-bodied and not in a vulnerable position. Most of the users at public facilities for the aged (*ryojin kensetsu*) in Japan reside there due to their frailty and dementia, so issues such as age, intelligence, and cognition should not be indiscriminately singled out by workers. As most people in Japanese society, in general, tend to have a low consciousness of racial, gender, age, intellectual and disability and diversity awareness, I feel that it would be best for staff at care facilities to be very careful about all sensitive issues of race, ethnicity, religion, political affiliation, nationality, gender, age, mentality/intelligence, and so forth. Preferably, I feel it needs to be taught to them while they are still in school. Ideally, I believe that "intercultural awareness," "professionalism" and "diversity" should be taught from kindergarten in Japan and reinforced each year through schooling, animation, children's programming and other forms of media and at home.

The men/boys at such facilities were also curious about my foreign body, and I felt that some of them occasionally peeked into the dressing room to catch a view of this much-talked-about *gaijin*. In addition, many male staff members were sent into the women's bath to help work there when it became busy. So it seemed to be cause for them to laugh, like immature prepubescent boys. But being immature does not excuse them, nor does it excuse the facilities that hire them or the schools that certify them. They need to be taught to behave more professionally.

It was bad enough being sexually harassed by girls, but when it happened with boys or young men working in the baths, it was distressing to me. When I mentioned what happened to my helper, she reported it to my care manager, who later lodged a complaint with the director of the facility. Sadly, after that, it seemed to go nowhere, as I have yet to receive an apology from anyone.

Here is what happened one day when I was assigned what I call a man-boy while I was in the bath. This man-boy was a man with respect to age, but he acted like an immature pubescent boy. He was a certified nursing aide, whom I expected to be a mature professional (as most of them actually are), but, instead, he was immature in his actions and demeanor. He washed my back and then dropped the towel on my naked lap and said in Japanese while laughing, "OK, now you wash your own breasts by yourself."

He continued laughing and then made eye contact with another young aide in the bath facility to get a male response, and they both laughed together. I wanted to ask, "What is so funny?" or "What are you laughing at?" But, in the end, I resisted asking, to avoid further humiliation. Now I wish I had asked.

I felt sexually abused in that situation: vulnerable and naked, unable to move at all, with nothing to cover my nudity. In those laughs and stares from both women and men, I felt ridiculed, objectivized and marginalized for my race and gender, as well as my disability and age. That should never have happened, and I hope they get it right soon. I am advocating for that!

Additionally, it should be emphasized here that saying similar things to a male user would be unheard of; it would be unimaginable, for example, for a male staffer to remark to a male user that he "envied him for his large penis." It would be even more shocking if a female staffer teased the man and laughed at his (smaller or larger-than-average) penis, so why should it be permissible to point out or to laugh at body differences among women, whether Japanese or non–Japanese? I think it would be inconceivable to say such a thing to a man, but what was said and done to me was just as bad, if not worse, I feel. It happened many times, especially among the girls, but also from those of a different sex and race.

We vulnerable, defenseless users/residents/survivors must put our trust and our bodies in the care of staff whom we expect to treat us professionally, and they are bound by law to do so. I want to say to directors, owners, boards of directors, presidents, administrators and teachers at schools training such students, and to the students themselves, that they should never point out or ridicule anyone in their care concerning diversities of gender, race, age, and body (size, color, shape, hair imperfections or quality, other kinds of physical or mental handicaps or imperfections, attractiveness or grotesqueness).

Management and oversight are key factors in maintaining a high grade of excellent service in public facilities. Fortunately, there are some checks in place to certify that users are indeed *not* getting abused in most places. Social workers regularly circulate around facilities in Japan, the United States, and elsewhere. I, myself, was personally approached in a Japanese facility by a social worker who asked me if I had experienced or seen any problems or things that were not good for me there. That was a breath of fresh air. While I did not seek this person out, when approached, I did not hold back in telling the story that I am also writing here in an act of advocacy for myself and other foreigners or for the aged in facilities in Japan.

I feel that individual staff members should strive to build their own sense of integrity and professionalism and try to gain respect from those in their care, as I indeed felt toward a man who sometimes gave me showers in the nursing home in the United States. We respected each other. He was a gentleman, proud of his good sense of women's needs.

I felt secure, safe and respected in his care, as he was a mature professional with a very good sense of humanity. As he was a male, with more strength than most women, I also felt sure that he would not allow me to fall, as others there had done in the past. I feel that it might be good for such longer-termed professional staffers to mentor the newer, less experienced staff and to serve as models for how to be professional.

In the United States, there were also many untrained young boys working in the nursing homes where I resided, as well as in hospitals or other facilities, who seemed to be quite young. Although I did not feel comfortable being cared for by them there, there were no specific events where I felt abused or harassed. I was unsure about their capabilities and felt physically vulnerable. But, at the time, I was happy to have any help at all, as the facilities were often understaffed.

I hope that this book will be translated into Japanese and that it might help others in similar situations in the future. But in reality, I do not expect much more than further laughter at my body difference within "a discourse of *gaijin* grotesqueness." I believe those staff members need to gain maturity and be instructed in diversity and intercultural awareness and commonsense behavior. Ideally, facilities will be more careful in future hiring interviews, screening for more mature staff.

It surprised me to find that various men hanging out or working in the women's bath at the day-service or short-stay facility I often used were the same men serving as the van drivers who had picked me up earlier that morning. Men from the office staff or the rehabilitation staff have also been sent into the woman's bath on busy days at one facility I used often. When I saw the male van drivers in the women's bath, I wondered, "What in heaven's name are those men doing in the women's bath?"

Personally, I feel it is cheap, unprofessional and inappropriate to have male staffers working in the woman's bath, especially the van drivers or office staff and other untrained staff, as if we female disabled or elderly no longer feel any shame about our naked bodies. Just because most of the users of these facilities are very old and may not have much sex appeal does not give anyone an excuse to ridicule them. In addition, many of those Japanese seniors actually feel more shame about their naked bodies than younger generations do, and the management and the staff should be sensitive to that.

I have also heard reports from some men users who felt severely sexually harassed with women staffers watching over them in the same bathing facility in Japan. I think that they should have only women staff helping female users and only male staff helping male users, even on busy days. In that case, the facilities may need to hire extra staff to ameliorate shortages on certain days.

Furthermore, I want to advocate for the Japanese government to establish some *ryojin kensetsu* (public housing for the aged) designed and subsidized specifically for foreigners to use in various places around Japan. Many foreigners in Japan, like myself, have devoted their entire working careers, over several decades, paying into the system, and as we come to age in increasing numbers, it would be nice to have our own homes to go to and live out our final years. It is not only issues of language, food, and customs (although those matter, too) but also a broader problem of exclusiveness, sexual harassment or abuse, consciousness, religion, worldview, acceptance, tolerance, maturity level, professionalism, and so forth.

When I went into short-stay facilities for five to ten days at a time, I often did not feel very comfortable residing with other seniors whose only remaining memory was that of having lost the war with the United States at a time when they were coming of age. Thus, to many of them, as a *gaijin* or outsider, a foreigner from the United States, I represented "the enemy," reinforced yearly by morning television dramas that culminate with the final months of World War II and its devastating aftermath in August. Many users thus were often not very kind to me. My presence may have served to help them deal with their negative feelings, but it did not serve me well at all. I felt especially uncomfortable in one particular facility, but better in another place that was much more friendly and accepting.

As expressed in the quotation by Roy T. Bennett at the beginning of this chapter, I feel that it is very important for people to accept, understand and love those who differ from them, instead of feeling hate and contempt. We can all learn from those who are different from us, and that should be the goal of meeting others.

CHAPTER 20

A Stroke of Balance

Taking the Best of All Worlds

In this chapter, I would like to discuss good practices and beliefs or philosophies of the differing East-West contexts of Japan and the United States, based on my experiences of being hospitalized and incapacitated in specialized care facilities and hospitals for more than a year. Various comparisons between the United States and Japan can shed light on areas in which improvements are needed, especially concerning such things as eating cultures, rehabilitation, and other beliefs and practices that I found quite different in the two contexts.

In an ideal world, we should be able to take the best parts of various systems while leaving out the worst parts of them all, in order to come up with better systems, so it is appropriate to look at what the West can learn from the Eastern model, and vice versa, starting by looking at what Japan has to offer, in terms of wellness and rehabilitation, upon surviving a stroke.

First and foremost, I advocate for improvements for all people incapacitated in facilities in the United States, in Japan and elsewhere. Below, I list practices and beliefs that I particularly feel need to be changed, based on my personal experiences. I advocate for those people (referred to as "users" in Japan or "residents" in the United States) staying in institutionalized care facilities, including hospitals and nursing homes and other facilities, for a long time.

1. **In Japan,** I hope to send a message to schools that certify nursing staff (such as *kaigo fukushi,* or certified nursing aides), directors, physician assistants, and similar health professionals. In addition, I would like to send a message to directors of facilities and hospitals, as well as head doctors, owners, and those who hire

them, to ensure that the staff they train or hire demonstrate maturity and professional attitudes and aim to develop integrity in working toward professional ideals of behavior.

2. **At facilities in the United States,** I hope to send a message to the owners, directors, and head doctors at facilities and hospitals to take care in hiring professional staff who are of the proper legal age and to pay them well. (In the nursing home in the United States, there were often teenage boys on staff, around whom I usually did not feel comfortable when I called for an aide to help me to use the toilet, for example.) I also feel that staff should not be allowed to work consecutive double shifts. At the very least, all beginner staff should be given some degree of minimal training anywhere— whether in Japan, in the United States, and elsewhere.

3. **"Institutional gossip":** When compiling reports, do not engage in institutional gossip. Respect the privacy of those in your care.

4. **Stereotyping residents/users.** Staff should never assume that one size/one pattern of behavior fits all. Staff everywhere should be careful not to construct all stroke survivors as "brain damaged," "demented" and/or "depressed." Instead, I recommend that they carefully consider each person individually, including elderly people with dementia or others in their care.

5. **Eating, diet and meal health.** Diets should vary between each patient, with more leeway and guidance given by the patient. Thus diet needs to be decided based on a partnership between the staff and the individual, working together. The goal should be for the stroke survivors to later prepare their own meals at home. Therefore, they should be directed in how to make wise eating choices.

6. **Daily exercise.** Like healthy people, stroke survivors and other infirm people or those hospitalized for extended periods need to spend time exercising daily, even if it includes time on machines, self-exercises or group exercises. Exercises should be practiced with a therapist first so they can be done safely alone later.

7. **Barrier-free Japan and elsewhere?** I hope and urge that future owners, planners and architects in Japan and elsewhere consider the needs of wheelchair users in construction plans. Rooms need to be made larger in homes, hotels and other public spaces to become a world-class barrier-free society, not just in Tokyo, where the Olympics and Paralympics of 2021 shone a spotlight, but throughout Japan.

These are practices that would be good to incorporate anywhere if we were to select the best of all worlds while leaving out the worst, establishing a better model to use to improve our own systems. I feel that the best practice begins with and includes the wise recruitment of staff who not only are well-trained workers but also have a personal maturity level that presupposes an ample amount of empathy, a component drastically needed in the care of the physically disabled. This goes for all staff, but it is especially important concerning male staff, I feel, based on my own personal experiences.

Chronological age often correlates well with maturity level, but not always—for this reason, the owners, head doctors and other hiring staff at various facilities need to carefully screen new staff. Of course, the most mature, reliable and professional staff members are those who have built up much past experience over many years in similar facilities.

CHAPTER 21

The Japan Model

I feel that "the Japan Model" can teach a lot to the United States and to the West, especially in terms of relaxation therapy. Allowing stroke survivors and other people hospitalized for extended periods to soak in hot-water baths or hot tubs, as opposed to just giving them showers, is a great practice, as baths are much more relaxing. Communal baths are a Japanese cultural norm and priority, making the cost more acceptable in their society. It is much more expensive to build a large bath, like a large hot tub, than simply putting in a shower room, as baths must also include spaces for showering and hair washing before the person enters the communal bath water, in a special wheeled bath chair, accompanied by trained staff. However, as with most things, it would be cheaper to build baths in the United States (and other places) than it would cost in Japan, even though there may be fewer natural hot springs outside of Japan.

Relaxation is extremely helpful as a first step in the healing process. Also, the Japanese method of massaging tight muscles and stretching with help from therapists, before having stroke survivors stand up and walk, is a great technique to adopt anywhere. It is very relaxing and helpful in walking.

In Japan, if anything, there is a tendency to be overstaffed rather than understaffed most of the time. Having enough staff to assist stroke survivors is very helpful. One of my first impressions of the stroke rehabilitation hospital in Japan was that it had more reliable staff than I had experienced when hospitalized and residing in nursing homes in the United States.

Food choice and eating guidelines do not seem to be well regulated in care facilities. I feel that nursing homes and hospitals in the United States should not force residents to eat so much food. Of course, stroke survivors need to eat certain types of food to regain their body mass and to rebuild muscles and brain cells, but many stroke survivor residents in the United States tend to be overweight, so I feel that each person should be considered individually and put on diets that match their specific needs. Many people in the United States need to lose weight or reduce their intake of certain types of food. Some are diabetic or have other food restrictions. Perhaps, when appropriate, some residents/users could serve themselves from a buffet-style setting, where they can decide on the type of food and the quantity that they feel meets their needs and tastes and choose foods that they prefer. This might help them as they prepare for more decision-making and independence when they go home. They might need some advice and help from nutritionists, doctors and other staff about how to choose foods for themselves. I would mainly choose salads, soups, vegetables and fruits, with few carbs, sweets or red meats.

The meals served in the Japanese hospital reflected the Japanese diet in general, which I feel is a very healthy diet. First of all, the quantity of the food is much less than the typical U.S. diet. Individuals have control over their total calories by requesting more or less rice. The size of the rice bowl determines the amount of rice one consumes. (I always used a small bowl of rice.)

In addition, I feel that the primary caregiver is the most important person to the stroke survivor and to others who are hospitalized or institutionalized for a long time. For that reason, this person (or these people) should be treated with the most care. It is very important to prevent your caregiver from feeling overwhelmed with the work of caring for you. Caregivers themselves must also be careful to rest or seek other help before they explode, burn out or do something drastic. The best solution to this big problem is to provide a backup support team to allow the primary caregiver time away from their responsibilities. They need their proper rest, even when they might say otherwise. Their break from helping you should be mandatory for both their and your own protection.

Another very important need for the stroke survivor and primary caregiver is to have a pattern of mutual communication, striving to understand each other. I was very fortunate in that my primary caregivers were several members of my close family in the United States and then my husband upon returning to Japan. In the United States, as I was residing in a nursing home, my family did not have total responsibility for all of my needs, as my meals, baths and other needs were taken care of in the facility. But that still left much room for emotional, spiritual and social care from my family. When I later returned to Japan, most of the caregiving work was taken over by my husband, along with paid helpers and those who took me out to day-service facilities three times weekly. Sometimes during long holidays, my husband had to do all of the work.

Being the recipient of such caregiving is very humbling. It requires expressing much gratitude and trying to do the small things that are within your capabilities while remaining safe. For example, I am able to transfer from the bed to the wheelchair, to the toilet and back, so I often go to the toilet by myself. Also, when my helper comes in the late afternoon, we often prepare meals together that I and my husband can eat for several days. Thus I try to cook meals that my husband likes, which are mainly Japanese dishes. He prepares the very simple breakfast and lunch meals. Where possible, I also try to do some light housecleaning and laundry, but it is difficult to do very much.

CHAPTER 22

Independent Accessible Rooms and Public Toilets

We have been born into a world designed and evolved to perfectly fit the needs of people who have fully functioning bodies with two legs and feet, as well as two arms and hands with ten fingers. By adulthood, most people have become very adept at doing many intricate things. We do not pay conscious attention to all of these things until we suddenly lose that ability. For example, try opening a small coffee creamer that comes in a plastic sealed case with just one hand (and without using your teeth) or even opening a milk carton with one hand without spilling it. Try tying a shoelace using one hand. Next, open a plastic water bottle with just one hand. I can open plastic bottles of drinks by holding the bottle tightly between my legs, but the problem is that due to squeezing it so tightly with my thighs to hold it in place, when it cracks open, it overflows, soaking my pants and legs, putting this task on my list of things I prefer to ask others to help me with. Try doing those things with just one hand. Better yet, I would like to implore able-bodied caregivers and family members to use only one hand (say, your left hand) for an entire day, and then you might come to understand the plight of a stroke survivor with one-sided weakness (hemiparesis) or one-sided paralysis (hemiplegia).

We stroke survivors very much appreciate having been able to survive the stroke, but we now have many new challenges that we ask the world to sometimes also consider to make our lives minimally easier. I am advocating for some changes to the status quo concerning public toilets, hotels, restaurants and other public facilities in my own country (the United States), as well as in my present country of residence (Japan) and other places around the world. I am hoping that some hotel and restaurant owners and other such people will read this book and take appropriate action. I don't like to rattle on and on, but the fact is, even though we've heard it before, things still haven't changed much. I know—I've experienced it.

I survived a massive hemorrhagic stroke some seven years ago, leaving me mostly wheelchair bound with the use of just one leg/foot and one arm/hand. Of course, there are many other people who face far more challenging situations than I do with fewer viable limbs. I depend on a wheelchair, an AFO (ankle-foot orthosis) leg brace, a cane and caregivers to help me travel. I am naturally a very outgoing, social person who thrives on going places and meeting up with colleagues, friends or family whenever possible. I am an otherwise very healthy American who resides now in rural Japan, an ocean apart from my family in the United States.

Recently I had a chance to attend my niece's wedding in the United States, where I needed to book a special, expensive wheelchair-accessible hotel room in Seattle. My siblings helped me to find and book the room for seven nights with my husband. It wasn't cheap, so I expected adequate treatment for disabled persons, as advertised.

It made me think about the minimum requirements for a good wheelchair-accessible hotel room. Furthermore, I used many public and hotel toilets while overseas and also came to consider "What is an excellent accessible public toilet?" This chapter addresses these two problems of accessible public toilets and hotel rooms for wheelchair users, such as most stroke survivors.

I would define the "perfect" wheelchair-accessible hotel room as a room that could be used by a physically handicapped person in wheelchair on their own, without the need for a helper to accompany them if they have one good hand. Here I will call such a room an "independent accessible room" to contrast it with a "dependent accessible room" that requires the wheelchair user to have a helper along to assist them. We physically impaired adults with robust minds like to travel independently, and in order to do so, certain minimum essentials are required, as highlighted below.

Carpeting

The carpeting in most hotels is poorly suited to the needs of disabled persons. I have always hated carpeting in hotels or homes (even before my stroke) for the simple reason that carpets are dirt traps and the cause of asthma, wheezing and allergies even for ordinary healthy people. I realized the dangers of carpeting after raising an allergen-sensitive child. Shampooed carpets tend to smell very badly, too, and they seldom resolve the allergen problem totally.

But for wheelchair users, carpeting goes beyond mere cleanliness or health problems. Hotel rooms with carpets potentially require the wheelchair user to have another person with them in the room, as it is very difficult for the wheels of the wheelchair to move smoothly across any sort of hotel carpeting without having someone else push the chair (few people use electrically operated wheelchairs). Thus hotel rooms with carpeting perhaps might be of the "dependent accessible" type, which means that they are *not* independent accessible.

Ample Space in the Room

The more floor space there is in the hotel room or bathroom, the easier it is to maneuver around in a wheelchair. It is all right if the bed is placed flush against a wall, as long as there is enough space on the other side of the bed for a wheelchair to approach. I always take my smaller, rented wheelchair with me when I travel, even though my larger one is more comfortable and easier to use.

Location of the Wheelchair-Accessible Room

Needless to say, the entrance to the hotel itself, the check-in reception area, and all restaurants, bars and other shops in the hotel should be barrier free, with ramps or slopes at the entrance and exit points instead of steps to maneuver.

Preferably, the "accessible rooms" in a hotel will be on the ground floor or nearest to the elevator if located on any other floors. Then, from the elevator to the accessible hotel room, there should be a non-carpeted pathway. I think the best surface would be a wooden floor. Linoleum or tile flooring would also be fine, but even a stone or concrete floor or any other smooth surface would surpass any kind of carpeting.

Roll-Over Room Entries

As for the inside of the room, there should be easy roll-over thresholds, extending from the hallway into the room and from the main part of the hotel room into the bathroom or toilet area and any other rooms or walk-in closets. There should be no steps or edges inside the entire room.

Baths

While baths are very good for relaxing stroke survivors, they are very difficult to get into safely for someone with paralyzed limbs and something that they would need help with. Such baths in a hotel wheelchair-accessible room, even with handles and so forth, are still quite dangerous. I have only occasionally seen a good accessible bath in a hotel. (See the photo on page 156.)

The Toilet

The seat of the toilet should preferably be a bit lower than an ordinary toilet to help in transferring from a wheelchair to the toilet seat.

When I first came to Japan in the early 1970s, most public toilets around Japan were of the "squat" variety, which require a lot of skill and well-developed leg muscles to use, even for a fully able-bodied person. It was particularly difficult on moving trains in Japan before they started using the Western-style sit-down toilets everywhere. It is no wonder that wheelchair-dependent impaired people were rarely seen in Japan before they began installing sit-down toilets. Now Japanese toilets have become very high-tech, many boasting health meters that provide heated toilet seats and bidet washlets. Some toilets available in Japan even are designed to check the quality of the user's stools and urine, among other things.

Handrails for a Wheelchair-Accessible Toilet

This is the most important feature of a truly accessible hotel room or a wheelchair-accessible toilet. There should be, at the minimum, a handrail on the right side of the toilet (usually connected to the wall), but the best toilets will also have a pull-down railing on the other side. (Sometimes the main handrail is placed on the left side of the toilet for people who have right-sided paralysis.)

A bath for handicapped people with arm bars in a good barrier-free hotel room in Japan (author's photograph).

The handrail should stand out from the wall by several centimeters (preferably twenty centimeters), and part of it should extend up vertically to about 1.5 meters (five or six feet) in an "L" shape. My home handrail beside the toilet stands out from the wall by about twenty centimeters. This is perfect, as those people with just one good hand need to maneuver first into a standing position so they can pivot around. They then need to free up their one good hand by balancing themselves, usually by anchoring their arm through the handrail or leaning their shoulder against the wall (or both).

I sometimes use my shoulder and chin to help balance myself on the vertical part of the handrail, in order to free up my good right hand, which then I task with lowering my clothing up down or down as needed, to safely and hygienically use the toilet. Sometimes, if I am wearing a dress or a skirt, I make sure to wear a belt over my clothing so that I can tuck the fabric into the belt, thus preventing it from falling or dipping into the toilet. Finally, I am ready to sit down on the toilet. After doing my business and cleaning up, the next task is to stand up and put my clothing back into order. I pull up my pants and/or lower my skirt, and then I finally pivot back onto the wheelchair, carefully double-checking to make certain that the wheelchair locks are securely in place, so that my chair will not roll away and drop me.

The Sink

The sink in the toilet room or the bathroom will preferably allow space underneath it for me to approach in my wheelchair without bumping my legs and still be able to reach the soap and faucets by leaning forward. A modern faucet with a motion sensor is the best-case scenario. The hand towels or dryers should also be placed within reach of an adult person or a child sitting on a very low wheelchair.

The Hotel Bed

The bed in any "accessible" hotel room needs to be low enough so that a person, even one sitting in a low-to-the-ground wheelchair, can easily transfer from their wheelchair to the bed and back safely. I feel that it would be best for the bed to also have a handrail on it like a hospital bed, but I have never seen such a bed railing in a hotel room. It would be ideal for transferring in and out of the bed, but it would also help someone paralyzed in half of their body vertically or horizontally to grasp a handrail once in the bed to help them turn over.

The fact that I cannot easily roll over in bed is the main reason that I am usually not able to sleep in such hotel rooms. This type of bed railing amenity would not be all that expensive to provide in rooms advertised as "accessible." (I have even thought of designing a portable bed railing that impaired travelers could pack in their suitcases. I considered submitting this idea to Quirky.com for patenting, but I am putting it out freely here for any engineer to design if they just inform me about it.)

Things such as the controls for the room lights, the television, the telephone and so on should all be on a nearby bed table, as in most regular hotels, so that there would be no need to get up after retiring to bed for the night. In addition, of course, all other usual hotel amenities should be included in the "accessible" room, such as lights, electrical circuits, lamps, closets, drawers and so forth.

* * *

The "accessible" room that I rented for seven nights when I came to the United States for my niece's wedding had a "roll-in" shower that I never used during the week I stayed there because it would have required the help of another person. I could roll into the shower in my own wheelchair, but I would have needed someone else to move my wheelchair out to prevent it from getting wet while I showered and then bring it back in when I had finished using the shower and had dried off and dressed.

When I first heard about a "roll-in shower," I pictured a shower wheelchair in the room provided by the hotel that I could transfer into from my own wheelchair; then I thought I would wheel in, take my shower, wheel out and then transfer back to my wheelchair. I also pictured a handrail inside the shower to make wheeling in by myself an easy task. I imagined that the hotel would have a waterproof shower chair for their "wheel-in shower." But at the hotel where I stayed, the customer was expected to use their own wheelchair to roll in and then transfer to a bench beside the shower, which, as I mentioned before, required the help of another person.

Even many married people prefer not to have to ask their spouse to help bathe them. I thought it would be easier to just wait a week until I got home to bathe. (In Japan, I am taken out twice weekly for baths at day-service facilities for the aged and the impaired.) Due to the problems noted above, I realized that it would be very difficult to use a so-called accessible hotel room on my own. I would still need to travel with a helper or ask a friend or relative living nearby for help. Otherwise, I would need to hire some local helper to assist me during my stay, but the cost of travel would then make it nearly prohibitive.

I would also have difficulty staying at a friend's or relative's house for the same reasons. This was indeed the reason that I decided to book the hotel for my stay in Seattle with my husband. I had never before stayed in a hotel in my hometown. The hotel had advertised the room as being "accessible," but, sadly, it was not very accessible for me.

This brings me to back to the question of "What is an accessible toilet?" I have partially addressed this subject above, but there are many sorts of public toilets, including those on public transportation or airplanes, as well as those in buildings, schools, restaurants, gas stations and other public venues.

On the long flight overseas from Tokyo to Seattle, with the help of my husband and the friendly Japan Airlines stewardesses, I was able to use the small airplane toilet once and then once again on the return flight. I am not sure exactly what kind of aircraft I was flying in. I believe it was a Boeing aircraft of some sort, but not its largest one.

I thought then that I would like to write a letter to Boeing executives, which I finally did, and I include part of that letter (sent on Friday, 20 September 2019) here:

Dear Dennis Muilenburg, CEO, and other Boeing Co. engineers,

I recently flew overseas from Japan to Seattle, U.S. and back in August, 2019 for my niece's wedding. I used an airplane toilet on that flight each way for the first time since surviving a massive hemorrhagic stroke in 2013, some six years ago. I and others impaired like me would like to travel much more if a few minor adjustments were made to the interior of your airplanes, as most commercial airlines these days use Boeing aircrafts.

First of all, I should mention that I am a relatively small American woman at just 5'1" (154 cms.) and about 60 kilograms (about 132 pounds), so compared to the average American, I am a bit on the small side. Even still, I felt the need for more space. The very tiny thin wheelchair that I changed into to be wheeled down the aisle of the plane to my seat near the toilets in the back of the airplane was very tight. I felt that the aisle could have had a few more centimeters on it. This plane had two aisles. It might be very difficult for typical American or other Western men who are usually twice my size or more to maneuver. This could be accomplished by making the seats slightly thinner or eliminating one seat across each row so that one of the aisles could be made slightly wider or just having one aisle instead of two aisles. I realize that fewer seats on an airplane would cost the airlines more, so I will leave that detail for you to work out. I suppose that a seat in the first class section might have ameliorated these problems somewhat, but, of course, cost is a problem for ordinary people like me.

I would describe my first flight overseas in wheelchair, five years before that, as "the flight from hell," even though it was a very comfortable flight with no turbulence and the landing was perfect in good weather. The problem for me was how to use the airplane toilet on that long ten-hour fight with my husband and son.

Before departure on my first overseas flight since the stroke in 2014, we all brainstormed on how to solve the toilet problem on the long flight. My sisters had decided, against my better sense, that I should wear a catheter. I finally gave in and agreed to allow a nurse to insert it. The problem was that I did not know how to take it out by myself and it leaked from the start at about thirty-minute intervals, wetting the diaper, my clothing and then the airplane seat.

Not only that but each time it leaked it was painful for me and I said so to my dear husband who also had to suffer with me that entire trip while my son sat on the other side of me feeling very ashamed of his mother. Thus I was both pained and shamed on that horrible flight and then the hour-long bus ride between the two airports in Japan and then a local 90-minute flight on which the problem continued. There were a few other problems as well on that flight, such as swelling in my leg that, the next day, in Japan was misdiagnosed as "economic-class syndrome" or "deep vein thrombosis." Fortunately, it was later correctly diagnosed as edema or swelling due to water buildup.

On this more recent trip from Japan to the U.S. and back last summer, in 2019, I was able to use the toilet as mentioned above, but I felt that the airplane toilet itself could be several centimeters wider too, especially for anyone larger than me. Just designating one toilet on each plane as a "wheelchair-accessible toilet" would be helpful. All of the wheelchair users could be seated near that toilet. On my last flight, this time I noticed that there were several easy to grasp large hand-railings around the outside of the toilet as well as inside of it too that greatly helped me to safely maneuver myself onto the toilet and back from the tiny thin airplane wheelchair. Still I required the help of two female flight attendants as well as my husband who had accompanied me for that purpose. I should also mention here that I am able to balance myself quite well on my one good leg while many impaired people cannot even manage that.

Even still, it was scary for me to have to transfer from the security of a wheelchair or an airplane seat onto something else to avoid falling down, especially in a moving airplane. Fortunately, on the way over to the U.S., I was able to hold my bladder for over eight hours. At first I tried to walk back to the toilet, right behind my seat, using my cane as I usually do for walking short distances, but due to the angle of the descending plane, the walk to the toilet area inclined steeply against gravity, making me have to give up my plan and return to my seat right away. Soon after that a flight attendant came by with the narrow wheelchair to transport me to the toilet and back after using it. It was a tight fit onto the airplane toilet, but I am very proud to say that I successfully made it both times.

It was a huge relief to finally use the toilet after so many hours in flight and two meals and it made the remaining several hours of the trip much more comfortable after that. By the return trip, having already successfully maneuvered it once, I felt confident and the transfer went very smoothly. Now I feel ready to fly again, but I would still feel the need to have my husband or another helper along to accompany me in case I needed extra help.

Most respectfully yours,
Laurel Nudelman Kamada

I have never received a reply to this message.

These are the main essentials that would constitute a good wheelchair-accessible hotel room and user-friendly accessible public toilet. Of course, any attempts to provide extra accessible accommodations for wheelchair users would be much appreciated and helpful. Most savvy wheelchair-dependent people will likely only use the better-equipped facilities. But my hope is that hotels, restaurants, airplanes and all other public facilities will continue to make the world an easier and more barrier-free society for wheelchair-dependent users in an ever-improving world, not only in our home country but abroad universally. I would also hope to be able to find online assessments rating the various facilities.

CHAPTER 23

Conditions Conducive to Stroke Recovery

For several years now, I have been researching the speediest and most efficient means leading to stroke hemiparesis recovery, especially walking and using the weakened hand. I have been talking to many people and asking many questions. I have also searched the Internet, read books and talked with professionals. Through all of this, I have come up with eleven conditions that seem to contribute to a speedier recovery, which I list and describe below, in no particular order:

1. **Being motivated to pursue goals.** The person is able to sustain a self-devised workout routine over a long period of time. She/he is driven to keep going against all odds steadily for many hours daily, sustained for many years. The person continues to try very hard in spite of pain and setbacks or without visibly recognizable progress markers.

2. **Having inner strength.** Motivation, drive, and the inner will to continue even in the face of challenges are important. The person must have great inner strength and a good sense of self. Quality of life, life itself, good health, self-confidence, and strength are vital.

3. **Having well-defined motivation to find wellness.** She/he has a plan, with clear goals, and is relentless in wanting to improve both physically and emotionally.

4. **Having a good therapist or helpers, along with a good home support team.** A supportive team of people helping to reach one's goals, both professional and private, is essential. Ideally one's therapist will help to build up "hope" and "achievable recovery goals."

5. **No major injuries or setbacks.** It is best if the stroke

survivor is able to avoid any major injuries or accidents during rehabilitation training, sustained over several years. (Some stroke survivors in rehabilitation whom I know have been able to make a total recovery in spite of incurring some injuries.)

6. **Being light in body weight or having a low BMI (Body Mass Index).** The lighter people are, the easier it is for them to work out with less fear of injury, compared to those with heavier body weights and higher BMI measures. Thus, being lightweight allows stroke survivors more efficiency and success in their recovery.

7. **Youthfulness.** Being young in age (for example, say less than 75 years young), or having "youthfulness" as an outlook and disposition, is a huge asset for nearly anything in life, and it certainly positively contributes to stroke rehabilitation, although, for many people, this is not a variable that we have control over.

8. **Perseverance.** Recovery takes several years to accomplish. During the extended time it takes to recover one's physical body strength after a stroke, life goes on around us and many changes occur. If those changes are positive or manageable or slight, hopefully, they will not cause large setbacks. However, some setbacks might even be assets in the recovery process, depending on how they are dealt with. Some changes might pose obstacles that are severe and could hamper recovery. Those stroke survivors able to flow through life's challenges while staying focused on their rehabilitation are the ones most likely to have total recoveries after several years.

9. **Being otherwise healthy.** Ideally the stroke survivor will be otherwise very healthy and take care of his/her health by eating well, exercising and keeping mentally and emotionally stable. She/he should find things to enjoy, such as hobbies and meeting with friends or family often.

10. **Having hope and support.** Ideally "hope" will grow spontaneously inside of the stroke survivor. Having others around, such as therapists, spouses/significant others/partners or other caregivers, family members, good friends, and doctors, will also encourage hope and provide much-needed support.

11. **Having ordinary financial stability.** Those who are financially stable, with no need to work at a job outside of the home, will be better able to concentrate on the rehabilitation process. Financial stability affords one more hours to concentrate daily on one's rehabilitation routine.

12. (Add your own good conditions for stroke recovery here.)

As for myself, concerning these important conditions, I have most of them already working in my favor. However, unfortunately, I lack low BMI, which many Asian people naturally have. I hope to keep up with the other factors while working to reduce my body weight and BMI. I hope to reduce fat but maintain muscle mass, contributing to a lower BMI. My weight usually drops a bit in the hot, humid season of summer in Japan, even if it is mostly just a loss of water weight. I am working on keeping my health in good shape while avoiding any accidents. I suggest that my stroke survivor readers and others work to fulfill these eleven conditions and add others that you think are also conducive to your own rehabilitation progress.

CHAPTER 24

Smell the Roses

First and foremost, enjoy the process of rehabilitation. "Smell the roses" is such a prosaic phrase, but, in so many ways, my experiences through this sudden and devastating stroke have helped me to stay positive. This book has shown how the process of stroke rehabilitation can be enjoyable and successful with the right attitude and approach. I believe it is important to remain highly motivated and to seek out one's own best path to recovery and to try to stay on that path always, even if it means asking for and receiving help from others along the way. Remember that it is all right to ask for help. (My brother tells me that "helping others is one of the best human activities" and that he felt honored and lucky to be caring for our aged mother.)

The path to recovery for stroke survivors often involves very hard going and requires a lot of difficult work and perseverance, and one should expect to endure pain and some setbacks. I advise stroke survivors not to forget to smell the roses along the way and express gratitude and give praise where appropriate. As recovery may take many years, it is best to enjoy the process and not be too focused on the final end goal. Expect also to find some wonderful new relationships and to make discoveries about your abilities and life itself. There are many state-of-the-art facilities for stroke rehabilitation around the world, and as a first step, I suggest researching the best place for your needs and within your budget, hopefully within easy access of your home, family and friends. In the meantime, try to assemble a support team of reliable friends and family. Do not waste time in researching all of your questions alone.

CHAPTER 25

Conditions of Stress in Stroke

I have tried to ascertain what caused my stroke. I was told by my sister, who I think heard it from my doctor in the United States, that the main cause of the massive hemorrhagic stroke, located in the basal ganglia of my right brain-hemisphere, was high blood pressure that had gotten out of control. I had been taking two different types of blood-pressure-reducing medicine twice daily at the time of the stroke, but the dosage of my medications had been deemed insufficient to keep my blood pressure under control, so the dosage was subsequently increased to three times daily. Besides my out-of-control high blood pressure, I had minor foot surgery (in December 2012) just three months prior to the stroke. Further, I may have a hereditary tendency to form brain aneurisms, along with hereditary hypertension and high blood pressure, as my grandfather passed away from an aneurism.

In addition, my stroke occurred a few days after a long overseas flight, which has always caused me extra stress, as I get very anxious in preparing for and going on such flights. I have heard of others collapsing (and sometimes dying) in airports due to the stress of embarking on overseas travel. For this reason, many major airports also have a small hospital with at least one doctor on duty during all times that the airport is open. The biggest lesson to learn here, which I would like to pass on to others, is that you should always keep your blood pressure under control. At one point I think that my doctor may have suggested increasing my blood pressure medications, with me wanting to hold back, knowing my liver was being badly affected by overmedication. I have thought that if I could go back in time, I might go back to that moment and agree to increase my medications. I wish I had known then what I know now, but in that case I might instead be nursing a liver problem today.

I feel that the best defense against strokes is to take preventative measures early, and one of the most proactive actions you can take is to reduce your stress levels, especially when you anticipate traveling. As mentioned in Chapter 6, I had thought I was doing all of the right things and was being careful with my health. But it proved not to be enough.

Following my stroke, moving my belongings out of Sendai was strenuous and took its toll. Long after I had returned home from the hospital in Japan, my husband and I made a busy car trip to Sendai, Miyagi, from Hirosaki, Aomori, in early December 2015, to try to beat the blizzardy driving conditions expected to come very soon. I needed to sift through my things there and eliminate half of them or more to move out of Sendai and send them back to Hirosaki. As both my husband and I had to retire at the end of that fiscal year (at the end of March 2016), we needed to move all of the belongings from our offices, where they had been amassing over our two entire careers, back into our house. I also needed to move out of my Sendai apartment. We had much more than would fit into our house, so instead of sending it all home, I needed to reduce my stuff by more than half. That was one of our main purposes for going to Sendai, but we could not complete the work in one trip, as it was immense, including cleaning out both my office and my apartment, meeting with my office staff, and getting my car moved and fixed. With the left side of my body nearly paralyzed, the climb up to the fourth floor of my apartment was very treacherous. (See the photo on page 167.)

First of all, there was only a very thin, much-rusted handle on one side in the best places. That is, from the bottom looking up, it was on the right side. So, coming back down, after several hours of work and no lunch, I had to descend backward with my husband's help. It just kept getting worse from there, as, when I had to round corners, the handrail would completely disappear and was totally missing in many areas, making the climb down (like the climb up) extremely dangerous. Miraculously, we made it safely to the car to begin our five-hour drive home, with my husband doing all of the driving, as with the trip to Sendai just the day before. We made it home safely rather late that evening. But we had to repeat that trip several more times. I realized that I needed to lose weight and strengthen my leg muscles, especially my left foot and my good right knee, which I relied on too much to compensate for weakness in the affected leg. But it was difficult for me to lose weight, as I was already eating the minimum and exercising at every chance.

We made a second trip from December 23 through Christmas and had an untraditional Christmas dinner in the hotel café, eating pizza and *tapas* with red wine, as the hotel Christmas dinner ended two days before Christmas, on December 23. Go figure?

I felt as if I was cleaning out my apartment after my death, as I had done decades earlier following the death of my Great Aunt Gussy. At that time, when I went with my mother to my Great Aunt Gussy's apartment to help clean it out, I felt as if we had violated someone's privacy, and at the time, I hoped that the same fate would not befall me at some future time and space. Instead, it was I, myself, cleaning out my own apartment there in Sendai, which seemed similar to the earlier experience, but I was glad not to have anyone else do that for me, except for

Perilous climbing for the disabled, with no handrails at most places in Japan: this is at my apartment building in Sendai, showing the dark stairwell. I had to climb up to the fourth floor four separate times that day (author's photograph).

my husband, who was helping me. It was an odd feeling, as, of course, I had not actually died. I had just come close to it.

After climbing up and down the four flights of stairs to my room twice and spending an entire day packing up boxes in my office, we realized that we needed to make another trip to continue the work, probably in the springtime, after the snow melted. We also needed to make a special trip for me to deliver my "last lecture" at the university where I worked and attend an after-party with a few students and colleagues. The packing-up work needed to be done, and I really appreciated my husband's close help and attention to details. I could not have done it at all without his assistance, even by hiring movers, which was the next step after I separated out the "throw-away stuff" from the "keep stuff" and divided it all into boxes to be moved home or discarded. That was tiring work, although my husband did all of the lifting and moving of numerous boxes down the four flights of stairs. I feel much gratitude for that.

We made a third trip to Sendai in the spring of 2016 to try to complete most of the work and get my car moved to be repaired as well. But we could not complete it, nor did we get an estimate from movers (they were already booked up, as it was their busiest season). I was also unable to give away my furniture and other still usable things that are costly to discard.

So, we needed to make a fourth trip to get the estimate and then a fifth trip on moving day, as we needed to coordinate the work. But my husband was burned out, and he wanted out of the work for good reason and told me that I should go to Sendai and do the work myself. That was impossible and totally out of the question, as I was then (and still am) totally dependent on him for the help. Once, on one of the earlier trips, after we had climbed up to my fourth-floor apartment, when he got tired and angry at me, he said, "*Sayonara*, good-bye," and then he just left me alone, sitting in a chair with my AFO on my foot and my cane, in the apartment, with no phone, no food and no water, no usable toilet, and no way to get down by myself. I cried at being left there for over an hour until he returned. I could not even go down the four flights of stairs without him, I realized. I could understand his not wanting to go there again, as I, too, felt pain and got tired just thinking about such a trip, but it was even more difficult for him, as he also had to drive five hours each way and carry many heavy boxes down four flights of stairs to his car and then run back up.

So it was still up in the air at the end of March 2016, and the deadline was fast approaching for me to move out. Of course, if I were able-bodied, I would have been able to take care of it all myself. But the reality of the situation, I realized, was that I am indeed very handicapped and climbing stairs is impossible without the help of my husband, who is well experienced in how to assist me without any handrails in many places. I would not be able to trust anyone else for that, except perhaps my therapist. The task was too intimate and dangerous to actually ask anyone other than family to assist me, even if I was willing to pay generously. It was impossible to ask for help with that. We had to do it ourselves.

I marked my 65th birthday (on January 16, 2016) while residing at a short-stay facility for a week, while my husband had business out of town. The staff at the facility kindly prepared my favorite dessert—chocolate mousse—for a birthday party in my honor and came into my room to get me when it was ready. The staffer first insisted that I put on earrings and lipstick and eye makeup, which she had noticed that I had brought along with me. I gladly complied with her request, as I always enjoy the chance to dress up. Then they snapped some photos of me (which I felt to be not very attractive).

The time came for my last lecture. I had another birthday ceremony of sorts, marking my 65th birthday and thus my retirement from work. I was asked to present my "last lecture" to the department/center along with four others also retiring in the same year, allowing us only twenty minutes each for our individual presentations. The presentation seemed to go off well, except that I ran out of time and was not able to state my conclusion or take questions and comments. I also missed getting any formal feedback, although at the after-party several people expressed interest in my work, which was a boost to my self-esteem. My colleagues and a few students attended the informal party in the school cafeteria, where I could briefly talk with a few people, including one of my closest students, Minako-san.

Davide, a foreign student from Italy, also attended the last lectures and the party. He had attended a class that I had volunteered to teach to foreigners about Japanese culture (both traditional and current culture). I was not given any extra reimbursement at that time for taking on the extra classes beyond my regular salary, although I had expected the administration to reduce my other load of nine courses during those two terms, but as they could not do that, I taught the classes voluntarily. I already had a full teaching load of eighteen classes; including the volunteer classes, I had charge of twenty classes that year. I enjoyed conducting the class very much, though, as I had taught it before elsewhere and had many materials and lesson plans already prepared for it. I enjoyed hearing the opinions of foreign students, and a few of my best Japanese students, including Minako, asked to audit the class so that they could connect with foreign students. They contributed Japanese perspectives, making it a win-win-win situation for us all. I felt sad at having to discontinue teaching it due to being overloaded with other work.

CHAPTER 26

Current Status

Moving Forward

After over four years of trying very hard to get back on my feet and walking again, I have not been able to walk more than around 300 meters for a half-hour while wearing a foot brace, using a cane, with a helper or a therapist nearby to spot me. But I am very grateful for being able to walk that much. I can circle around my house fifteen times or so with the help of the leg brace and a cane. I am very proud of that accomplishment, remembering how I asked my first physical therapist, Aaron, in Seattle, to help me walk. Now I have confidence in climbing stairs up or down if there is a handrail, as well as walking quite a distance if I should ever need to (with the leg brace on and using a cane or handrail).

As I revise this now February 19, 2020, it has been nearly seven years since the stroke, and my condition is unchanged from what I wrote above at the four-year mark. If anything, I have gotten used to my condition even more than before and am quite complacent with where I am right now in my journey. I am satisfied that I was able make a successful trip back to my hometown last summer in 2019. It involved a flight across the Pacific Ocean from Japan to the United States. (As of August 23, 2020, seven and a half years after the stroke, I am still doing very well and am also being careful to avoid getting ill from the pandemic caused by the new coronavirus.)

One-Handed Spasticity

My left hand is still curled and spastic, even with taking a low dose of anti-spasmodic medicine to relax muscles and self-stretching the hand open several times daily. Even now, my left hand is not very useful to me, as I cannot type like before, using both hands. I also cannot bind my hair by myself and perform easy things like that which require two dexterous hands. Still, I have come up with some methods to make my right hand more useful.

Coordinating Two Hands Together

My father used to ask us to ponder the riddle "What is the sound of one hand clapping?"

I have thought about that sometimes these days. One hand, my good right hand, does the difficult work, and the other hand is often needed just to give some torque, or pull. For example, when trying to tie a shoelace, the good (right) hand can form the bow, while the other (weak) hand or a tool is needed to give some pull or resistance. So if I cannot use my left hand for that, I try to find a tool, like a hook or something to provide the torque. One of my goals is to be able to bind my hair by myself, so I can wear my hair long. My home therapist often used to commend me for "using my head." But using my creative facility is the easiest thing for me, as my cognition is the only thing that seems to still be intact, rather than my body. I am constantly trying to figure out creative ways to accomplish things better with just one hand and one leg, without incurring further injury.

For now, my hope is just to wake up to find myself totally recovered or to see my total recovery gradually occur over time. It is like trying to lose weight. I can easily visualize it, but it is not something that suddenly happens. It is very slow and gradual and hardly noticeable. But with perseverance, the goal may be realized.

"The More I Seem to Remain the Same, the More I Change"

I wonder if I am actually changing more than I realize. Friends and acquaintances whom I saw in Tsukuba in May 2016, who had not seen me for over a year, told me at that time that I had improved, but I could not really see it. Perhaps I am making slow progress, which is so gradual that I cannot notice it. Only if I compare myself with photos taken of me three years ago, when my face drooped a lot, can I realize that I must be making a bit of progress, as my face droops much less now. But my face is crooked enough to have made some small Japanese children, who did not know me, cry when they saw my face when I smiled at them. It happened at the grocery store in rural Japan awhile ago. I was saddened at their behavior and that their parents allowed them to behave so rudely. I suppose that it must have been a double or triple whammy for them, seeing someone who is not only a *gaijin* (foreigner) but also handicapped in a wheelchair and who has a crooked face. I am determined to say something the next time a child begins to cry upon looking at my crooked smile. At least it was an attempted smile, and I do not bare teeth as if to bite them. It made me feel like a deformed, horrible monster straight out of hell or something.

A Total Recovery?

I hope to recover enough to be able to use my left side again, as has happened with a few people I know. I hope to use my left hand and my left foot for walking. I am still waiting for that miracle of a total recovery to occur, even after some of my therapists and doctors have told me that it is most likely not going to happen. Through my informal surveys talking to others, it seems that, on average, it can take eight years to a decade to heal from the physical effects of a stroke (if at all), if one is young enough to enjoy the recovery and if their original brain injury was slight or moderate. It might be less obvious in those people who are over the age of 75, with age-related issues also to manage. That gives me perhaps few years more to work on my recovery, even though it is often said that the progress made in the first twelve or eighteen months after a stroke is the most that will be made. Beyond that, not too much is expected, but I choose to disagree with this stereotypical notion.

I think that the first year of recovery just indicates the degree of severity of the brain injury and that other progress can continue for as long as one is motivated and works hard at it. Most of those people in my informal survey who fully recovered were younger than seventy, it seems, but please do not let my writing/saying that limit anybody who reads this book. I think that *everyone*, no matter their age or the severity of their brain injury, should continue to pursue their total recovery, if at all possible. I myself will certainly pursue my recovery until my death. I am in this for the long term and may outlast many of my therapists, helpers and caregivers. Most of those who recovered their ability to walk have worked very hard at it. I am hoping to be one of them, and I encourage my readers to try hard also to be one of them. As I used to tell my university students, "Set your goals and fiercely work to achieve them. Try again and again if necessary, but never give up." Anat Baniel, in her book *Move into Life* (2016), stresses that we should be flexible with our goals and allow some deviance from the original objective. (See Chapter 23 for my "conditions conducive to stroke recovery.")

My next strongest hopes are that if I cannot become totally healed on my own, I may someday be able to purchase or to use a reasonably priced robotic suit or exoskeleton to assist me in walking. In Japan, the research in this area is being supported by public funds, so I am hopeful that I will be able to afford one of those to free me up to walk again. They are also being developed outside of Japan, and hopefully competition will speed the process up and encourage quality products that might benefit me and others like me soon, perhaps within the next few years.

I think that the state-of-the-art robotic suit is one being designed in the Bay Area in the United States called Ekso at the Ekso Robotics Company.

Robotics Technology for Re-Walking in Japan

Since I reside in Japan, having robotic technology available here is vital to me, as it is more accessible than such technology in the United States. I am very happy to report that there seems to be promise for the Hybrid Assistive Limb (HAL) robotic suit being designed at Cyberdyne Studio in Tsukuba, Japan.

I am placing my hopes in robotic aids for walking, and if I could afford it, I would buy a robotic suit or invest in a future robotic limb product that might have universal appeal and need, even beyond the level of the ubiquitous smartphones.

Smartphones are fun gadgets to own, but a robotic suit may become a necessity for many of us, like a wristwatch, a computer, a hearing aid, eyeglasses, a pacemaker, an automobile, a bicycle and so forth. It is already needed—certainly for stroke survivors like me, impaired on half of our body vertically, but even more so for quadriplegics or others with spinal-cord injuries who are impaired horizontally, usually below a certain injury spot along their spinal cord or neck. I long wished to try out such a robotic suit to weigh the advantages of using it against the disadvantages concerning my ability to walk and to get around safely and painlessly. I waited anxiously for the day to come when I could be fitted with such a suit.

At last, I *did* actually have a chance to try out a Hybrid Assistive Limb (HAL) in Japan (see Appendix IX). There must be hundreds of thousands or millions of others like me (and more increasing daily) around the world. I just wish such devices would become common and affordable. The government of Japan is planning to make the use of such suits available through use of the national insurance for those people with extremely difficult neuromuscular conditions, such as ALS. At this point, that consideration does not include stroke survivors. I cannot understand why it would not include everyone with a walking deficiency who might benefit from it. I want to say the following to all of those robotic engineers:

> Come on. Let us see what you have designed. I will be very happy to try it out for you and to promote any of your good products. I love technology and technicians. I want to encourage you all to keep on going to the next level with devices to better aid stroke survivors and other disabled people.

You can see me using a robotic limb at Cyberdyne on Youtube. Please search "Laurel's Robot therapy 1." There are several short videos from 1 through about 9 or 10. "Laurel's robot therapy 5" is one of the best to show me walking with a leg limb. I was so excited about it that I could hardly speak.

The Path to Stroke Recovery

Through my few years of researching and asking people questions about stroke recovery, I feel that one of the most important aspects of recovery is reconnecting pathways from the brain to the muscles and tendons in one's limbs. This is not so easy to do in reality, though. There are various methods proposed by many people regarding how best to do that, but I think each person needs to find their own way there. I personally am trying to become more mindful of my body during my walking sessions and am trying to work out stretching my hand too. Hard work and dedication are also needed to speed up the recovery process. Lastly, as stated above, recovery depends much on the severity of the original stroke damage, including the brain location, extent of the damage, age of the survivor, and so forth.

I feel that communication and interaction with others and doing rehabilitation exercises is the starting point. Just as is the case for able-bodied people, the most important thing to help us get though our regular, mundane, stressful, and difficult daily lives is to love and to be loved by friends, family, and co-workers. There are few very precious people on this Earth who truly love us and whom we truly love, so we need to appreciate those most beloved people and let them know. It may be difficult for some people to express their love to others or to simply say to them, "I love you." Or "I appreciate you." Or "Thank you."

Certain practices and philosophies of rehabilitation care for stroke survivors would be good to incorporate at hospitals and facilities around the world. Simply stated, I feel that it is best to train aides and other staff to be interculturally aware and professional in their words and actions. Users/residents should be treated with respect, and they should not be assumed to be brain damaged or depressed like the stereotypical disabled stroke survivor. Judgments should not be passed without rigorous observation and dialogue. Also, I believe that survivors should be able to play a more active role in their own recovery and rehabilitation process.

Final Words

This is a hard book to finish. I want to keep writing, because the story is not over, but it helps me to view this book as more of a beginning. I hope you can view it that way as well. Certainly, for me, much has happened on the road to recovery—so many small advances, along with much larger crystallizations of thought and understanding, have occurred, which have facilitated physical and emotional wholeness. For stroke survivors, things will never be the same. We are constantly striving, constantly adapting, and constantly implementing workarounds to make our day-to-day lives more full and rewarding. So, moving through and beyond recovery, let's keep in mind that much of our progress is measured in our outlook, our attitude. Nobody can take this away from us.

Many people, especially when young and still healthy, think that they will keep living healthily on and on, forever maybe. But it is not going to happen for any of us. It does not help to look young (even some thirty years younger than our real age), or to be active or in good shape, or to pair up with a much younger partner, lover or spouse. Those are all superficial things that are drastically different from the truth revealed in images taken from inside our veins, hearts or brains, and so on.

On the road to recovery, in 2015, twice I planned and carried out long train trips alone to conferences out of town, across Japan. Like a bird out of my cage, after a year of being closed in, I was super-determined with a never-give-up *gambaru* spirit. I wanted to show that I was back to my normal self after residing for an entire year in nursing homes and hospitals, but it was not as easy to accomplish as perhaps I had initially imagined. I needed much help from others.

First of all, I attended an academic conference far away, out of town in Tsukuba, which I went to by the *Shinkansen* (bullet train) and local trains to present an academic paper. I asked an agency to help escort me there and care for me at my destination and then bring me back home, but, as they were understaffed, they could only take me there, drop me off, and then say "*sayonara*" at the station, leaving me alone. The rest of the time, I was helped by friends there, unsolicited. I made my way back home by myself with the help of the train staff. I thought that it was a great experience, but I was later told by one man that I had "inconvenienced" those people who stepped forward to lovingly help me, from their hearts. I thought that they wanted to help me, and calling their loving actions an "inconvenience" seemed to me to be leveling an insult against them. But some of the conference executives kept me from attending the conference the following year. I felt excluded, being asked not to attend the conference unless I could procure a full-time helper, which I could not find, even though I was willing to pay for one. I felt very sad at missing the event, as I had been an active member and volunteer executive with the organization since nearly its beginning, some thirty years before, and I had made it a practice to attend yearly, to reunite with my colleagues at nearly every conference. It was an important part of my life and my identity over my several decades in Japan. Perhaps in the future I will take steps to be more proactive in anticipating roadblocks on such a trip, including trying to hire an aide (if that could be arranged). I don't want to lose the connection I had with this community, especially with the bilingualism, teaching children, and gender and language in education special interest groups there, among others. So, again, workarounds will be necessary. We live in an imperfect world.

Next, I traveled to the Association of Foreign Wives of Japanese (AFWJ) convention in Sendai, Japan (a gathering of very supportive wives of Japanese), when an organizer offered to escort me there and back by train. I was also on the organizing committee, as I had lived in Sendai (the venue city of the convention) during the early planning stages, before the stroke. I likely did inconvenience some people there whom I asked to help me wheel around quite a bit, but I also enjoyed being able to meet up with those foreign wives who are like my sisters in Japan.

I had wanted to show everyone that I was fine and back to my old self, except in a wheelchair. I gave short presentations at both events (and then later at a short-stay facility to the rehabilitation staff) about my stroke experience, which became the background for this book. Up to a point, I may have shown that I was back to my old self, but I could not have attended those two events without a lot of help from others.

And it is important to realize and recognize that people with good will who are trying to help often do not know the correct ways to assist handicapped people. They may feel insecure or simply afraid to step in and help. We should always keep this in mind on our road to recovery.

The final message I'd like to leave with you, as a stroke survivor, is one of encouragement. Please work fiercely to enjoy the process of rehabilitation, as it may last longer than you initially expected. Enjoy your relationships by fully participating in the process itself and not remaining too fixed on the end result. If possible, seek out people with a good sense of humor to make you laugh, even if you find yourself laughing at yourself. Never miss the chance to laugh wholeheartedly. Laughter is healing, and it feels good.

I have found, when examining various types of recovery, that a common important feature in maintaining health is not only paying attention to one's physical body but also staying mindful and being sensitive to your emotional and psychological needs. There are many ways to do this, some of which I have discussed in this book, along with others you will discover on your own path to wholeness. I encourage you to be brave, step out in faith, and challenge yourself, but always remember that hard work only reaps benefits over time, so be patient. This will take time. I wish you all the very best. Go for it!

Haiku of Completion

I end with a haiku I wrote after finishing my final draft of this book project. This haiku expresses my feelings as I completed the first draft, taking over five years to complete it from start to finish.

My Work Is Finished

Work finished by fall
Why so drained, lonely, and sad?
Hobby, sport, "Good-bye"

Good Practices in the United States (Harborview)

Harborview Medical Center in Seattle, Washington, has some excellent practices in place, which I benefited from greatly, and which the facilities in Japan could well learn from. Below I list some of what impressed me after my stay in its rehabilitation unit:

1. Using blackboards in the stroke survivor's room as reminders for patients.

2. Providing notebooks for stroke survivors with answers to all of their questions and concerns, as well as an introduction to the facility and the staff.

3. Introducing staff personally, one by one.

4. Including residents in meetings about them.

5. Spending more time on actual rehabilitation exercise and training.

6. Using an AFO (leg brace).

7. Using the gait belt for safety.

8. Offering stroke survivors baths instead of showers (as in Japan).

9. Making Wi-Fi available for residents so they can research their own conditions and stay connected to the outside world.

10. Maintaining a positive attitude: "Life should be happy and fun," with activities, movies, and so forth.

No matter where they are, staff in care facilities should keep in mind that there is never a "one size fits all" approach. They should allow for individual differences, instead of stereotyping all stroke survivors as having the same problems and needs.

In addition, facilities should incorporate more "flexibility" into their practices to allow greater freedom and enjoyment. I feel that greater flexibility would also contribute to better healing.

Below are some areas that could improve in Japanese facilities.

1. As mentioned in earlier, providing Wi-Fi to the residents would allow them to re-adapt more quickly by keeping their social networks and contacts intact. It would also give them a chance to research their condition, as there are many good sites for support, recovery and information about strokes available online. Furthermore, Internet access provides residents with entertainment and enjoyment and freedom, which contribute to healing.

2. I feel that the use of "gait belts" is a practice that could greatly contribute to the safe care of stroke survivors in various facilities in Japan, where they are not generally used. They are helpful for untrained staff and are much safer for stroke survivors than trying to catch them by the scruff of their pants or an injured arm.

3. I feel that Japanese staff need to raise consciousness to "respect diversity" much more than they currently do. Staff should never discriminate on the basis of gender, race, ethnicity, ability, beliefs, age and so forth. This should be taught as a lesson to future staff at schools certifying nursing staff, as well as boards and directors of facilities, doctors, and rehabilitation staff. Consciousness training, including intercultural awareness, diversity, and professionalism, would greatly help solve some of the problems I witnessed in Japan at facilities for the aged and the impaired, especially concerning bathing practices.

4. Care facilities should employ same-sex aides in baths, particularly for women.

5. No one should prevent residents from eating as they choose. Permit them to make individual eating choices like at home. Allow occasional snacking.

APPENDIX II

Good Practices in Japan

Hirosaki Stroke Rehabilitation Center Hospital (Aomori Prefecture, Japan) had many good practices and beliefs that I believe the United States could learn from. Here are a few examples:

1. The nutrition and weight management advice and teaching in Japan, in my opinion, far outshines what is found in the United States. Weight loss alone, as a healing strategy (especially by restricting the diet), is not a good thing. Survivors should have tailor-made diet protocols and be guided to make their own eating choices so when they return home, it will become second nature.

2. Japan facilities offer baths instead of showers, because baths aid in relaxation and muscle flexibility. Baths also help residents to maintain body warmth throughout the cold nights. I realize this practice could be economically prohibitive to institute in the United States, where facilities often have no bath capability, but it is something worth pursuing.

3. Daily massage is provided to stroke survivors for relaxation and to reduce pain in tightened body muscles and tendons. It also warms up the body for rehabilitation and walking exercises.

4. Japan infrastructure allows stroke survivors (and others with chronic or long-term disabilities) to access treatment by way of program availability and monetary subsidy. This system allows for nearly seamless ongoing care, a situation not readily available to Americans.

Safe Aids in Mobility— the Harness Walker

The harness walker, called the *second step gait harness system*, is one of the most secure and safe aids for walking that I have seen. Second Step Inc. is the company that supplies this harness. They claim on their website that they "foster independence and maintain dignity." They also write, "Patients cannot fall using this System as the harness is designed to support their full body weight if necessary. No walker or cane can compare to the safety of this System." Although I did not go as far as purchasing one and having it sent to Japan from the United States, it looks very appealing to me. Perhaps someday I may get the chance to try one out or purchase it. However, this device seems to be too large for Japanese homes, public facilities, automobiles and so forth. It would be good if someone could develop a slim, collapsible version. I believe there may be similar such harness walkers available in Japan. (I actually *did* have a chance to try out another type of walker with a harness while at Cyberdyne Studio in Tsukuba, Japan, although it was made by a different company in Japan. It seemed very stable, although I never tripped, causing me to rely on the harness to catch me. So, I do not know its full capacity.)

Information and Networking
Websites for Survivors

There are several good facilities, websites and other resources that I would like to briefly introduce here and hopefully add to, as time goes on.

Free Magazine and Web Information
(Sponsored by the American Stroke Association)

A great site offering this kind of information can be found at stroke.org. You can receive a free online or print publication sent to your home (U.S. addresses) about strokes and stroke rehabilitation called *Stroke Connection Magazine*. This free online and hardcopy magazine is a good place to find information and to read inspirational stories and make connections, and can be found here: https://www.stroke.org/en/stroke-connection.

Online Stroke Community

The opportunity to engage with others experiencing similar medical circumstances has been shown to offer a great benefit for peace of mind as well as promoting recovery. It can be a means of connecting with other stroke survivors in English or other languages in which you are fluent. Stroke.org also offers an online community.

The American Stroke Association (with the board of directors mostly situated on the East Coast of the United States) provides free information on stroke prevention and rehabilitation, as well as networking for stroke survivors. The organization assists survivors, their families and friends, and healthcare professionals in the field. They aim to reduce the incidence and impact of strokes and offer support. This association is designed for English-speaking Americans residing in the United States but is a worldwide online network. They also try to market some of their products and to recruit sponsors and donations to their cause of stroke awareness, prevention, rehabilitation, cure, networking, and so forth. I believe that it is a donation well directed.

Other Networking Options

Flint Rehab (www.flintrehab.com) offers networking with other stroke survivors and a variety of information. The website is very easy to use, and the members are friendly (mostly Americans, it seems). Their "MusicGlove Hand" product looks interesting, and I will ask my rehabilitation facility to purchase it and, if possible, to try it out first to see if it does what it advertises.

I happened upon another website for stroke survivors called Spokes Fighting Strokes (spokesfightingstrokes.org). It is a community, based in the United States, for stroke survivors who want to use pedaled tricycles for getting around and for sport trips. They have get-togethers and events, races, and so forth.

For Gardening Lovers

Accessible Gardens is a great website for stroke survivors and other people interested in planting and caring for gardens even while in a wheelchair, vision impaired or experiencing other impairments. Gardening can be an excellent hobby for anyone with disabilities, and I have found this website to be especially helpful. Find it at accessiblegardens. org.

My relatives are the creators of this website: my aunt, Shirley Sidell, a professional photographer who is garden-crazy and involved in many garden projects, and her son, my cousin, Ronald Sidell, who became a quadriplegic due to a serious case of Guillain-Barré Syndrome. They have put a lot of energy into the website.

Other Special Needs Equipment

I happened upon a website for special needs equipment while searching for a tricycle wheelchair for adults, with pedals. I thought it would be good exercise as well as providing mobility, not just for children but also for adults. But the cost of purchasing it and shipping to Japan was prohibitive. However, I thought that some of the company's products were very nice and worthy of mention here for those residing in the United States. The website, Adaptive Mall, gives hands-on experience with many wonderful children and their families, supplying appropriate adaptive equipment to children, their parents, and caregivers. Their services find the best equipment to support the children at their highest functioning level.

In addition, a pedal wheelchair made by TESS Co., Ltd.—the Cogy wheelchair—was developed in Japan. This wheelchair, which was designed for people who have trouble walking but can still move their legs, is pedal-powered, says the firm's representative director, Kenji Suzuki. I'm not sure if it works with one leg completely paralyzed, as in hemiplegia, but it's worth looking into. Apparently, the pedal wheelchair now comes in two sizes: medium and large (though a small one may be coming soon or is already available in Japan).

I was able to try out another pedal wheelchair at my rehabilitation facility in Japan and was very impressed with the product, although I still have many lingering concerns about it: The design is very nice, and it is beautiful and "sexy." It also maneuvers very well, at least at my "indoor" rehabilitation facility, which is very spacious. I feel that by using this product I would be able to make my way over several kilometers to the closest stores from my house on good pavement.

The problem with it is that I would only be able to use it outdoors and in dry conditions, such as spring and summer, on smooth paved roads. It is too large to be of much use inside a Japanese home or shop, restaurant, and so forth. It is also difficult to strap into alone. Following are some of my other concerns about this wheelchair:

- If it were to be used outside, how would it handle over ruts in the road, gravelly or grassy surfaces, and steps?
- Would I be able to easily transfer from the wheelchair to a toilet and back, and to my bed and back, by myself, unaided? It seems a bit difficult getting into and out of it right now for me. The feet need to be strapped in well by someone else. I think I could make it to the closest store to my house, but would I be allowed, if physically able, to enter stores, restaurants and other public places in Japan (or elsewhere) with it?
- Is there a way to easily clean off the tires before entering a house or shop? It seems too big for some entryways in Japan; electric doors may be a problem too, as well as circling push doors.
- How would it maneuver up steps into buildings and homes?
- Could it be locked to prevent theft?
- Does it have brakes to keep it from rolling away?
- How would I fix flat tires on it by myself?
- I would like to rent one for a while, but is it available? And what would that monthly rental cost be?

These are just a few of my concerns.

I am thinking that the perfect walking aid for me might actually be "a walker" with a seat on it and a place to put groceries and a drink holder. It should fold up to carry on a bus or plane. I am even thinking of a cane with a chair to sit on. My therapist has recently recommended that we no longer use a 4-pronged cane, but rather a simple one-stick type of cane instead. I am not sure why. If it had a seat on it, perhaps it might do, but now it seems a bit unstable. I want something versatile, small, light, collapsible, and stable. I want something I can sit on to rest like a walker and that I can carry my stuff on. It should have wheels and be able to brake/stop, with only my right hand. Its purpose would be to free me from needing someone to push my wheelchair. Instead, I would walk, but if I got tired, I would need to rest and sit down. I want something that would be easy to take onto buses, trains, and planes and in a car. Possibly it could be a wheelchair/walker or a tricycle pedal walker, or something similar, but it needs to be light and very portable. I still have yet to find the best walking aid for me.

Facilities for Re-Walking (Project Walk)

Besides Harborview Medical Center in Seattle, Washington, through my Internet searches and contacts, I have learned about other very good places for rehabilitation and learning to walk again. One of the best programs appears to be one called Project Walk Recovery Foundation. Available resources can be found here: https://www.guidestar.org/profile/20–2722055.

Project Walk Recovery Foundation claims to be an "activity-based rehabilitation method," involving self-awareness through movement. They advocate the regrowth of brain connections. They state on their website, "Brain axonal sprouting is thought to be increased by physical training and training helps to reorganize the nervous system."

This project aims to get people out of their wheelchairs to do things they could not do before with real results, with their highly trained staff and published research. They seem to have high-tech specialized equipment.

Project Walk recovery institutes seem to be mostly directed toward "paralysis recovery" such as spinal cord injury (rather than specifically for stroke survivors). They have several facilities around the United States and offer franchise opportunities for people to start their own facility in their hometown if there is not one there already. Their main center is based in San Diego, California. Project Walk Recovery Foundation is geared more toward people with spinal cord injuries, multiple sclerosis, ALS, muscular dystrophy, cerebral palsy, and many other illnesses and injuries and children's conditions that involve neural-muscular impairments to walking. As a stroke survivor, my left side is very weak, but it is not paralyzed. Thus I do not see myself (nor should I be seen) in the same way as those people with spinal cord paralysis. In the case of stroke hemiparesis, the weakness occurs vertically (from head to toe) on the body side opposite to where the brain injury occurred. Nevertheless, I believe that these facilities could also benefit stroke survivors.

Project Walk Recovery Foundation centers help adults and children alike with conditions that include walking deficiencies. If you are covered by insurance or have other means, and if you happen to live near one of their centers, I recommend checking it out further. If I find the means, I would definitely like to go to one of their facilities someday.

Strategies to Walking Recovery

Nancy Mairs is a writer and speaker about disability. She has been disabled since before she was diagnosed with multiple sclerosis (MS) at age 28, some three decades ago, and is wheelchair bound. I like her wry sense of humor and her attitude toward being disabled, or "waist-high in the world" (in a wheelchair), as she puts it. Many of her writings and speeches are available on the Internet. Please check out her well-known essay "On Being a Cripple" or read her books, including *Waist-High in the World: A Life among the Nondisabled* (1996). Mairs has many other postings available for free online, where you can get a feel for her writing style.

While I do not agree with all she writes (such as her thoughts regarding suicide), we share many of the same priorities, such as the need for a more barrier-free accessible society, both at home and around the world. We are both "waist-high in the world" in wheelchairs (although, being short in stature, I have never been much more than "shoulder-high" in the world); we are also both independent women with very kind caregiving husbands by our sides helping us to get around. I was impressed by her writing about her experiences of living with MS, which are detailed in *Waist-High in the World*.

*　*　*

The Feldenkrais Method* is a form of somatic education (involving movement, awareness and bodywork) developed in the 1940s in response to the founder's (Moshe Feldenkrais') soccer knee injury, which was further damaged later after slipping. This method uses "gentle movement and directed attention" to improve mobility and enhance human functioning. The website dedicated to this method claims that one "can increase one's ease and range of motion, improve flexibility and coordination, and rediscover one's innate capacity for graceful, efficient movement." These improvements will often generalize to enhance functioning in other aspects of one's life. Feldenkrais applied techniques he learned from judo, physics and engineering, which he devised into his self-healing method and then taught it to others. "In order to sense, one must move, feel and think" (Feldenkrais, 1972).

> The Feldenkrais Method is based on principles of physics, biomechanics and an empirical understanding of learning and human development. By expanding the self-image through movement sequences that bring attention to the parts of the self that are out of awareness, the Method enables you to include more of yourself in your functioning movements. Students become more aware of their habitual neuromuscular patterns and rigidities and expand options for new ways of moving. By increasing sensitivity the Feldenkrais Method assists you to live your life more fully, efficiently and comfortably. (https://www.lessonswithease.com/what-is-feldenkrais/)

One of Feldenkrais' main ideas was "awareness through movement," which emphasizes "learning which movements work better and noticing the quality of these changes in your body." Through increased awareness, you will learn to abandon habitual patterns of movement and develop new alternatives, resulting in improved flexibility and coordination. The ability of the brain to change structurally and functionally based on experience is the essence of the Feldenkrais Method (from the Feldenkrais Method website, accessed 12 June 2016).

*   *   *

One of Moshe Feldenkrais' most well-known disciples is a fellow Israeli, a woman named Anat Baniel, who practiced in New York City starting in 1982. Through her training as a clinical psychologist, a trainer and a dancer, along with her Feldenkrais experience and her work with children and adults, she devised her own method, called the Anat Baniel Method (ABM). The ABM includes her Feldenkrais training, along with other university training and years of hands-on work with adults and children.

I first learned about the ABM as the method used by Jill Bolte Taylor's mother to help guide her daughter to a complete stroke recovery in eight years. ABM includes Baniel's "nine essentials" for improved movement and faster rehabilitation. Please see www.anatbanielmethod.com or read Anat Baniel's book, *Move into Life: Neuro-Movement for Lifelong Vitality*. She developed the concept of NeuroMovement®: "Movement is the language of the brain" (Anat Baniel, taken from the Internet, August 2016).

The "nine essentials of Anat Baniel" (2013) are, briefly summarized, as follows:

1. **Move with attention:** One should exercise "mindfulness" when in training and moving.

2. **Use slow movements:** Slowing down one's movements helps one to learn more and better.

3. **Employ variation:** Vary the patterns of doing things to allow for more brain stimulation.

4. **Use subtlety:** Move using slow movements. Break down each larger movement into even smaller parts to increase brain stimulation.

5. **Maintain enthusiasm:** I take this to also mean "motivation."

6. **Have flexible goals:** With goals less rigidly defined, the greater you will succeed.

7. **Keep the learning switch on:** Be ready to learn the entire time. Be switched ON.

8. **Keep imagination and dreams:** Allow yourself childlike dreams and imagine yourself being better than you already are. Be creative. Dream and have fun in the process. Keep a good sense of humor.

9. **Remain aware:** Keep yourself aware and at attention in order to retrain the brain and develop and repair more positive brain connections. Be aware of your movements and your body.

Robotics Rehabilitation
Ekso-Skeleton Suits in the United States

Ekso Bionics promotes walking rehabilitation with the use of robotic exoskeleton technology. On the company's website (eksobionics.com), the following is stated:

> Ekso Bionics® (EKSO) is a worldwide pioneer in the field of robotic exoskeletons. For over 10 years we have been committed to developing the latest technology and engineering to help people rethink current physical limitations and achieve the remarkable. Our products unlock human strength, endurance, and mobility potential, with broad applications across medical and industrial markets. We have yet to imagine all human robotics applications and remain committed to forming strategic partnerships for cutting-edge innovation. Ekso Bionics is headquartered in Northern California, (the Bay Area), USA, and is listed on the OTCQB under the symbol EKSO.
>
> Ekso Bionics uses the power of smart exoskeleton technology machines to empower people. Our therapeutic devices can help stroke patients during rehabilitation learn to walk again and provide those with spinal cord injuries the chance to stand and walk. The Ekso device, so named because it resembles an exoskeleton, helps the wearer walk of their own accord, by picking up small upper body movements and translating them into strides.

According to Nasdaq, "Ekso Bionics is a leading developer of exoskeleton solutions that amplify human potential by supporting or enhancing strength, endurance, and mobility across medical and industrial applications. Founded in 2005, the Company continues to build upon its unparalleled expertise to design some of the most cutting-edge, innovative wearable robots available on the market. Ekso Bionics is the only exoskeleton company to offer technologies that range from helping those with paralysis to stand up and walk, to enhancing human capabilities on job sites across the globe." The company also provides research for the advancement of R&D projects intended to benefit U.S. defense capabilities.

According to Intechopen.com, "In 2010 Berkeley Bionics unveiled eLEGS, which stands for 'Exoskeleton Lower Extremity Gait System.' eLEGS is another hydraulically powered exoskeleton system, and allows paraplegics to stand and walk with crutches or a walker." The computer interface uses force and motion sensors to monitor the user's gestures and motion, and it uses this information to interpret the intent of the user and translate it into action. Users can "put on and take off the device by themselves as well as walk, turn, sit down, and stand up unaided," per Berkeley Robotics & Human Engineering Laboratory.

The Intechopen.com article goes on to say, "In 2011 eLEGS was renamed Ekso. Ekso weighs 45 pounds (20 kg), it has a maximum speed of 3.2 kph [2 mph] and a battery life of 6 hours." It is suitable for users who weigh up to 220 pounds, are between 5 feet, 2 inches and 6 feet, 4 inches tall, and can transfer themselves from a wheelchair to a chair. According to Renown.org, Ekso allows the user to "walk in a straight line, stand from a sitting position, stand for an extended period of time, and sit down from a standing position."

The Ekso Bionics website states, "The Ekso GT with smart Variable Assist™ (marketed as SmartAssist outside the U.S.) software is the only exoskeleton available for rehabilitation institutions that can provide adaptive amounts of power to either side of the patient's body."

A 2015 article from LiveScience.com likewise made the following announcement:

> HARMONY, a first-of-its-kind, two-armed, robotic rehabilitation exoskeleton is upgrading rehabilitation. Developed by researchers at the Cockrell School of Engineering at the University of Texas at Austin, HARMONY is a two-armed, exoskeleton that fits over the entire upper body, connecting to the patient in three places."
>
> "This robot is designed to deliver physical therapy and aid neurological disorders such as stroke or spinal cord injury," said lead developer Ashish Deshpande. HARMONY uses mechanical feedback and sensor data to provide therapy to patients with spinal cord and neurological injuries....
>
> The researchers expect the exoskeleton will be customizable to an individual's therapy needs, reducing recovery time. And, using HARMONY's sensors and software, the system will allow therapists and doctors to deliver precise therapy while tracking and analyzing data. With HARMONY now complete, the team continues to develop the software and prepare for upcoming trials on patients. (https://www.livescience.com/50918-robotic-exoskeleton-to-be-used-for-rehabilitation.html)

An article titled "The H2 Robotic Exoskeleton for Gait Rehabilitation after Stroke" concluded, "The developed exoskeleton enables longitudinal over ground training of walking in hemiparetic patients after stroke. The system is robust and safe when applied to assist a stroke patient walking."

I have yet to try any of the U.S.-developed robotic suits, but I would very much like to test them out, and from the look of the companies' website, I feel that these robotics hold much future promise. I very much hope to be able to use such a device while I am still relatively healthy, but getting to their studios or facilities in the United States poses some challenges for me. I would like to see the American and Japanese teams and others join forces to advance their technologies further and faster.

Robotic Rehabilitation Technology in Japan

As I now reside far from the Ekso Bionics facilities in the United States, I was delighted to find a robotic suit being developed in Japan in a city called Tsukuba, about one hour from Tokyo by local train. The nickname of Tsukuba has been "Science City," as many scientific institutes sponsored by the Japanese government were moved there from Tokyo in the 1980s. My husband and I lived in Tsukuba for several years early in our marriage, in the late 1980s, while my husband worked in one of the national science institutes there in geology research and I taught English at Tsukuba University and other places. Tsukuba is also the place where our son was conceived and born. I had long wanted to return to Tsukuba for a visit.

I was finally able to go to the Cyberdyne Studio in Tsukuba in 2016, where they are developing a robotic device called Hybrid Assistive Limb. I was able to try both the arm and the leg limbs for my weak left side.

As an online article states, "Japan's Cyberdyne may share its name with the company responsible for nuclear destruction and the killer robots of the 'Terminator' movie series, but the similarities end there.... The real-life Cyberdyne is in the business of revolutionising lives" (see phys.org/news/2010–12-japan-robot-disabled.html).

The Hybrid Assistive Limb is also known as HAL, which, in another sci-fi-related coincidence, is the name of the devious computer in Stanley Kubrick's *2001: A Space Odyssey.* The exoskeleton device gives power to its wearer by anticipating and supporting the user's body movements using sensors monitoring electric signals sent from the brain to the muscles.

The online article goes on to say, "Some 50 hospitals and homes for the elderly in Japan are using a lower-limb version of HAL to assist disabled people. Rental fees for both legs are 140,000–150,000 yen a month (approximately 1,600–1,800 dollars). It aims to begin sales to consumers from 2015."

Robotic Suit in Japan: Some Limitations

At this time, the HAL robotic limb can only be worn indoors. The government of Japan has recently decided that the national insurance can be used for it, but only by sufferers of ALS, and it does not include stroke survivors. But please seek out more information on Cyberdyne's Japanese website or check out their English website at www.cyberdyne.jp/english/products/HAL.

I suggest that you request an appointment very early, as there seem to be users who come in to regularly train with HAL, and it can be difficult to book a slot that you want, especially on weekends, as it was for me. On the Cyberdyne website, HAL is said to be "the world's first cyborg-type robot, by which a wearer's bodily functions can be improved, supported and enhanced. Wearing of HAL leads to a fusion of 'man,' 'machine' and 'information.' HAL assists a physically challenged person to move and enables him or her to exert bigger motor energy than usual. HAL is also considered as the system that accelerates a motor learning of cerebral nerves."

My Experience Walking
Wearing a Robotic Suit in Japan

It so happened that the Association of Foreign Wives of Japanese (AFWJ), of which I am a member, was to hold its annual convention in Tsukuba in May 2016. I spent a few months planning for a tour at Cyberdyne while attending the 2016 AFWJ convention. I was late in trying to reserve an appointment at Cyberdyne and was finally put in the last time "training" slot available before I needed to leave Tsukuba on my final evening there in order to catch the last *Shinkansen* (bullet train) back to Tokyo and onward from there home. I was later moved back by one hour due to a cancellation. I felt I needed more time, but I was so excited that I was able to get into any slot at all at Cyberdyne.

My experience trying out the Hybrid Assistive Limb (HAL) was fantastic for me. I was so excited and nervous about going there, and I did not want anything to come between me and my planned experience. It felt like when I was about ten years old going to Disneyland for the first time, experiencing uncontrolled excitement. It was just too important and essential for me.

On the day of the Cyberdyne tour, several other AFWJ members kindly joined me to go there first for a group tour, which I greatly appreciated. Then they stayed on to cheer me on during my individualized training session when they saw me standing up and walking.

The first thing I was instructed to do at the Cyberdyne Studio after the conclusion of our group tour was to remove my trousers and put on a pair of theirs, which included a slot opening for sticking the electrode pads onto my leg. They next had me remove my solid leg brace and place my feet into some soft shoes with a HAL device attached to them. Then they connected a sling around my waist and legs. After that, I was asked to take hold of the walker and stand up, which I did. The top part of the walker electronically lifted me upward a bit. I noticed that the walker had no brake stoppers on it. Mostly through my experience I have found those types of walkers difficult to steer and to brake, and my therapists in Japan where I work out usually do not recommend them for me, as I have trouble steering with just my right hand. After standing up, I started walking forward slowly, as I usually do in practice, but now, instead of using my rather unsteady cane to aid my walking, I used their walker, which I could lean on with the upper part of my body and my right hand. This was when I felt the most nervous, although I realized that it was extremely stable and safe with the upright walker, the sling, and several therapists helping me as I stood up and started walking. A girl staffer at Cyberdyne was serving a buffering and braking purpose by walking backward in front of me, going at my pace, so I did not need to use any brakes myself or worry about steering. In addition, there were two other male therapists nearby to spot me, making me feel very secure. So I could easily move forward, circling around a large open space.

Due to all of that support, it was difficult to tell how much the lower-body leg robotic HAL was actually helping me to walk. I felt that I walked well because I already know how to walk well, as I practice walking nearly daily with a leg brace, and I have developed the proper walking muscles for that too. I later heard that the therapist there had told one of the members of our group that I was "the perfect candidate subject for trying out the HAL there."

Later, when I tried out the arm HAL on my weakened left arm, I felt the effect there was greater, as I am not normally able to lift my left arm on my own at all. With the robotic limb, I could lift my weak left arm as it jerked up, up, up several times. The time was too short for me to really know the effect of the HAL very much. But I was awed by the exciting experience and felt like Arnold Schwarzenegger in his role as the Terminator when I exclaimed, "I'll be back." That is to say, "I hope that I can have a chance to return there someday soon to try it out again."

I felt that it would be best if we could bring HAL to Hirosaki in northern Honshu, where I live. When I attended my rehabilitation session the next day, back home at the facility I often use, I told my therapist about my experience in Tsukuba trying out HAL. I was surprised to hear from him that they had considered renting HAL at that facility that I use twice weekly. I am not sure why they have not obtained it yet, but I assume that it must have been beyond their budget. In my next visits to that facility, I want to further encourage them to rent HAL if possible. I have since discovered that another facility in my city is renting HAL for the lower body. I have yet to go there to try it out again but hope to soon.

Reimaging and Strengthening Pathways from the Brain to the Muscles and Tendons

The technology, the hypothesis and the vision for Ekso in the United States and for HAL in Japan at Cyberdyne Studio are truly admirable and awesome. The notion that all movement in our muscles originates from electrical impulses sent out from the brain seems to be at the heart of this technology.

I believe that this process has an overlap with the Feldenkrais Method or the Anat Baniel Method, but the "approach" to making brain-body connections differs. ABM uses nine essentials such as slow, mindful movements, while HAL uses brain impulses to move an electrical-robotic arm or leg. HAL helps to pick up those messages sent from the brain to the leg for walking or to the arm to raise it, for example. Then it helps make the movements electrically linked to an apparatus connected to the arm or leg, like a cyborg.

I think it can be concluded that "one of the basic keys to recovery from stroke hemiparesis must certainly be reimagining and strengthening the pathways from the brain to the muscles needed for walking or using an arm." The biggest remaining problem is then "how" to reimagine those pathways, which may differ from person to person. I am still in the process of trying to decipher just how to reimagine my own brain pathways so that I can move beyond the wheelchair and literally get back on my feet. I am earnestly working on doing that these days. One such stroke survivor is Ms. Negishi, whom I see regularly at a day-service facility in Japan. She walks very well, with a tight leg brace on her weak leg. She told me that she has spent four hours daily on her own rehabilitation, such as walking, for some ten years now. I have been trying to talk with her about her journey toward mobility. First, she is much leaner than I am. I would guess her weight to be less than 50 kilograms, compared with my 60 kilograms. She also has built up very strong muscles in her body, especially in her legs. Another user at the same facility impressed me with her ability to get some movement out of her weakened hand. So I am now trying to learn secrets of success from my peers when I go out for day-service training. In addition, I have found many interesting and informative videos on YouTube that you can view, particularly on robotics. Please search "stroke + robotics" and add any key words to your YouTube search field.

Amazing Robotics Vision: Open Letter to Robotics Technicians

I was so moved by the potential for robotic suits that I wrote a letter to the Cyberdyne founder in Japan:

Dear Professor Sankai Sensei
(and to other robotics technicians and designers),

I recently visited Cyberdyne Studio on May 29, 2016 and I want to let you know that, as a stroke survivor in wheelchair with one-sided weakness, I was greatly impressed and excited about trying on the arm and lower body HAL. It helped me walk and to raise my weakened (left) arm. It was like a dream come true for me. I am hoping that you will continue to improve the device until it becomes possible to produce them at a very low reasonable cost for ordinary people around the world to simply strap on and use by themselves, both indoors and outdoors.

I was thinking that the very large walker could be improved by designing accordion-like units (like a folding fan or a folding umbrella) for maneuvering tight spaces, such as in most homes and public spaces in Japan. Please continue the work to make your product a replacement for the wheelchair or walker. I now must use a wheelchair most of the time. To walk for exercise, I strap on a *sougu* (an AFO or a leg brace) and I use a cane, but I can only walk about 300 meters maximum or about a half hour before getting tired, as yet.

As I live in rural Hirosaki City, Aomori Prefecture in northern Honshu, Japan, it was a very difficult full day trip to Tsukuba and to Cyberdyne Studio, but I am very glad that I was able to make the trip there and have had the chance to experience trying on the HAL and experience firsthand the newest technology offering great hope for us with compromised limbs. There must certainly be hundreds of millions of us stroke survivors around the world who would be greatly helped if you could make a product that could be used to help us walk again and to use our weakened hands or legs. Such a person would win a Nobel Prize for the contribution, I feel. I think that the world is waiting for this technology to be spread around and I challenge you to be the first to make it universally available. I have also heard of an EKSO skeleton being developed in the U.S. and something else like it in Europe, I think. It may also be in developing stages in other places such as Russia, China, India, and elsewhere. If it can be simplified a bit and produced cheaply enough, it would be the next generation of walking devices, not only for stroke survivors, but for many other illnesses as well, children's diseases, and the millions injured by accidents, war or violence. I am so much looking forward to that next step.

Yours respectfully,
Laurel Kamada

I never received a response from Sankai Sensei. I include this letter here because I am advocating these notions as an open letter to all technicians everywhere working on such technology (including the Ekso producers in the United States) and also to the hundreds of engineering students at Tohoku University who were in my English classes from April 2009 to March 2013 and to those engineers there before or after that time as well.

Summing Up Keys to Rehabilitation

When I first applied for a training session with HAL at Cyberdyne, I was told that it was not yet meant for those who are disabled like myself. I felt very disappointed upon hearing that because, first of all, I did not feel myself to be "*dis*abled." I felt "*en*abled," as I have put in years of hard work "enabling" me to walk well with a leg brace and a cane. Also, I felt that the purpose of the robotic device/invention should be to aid people like myself. The company appeared to be ignoring a whole sector of diverse physically challenged ("disabled") persons who are eager to be included in its trial and usage. I felt it should be the other way around: I hope that this valuable breakthrough technology will become more readily available in time. As it turned out, I was eventually allowed a "training" slot on a weekend afternoon. I very much appreciated that, so that I could try it out during my short trip to Tsukuba, which is not likely to happen again during my lifetime. I also hope to try out the Ekso device in the United States someday, if possible.

While I have yet to experience a complete recovery over the seven or so years since my stroke, I want to work more on "mindfully" reconnecting my brain pathways to my muscles and to consider how the muscles work to help me walk. If I continue to practice these techniques, even by myself, I, too, might have a total recovery. I am setting that as my goal. If I reach my goal, I may write a sequel memoir.

Through my research on stroke rehabilitation combined with my experiences, I would sum up the most important aspects of stroke rehabilitation success as follows: In order to regain function in one's weakened limbs, one needs to rebuild muscles and practice how to balance and gain stamina. Relearning proper balance when walking requires rebuilding muscles that deal with the subtle differences in movement that compensate for lost balance, such as when one nearly trips or one tries to go through a course with obstacles. Much of this is established in our early childhood, I feel. How many times did you scrape or skin your knees and elbows, having taken a fall, as a child? I feel that one must first rebuild pathways from the brain to the various body parts and muscles being called upon in walking, as stated above.

This abstract notion is not easy to accomplish unless it is practiced consciously and repeatedly over a long period of time. But we just get older, and we have "aging" as another obstacle in our path of recovery to overcome. Each person needs to find their own ways to rebuild their brain pathways. Those who succeed have all worked very hard at it over a very long time, often with the help of others and physical aids such as leg braces, canes, handrails, and so forth. Therapists give survivors "hope" by letting us/them realize that "it is indeed possible to walk again." (See Appendix VII.)

My Personal Best of Walking (Distance and Speed)

While working out with a robotic arm or leg, stroke survivors can work to build up their proper muscles, learn balance, and increase muscles that adjust for balance and imbalance; they can also gain stamina by practicing the movements daily. Decades ago, in my 20s, when I would go mountain ice climbing in the northern Cascade mountain range (about 60 miles east of Seattle), I learned that "the best training for mountain climbing is simply mountain climbing itself." It is not jogging, working out in a gym, or weight training. Putting that idea into practice now, I think it is fair to conclude: "The best practice for walking is walking itself." It is not just working out on machines. With this thought in mind, and after my suggestion, my therapist recently, instead of having me work out on a machine for half of the session, has been concentrating on having me do more walking. He recently doubled my walking distance to 300 meters at each session, and he is also trying to have me quicken my pace by timing me over an established distance of about 65 meters. My first time was about 3:20, walking with a leg brace and a cane. I reached "my personal best walking distance" of about 300 meters on July 4, 2016, by walking down and back a very long corridor in one shot, without resting, twice. My goal is to be able to walk 1, then 2, and finally 3 miles. And then I hope to be able to walk that distance outside on the street. Admittedly, these goals might be very hard to reach.

Poetry, by Laurel Kamada
A Calendar of Poetry and Haiku

Poem for Winter, January 2017

(This poem was written while I was still recovering in Japan, toward the end of that hospitalization, in around January 2015.)

"Waiting Is a Long Bad Poem"

Waiting is a long bad poem.
Waiting is the loud silence of ringing in my ears.
Waiting is the clock whose second hand has stopped. Waiting is time stopped.
Waiting is the fret and worry of what may have happened to you.
Waiting is my impatience causing anxiety.
Waiting is uneventful space of emptiness.
Waiting is creatively trying to brainstorm Plan B when there is no Plan B.
Waiting is forever needing to use the toilet before you arrive to take me away.
And you admonish me for not being ready while waiting for you.
Waiting is forever.
Waiting is rehearsing in my mind what I will say to you when you arrive.

Poem (Haiku) for February 2017

I feel like this now:
My ass hurts, as does my neck.
Husband is angry.

Poem (Haiku) for March (written March 27, 2016)

"Waiting for Spring"

Awaiting respite
Stuck in this damaged body
Spring's warm fragrant breeze

Poem (Haiku) for April

At one of the day-service facilities that I attended, where the average age of the users was around 78, they had us doing what they called "Relax Exercise," which I felt to be an oxymoron. That is what prompted me to write this haiku.

"The Oxymoron"

Relax exercise?
To relax and sleep, but never
The oxymoron.

Haiku for May

"Weather Signals"

Spring about over
It passed through here unnoticed.
Gone on arrival.

May 2017

"Summer Heat"

Winter changed to sweating hot.
Now I complain, It's too hot
for a few more months.

Poem (Haiku) for June (written March 26, 2016)

"*Seattle*, a Poem Unpenned, in My Heart"

"World's best place," I say.
Eyes wide, they all say, "Really?"
"Got Family there."

Poem (Haiku) for July (March 29, 2016)

"But More Abnormal"

Seen as abnormal
Slumped over like Steve Hawkins
With a robust mind

Poem (Haiku) for August and September

"Tokutarou"

Summer 'bout over
Time moves away like blossoms.
Then come all the leaves.

October (Haiku)

"Halloween Time Is Here"

Rain in Seattle
Costumed kids with candy bags
Ghouls and stroke rehab

November: Essentialist Poem—Zaz

What is zaz? A feeling of being in a poetic state of mind? But my poem is an essentialist poem, with only feelings of languidness, inactivity and tiredness, lethargy. Also known as "writer's block" or "neck ache."

"ZAZ, A Poem"

I cannot make any progress here now.
Everything that can be said lies between A and Z
so my poem or story is just az za, za, za, za or zaz. Zaz, zaz.
Feeling zazzed up now, but not very razzed about it all.
Just waiting for the evening to crawl into bed
after taking my after dinner medicines
after eating dinner to be eaten with no appetite.
Did you say, "no appetite"? Quick put her on antidepressants
before she opens a window and jumps out
into the garden on the first floor, or maybe just to let the bugs out.
It is stifling in here anyways, so natural to open the window,
and suicidal to leave it closed. But why is her window closed?

Winter: Poem for December (May 2016)

"Thanatopsis of the Deadline"

I have too much work to do.
But at least
I do not have any deadlines
except when I die
and they have to lay me out on a line.
That will be my **dead**line.
But I will need to have completed
all of my work before that "deadline."
Just thinking of Japanese funerals
makes my eyes water.
Not from the pathos of it all,
but from the heavy incense.

Messages from Others Around Me for Stroke Survivors

I have asked several people whom I come into contact with at a day-service facility in Japan, and who have much to offer stroke survivors, "What are your impressions about your experiences here?" I have paraphrased some of their comments below, which they have shared with me.

The director of the facility, Dr. Ishitoya: This is a facility for medical rehabilitation, nursing, and care for the elderly. There are four physicians who work here, including myself. We have a rehabilitation section here with professional physical, occupational and speech therapists, including experts dealing with one-sided stroke-related paralysis and weakness. When I see those users working out and looking so cheerful, it makes me feel very happy. Rehabilitation is not just working out on machines by oneself; rather, it involves teamwork with the entire staff, working together toward being able to lead a life of independent movement.

Kudou Kazuto, my physical/occupational therapist at the day service: Do not give in to your illness; perseverance is powerful, so let us continue to do rehabilitation together.

Kabutomori, an OT/PT at the same facility: Try your best and never give up. Let's accomplish your goals together.

Toyama Miyuki, a PT therapist at the same facility: Today is the first day of the rest of your life. You should move forward step-by-step.

Misaki Nakanuma, an occupational therapist at the facility: Whenever I see how Laurel always positively works on her therapy, I strongly feel that I also need to grow daily in my work as an occupational therapist. Please continue to do your best as a good example for everyone.

Kumiko Negishi, the woman user there whom we call "Superwoman": Do not let others define what you can or cannot do. No matter how impossible it might seem, do what you feel you need to do, even if others object. Do not allow others to hold you back.

Hidemi, a stroke-survivor user at the facility who I met there (She had a very massive hemorrhagic stroke that left her vision impaired, along with a disfiguring drooping face and difficulty eating and walking; however, she impressed me with her ability to raise her weak, affected hand high over her head and to open her fingers of that hand): "Continue to stretch out your weak limbs, such as your hand, even if it feels painful or uncomfortable. Keep going at it daily." Hidemi often feels down about her severely drooping face, as she must have been beautiful before the stroke, but I tell her, "Do not worry about that. You are still beautiful. Beauty is not something seen in the face; it comes from the heart, and your heart is pure and beautiful. Thus you are beautiful." I also tell her, "Do not dwell on the things you have lost or can no longer accomplish. Celebrate the things you can still do or have recovered. Have gratitude for the things you do have, such as your robust cognition and memory."

Selected Glossary

This glossary (listed in alphabetical order) presents several uncommon vocabulary terms used in this book, along with their definitions.

Hemiparesis (n.), hemiparetic (adj.): Hemiparesis is a condition of weakness on one side of the body vertically from the top of the head to the toes and fingertips. In contrast to a hemiplegic person, who is paralyzed on one half of the body, hemiparesis refers to weakness, but not always paralysis. Often the brain can be retrained to regain some movement in a hemiparetic limb.

Hemiplegia (n.), hemiplegic (adj.): Hemiplegia is the condition of being paralyzed on one side of the body vertically from the top of the head (including half of the face, tongue, lips and neck) to the toes and from the shoulder to the fingertips. It is generally caused by strokes or a brain injury.

Neuroplasticity: This is a concept in which the brain is theorized to remake and retrain itself, usually by forming new connections in the brain. Practice and repeated movements or exercise is thought to stimulate this brain process or learning (see Doidge, 2007). The concept of neuroplasticity is very exciting for me and other stroke survivors, as it is the best hope for those of us with brain injuries to retrain our brains to recover what we have lost. I believe that the theory is rich and promising, but we are still left with trying to find "the best method" for more quickly and efficiently retraining the brain to grow more connections.

Many methods are being promoted and used by various people to utilize concepts of neuroplasticity. Some methods emphasize repeated practice, which I agree with. Other methods suggest very gentle movements for the injured body parts such as knee joints or other sensitive areas, which seems to work better with selected individuals. I personally feel that borrowing from several different methods might be a good way forward and that each person might have their own individual methods. Some use aids such as robotic limbs or frequent physical and occupational therapy. I am still searching for other new methods to try out.

Paraplegia (n.), paraplegic (adj.): A paraplegic person is someone who is paralyzed in the lower half of their body. Generally it means that both legs are paralyzed, but paraplegics usually have the use of their arms and upper body. Often paraplegia is caused by an accident resulting in spinal cord, back or neck damage. The Paralympics has used the prefix "para" to indicate people with some body impairments. But with aging populations around the world, I think that more people may become impaired due to strokes, which cause hemiplegia (see definition above) rather than paraplegia. So perhaps someday there will be "hemi" sports events.

Perseveration (n.), perseverate (v.): This term is often used for some stroke survivors who tend to repeat themselves and to obsess over a particular idea or thought. In its verb form, "to perseverate," it means to do or to say something repeatedly, or to go the limit, to be stubborn.

Quadriplegia (n.), quadriplegic (adj.): A quadriplegic is a person who has paralysis in all four limbs; in this case, both hands and both feet are usually paralyzed. However, there might be slight movement in one hand, and the head and face are usually unaffected. Causes include neck or back injuries and certain illnesses, syndromes or conditions.

Sublexion (n.), sublexed (adj.): When an injured joint is starting to be pulled out of its socket, it is said to be "sublexed." Often, a shoulder joint becomes injured and sublexed in stroke survivors. It can be quite painful, and care is usually taken to prevent further injury to the joint by using a sling and a gait belt. A shoulder sublexion can be made worse just by the weight of the arm hanging down and the pull of gravity on it. Thus the arm sling might help, but it might also cause the person to avoid usage of that arm if the sling is used too often.

Bibliography

Baniel, Anat. (2016). *Move Into Life: Neuro Movement for Lifelong Vitality.* San Rafael, CA: Crowning Beauty Publishing Company.

Baxter, J. (2003). *Positioning Gender in Discourse: A New Theoretical Methodology.* London, UK: Palgrave Macmillan.

Bolte Taylor, J. (2009). *My Stroke of Insight: A Brain Scientist's Personal Journey.* New York: Penguin Group.

Feldencrais, M. (1990). *Awareness Through Movement.* New York: Harper One.

Mairs, N. (1997). *Waist High in the World: A Life Among the Nondisabled.* Boston: Beacon Press.

Merriam-Webster. (1992). *Dictionary of Quotations: Quotables from Notables.* Springfield, MA: Merriam-Webster, Inc.

Merzenich, M. (2013). *Soft-Wired: How the New Science of Brain Plasticity Can Change Your Life.* San Francisco: Parnassus Publishing, LLC.

Miller, R.A. (1982). *Japan's Modern Myth: The Language and Beyond.* New York: John Weatherhill.

Nudelman, E. (2014). *Out of Time, Running.* Hartford, VT: Harbor Mountain Press.

Sergeant, P. (2011). *English in Japan in the Era of Globalization.* London, UK: Palgrave Macmillan.

Sunderland, J. (2004). *Gendered Discourses.* London, UK: Palgrave Macmillan.

Index